RODALE'S

SUCCESSFUL ORGANIC GARDENING™

CONTROLLING PESTS AND DISEASES

Rodale's Successful Organic Gardening™

Controlling Pests and Diseases

Text by Patricia S. Michalak

Insect and Disease Guide by Linda A. Gilkeson, Ph.D.

Rodale Press, Emmaus, Pennsylvania

Our Mission

We publish books that empower people's lives.

RODALE BOOKS

If you have any questions or comments concerning this book, please write to:

Rodale Press
Book Readers' Service
33 East Minor Street
Emmaus, PA 18098

Library of Congress Cataloging-in-Publication Data

Michalak, Patricia S.
Controlling pests and diseases / text by Patricia S. Michalak ; insect and disease guide by Linda A. Gilkeson.
p. cm. — (Rodale's successful organic gardening)
Includes index.
ISBN 0–87596–611–X hardcover — ISBN 0–87596–612–8 paperback
1. Garden pests—Control. 2. Plant diseases. 3. Organic gardening. 4. Plants, Protection of. I. Title. II. Series.
SB974.M53 1994
635.049—dc20 93–6103
CIP

Printed in the United States of America on acid-free ∞, recycled paper ♻

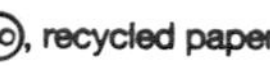

Rodale Press Staff:
Executive Editor: Margaret Lydic Balitas
Senior Editor: Barbara W. Ellis
Editor: Nancy J. Ondra
Copy Editor: Carolyn R. Mandarano

Produced for Rodale Press by Weldon Russell Pty Ltd
107 Union Street, North Sydney NSW 2060, Australia
a member of the Weldon International Group of Companies

Publisher: Elaine Russell
Publishing Manager: Susan Hurley
Senior Editor: Ariana Klepac
Editor: Margaret Whiskin
Editorial Assistant: Libby Frederico
Horticultural Consultant: Cheryl Maddocks
Copy Editor: Dawn Titmus
Designer: Rowena Sheppard
Picture Researcher: Anne Nicol
Illustrators: Barbara Rodanska, Jan Smith
Macintosh Layout Artist: Edwina Ryan
Indexer: Michael Wyatt
Production Manager: Dianne Leddy

A KEVIN WELDON PRODUCTION

Distributed in the book trade by St. Martin's Press

4 6 8 10 9 7 5 3 hardcover
4 6 8 10 9 7 5 3 paperback

Opposite: Common spangle galls
Half title: Green lacewing
Opposite title page: Lady beetles
Title page: Monarch butterfly
Opposite contents: Hoverfly
Back cover: Pyrethrum daisies (top), lacewing (bottom)

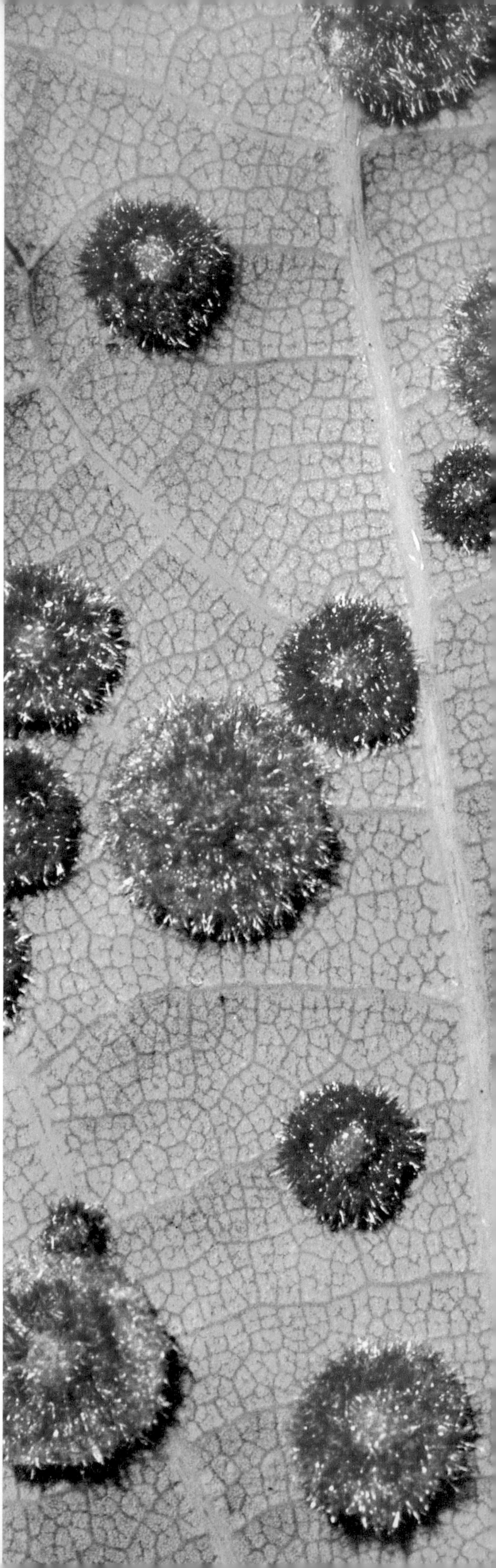

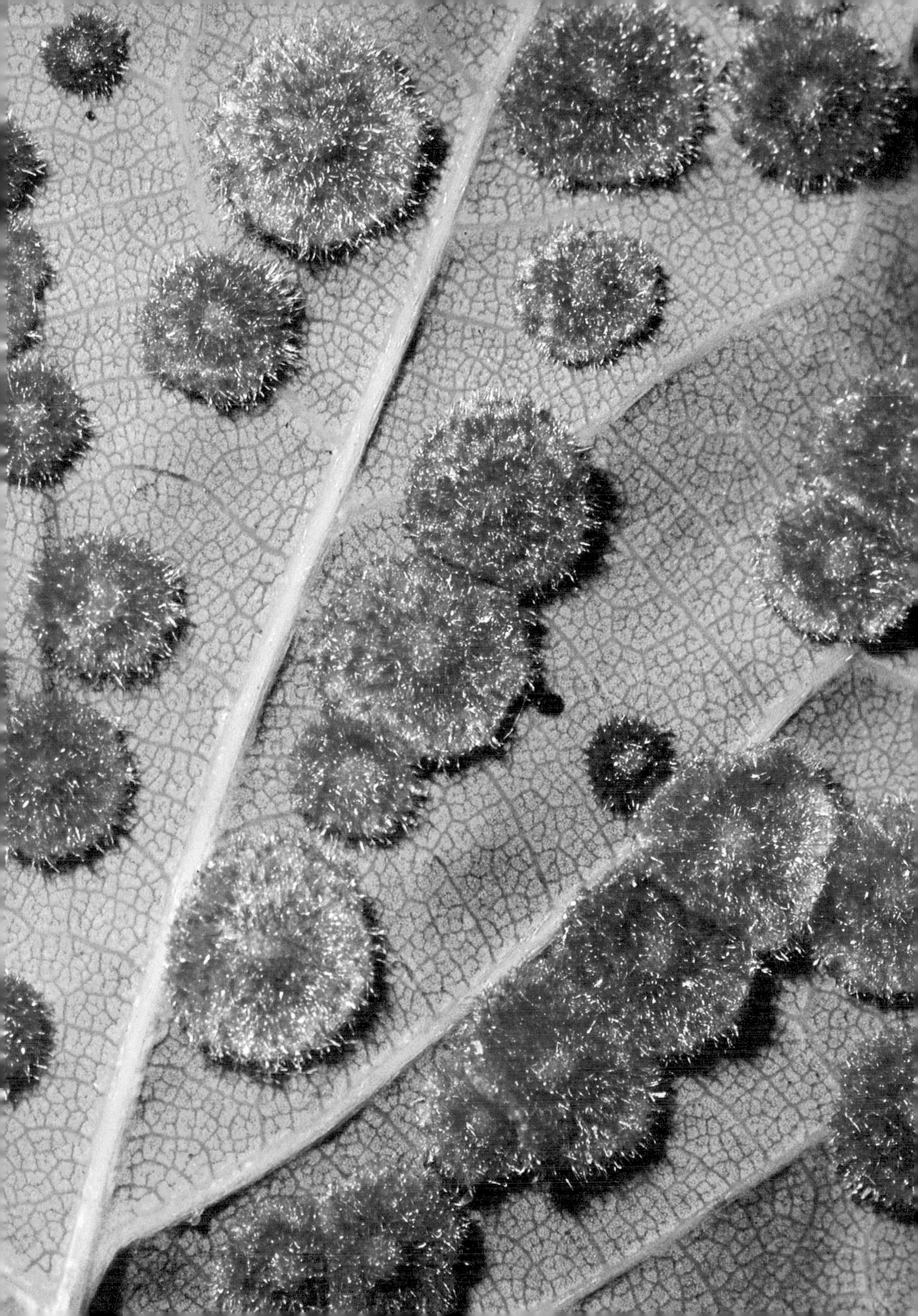

Contents

Introduction 8

How to Use This Book 10

Preventing Plant Pests and Diseases 12

Your Healthy Garden • Buying Healthy Plants • Improving Your Soil • Watering Wisely • Planning Crop Rotations

Identifying Garden Insects 24

What Is an Insect? • Beneficial Insects • Diagnosing Insect Damage

Managing Insect Pests 32

Preventing Pest Problems • Keeping Pests Off Plants • What to Do If Pests Appear • If All Else Fails

Identifying Plant Diseases 44

What Is a Disease? • Diagnosing Disease Problems • Common Signs and Symptoms • Disease Look-alikes

Managing Plant Diseases 54

Planning for Disease Prevention • Minimizing Disease Development • What to Do If Disease Appears • If All Else Fails

Identifying and Managing Animal Pests 64

Beneficial Animals • Deer • Rabbits • Birds • Moles and Gophers • Dogs and Cats • Woodchucks • Meadow Mice

Insect and Disease Guide 76

Index 156

Acknowledgments 160

Introduction

You've spent hours, days, or weeks getting this year's garden ready. You thumbed through the catalogs until they were limp and tattered, looking for new and interesting crops to try or for the latest perennial cultivars. You dug and raked and planted until your back ached, then you set out all of your precious seedlings and stood back to watch them grow.

This is going to be a great year, you think, as you stroll through the garden, admiring your handiwork. But wait—what's that black spot on the bottom of your first ripe tomato? And what are those white patches on the bee balm leaves? And what happened to your new planting of beans—it looks like a tiller went berserk in the middle of it! Welcome to gardening in the real world, where insects, diseases, and animal pests are ready and waiting to compete with you for dinner.

Fortunately, you have a lot of strategies at your disposal for outsmarting these critters. *Rodale's Successful Organic Gardening: Controlling Pests and Diseases* is chockfull of techniques you can use to prevent and control damage caused by pests and pathogens. Buying healthy plants that are well adapted to your garden conditions is one part of the pest-control plan. You'll also learn how you can adapt everyday gardening techniques to help make plants less susceptible to problems.

One important rule to remember is that not all insects are pests. Your garden is home to a wide variety of beneficial insects that get their food by dining on plant-feeders. Some of these beneficials—like praying mantids and lady beetles—are large enough to see; many are so small and fast that you may never have noticed them. You can protect and encourage these beneficials to stay in your garden by meeting their basic needs of food, water, and shelter.

If you've been gardening for any length of time, you also know that not all pests are insects. Deer, rabbits, woodchucks, and other animals will claim their share of the harvest if you let them. As with other garden problems, the best control for these critters is prevention. Installing effective barriers between animals and plants will keep damage to a minimum. But don't condemn all creatures to a life outside the garden gate; some, like bats, birds, and toads, are actually on your side. These and other beneficial animals will help keep insect pests to tolerable levels.

In most cases, you'll find that plant diseases are the least common problem you'll have to face. Once they get started, though, they're often tough to stop; here again, prevention is the key. You'll also need to learn how cultural problems, like nutrient deficiencies or waterlogged soil, can cause disease-like symptoms. Starting with healthy plants and using a combination of good gardening practices will go a long way toward keeping these kinds of problems at bay.

So don't despair—help is here. Try these techniques for creating a naturally healthy, ecologically balanced garden. Learn to live with a little damage, and let insect and animal predators keep the pests under control for you. Pretty soon, your garden will turn from a battleground into a beauty!

Opposite: Not all garden pests are as showy as this colorful caterpillar! It can take a close inspection to spot the many pest insects that are small and well camouflaged in dull greens or browns.

How to Use This Book

Pest and disease problems can discourage even the most experienced gardener, but it doesn't have to be a losing battle. This book is your guide to keeping your yard and garden naturally healthy, without having to resort to synthetic chemicals or high-priced garden gizmos. Here, you'll find plenty of common-sense advice for some of your most perplexing garden problems.

Rodale's Successful Organic Gardening: Controlling Pests and Diseases is divided into two main sections. The first section gives you the how-to information you need to prevent and control pest insects and animals, as well as plant diseases. The second section is the "Insect and Disease Guide," which starts on page 76. These pages are your handbook for identifying and dealing with pest insects, beneficials, and diseases that you may come across on your garden plants.

"Preventing Plant Pests and Diseases," starting on page 12, tells you how to use common garden practices to keep problems from developing. Buying healthy plants, improving your soil, watering correctly, and using crop rotations are all important steps in the prevention process. A well-planned and well-maintained garden provides the best possible conditions for growth, so your plants will naturally be more healthy and less attractive to pests.

When insects do show up—and they will at some point—you'll need to figure out if they're harmful or helpful. "Identifying Garden Insects," starting on page 24, will tell you what you need to know about basic insect biology—what makes insects different from other creatures, how they feed, and how they reproduce. You'll also learn about the helpful beneficial insects, which work with you to keep pests at tolerable levels. If you do spot damage, you'll find out how to determine who the culprit might be.

"Managing Insect Pests," starting on page 32, takes you through the steps of planning an effective pest control strategy. You'll find specific tips for preventing pest outbreaks and ways to keep pests off your plants. If pests do appear, try these safe and easy techniques for removing or luring pests away from plants. And if pests get out of hand, read about the strong but organically acceptable controls that you may decide to use as a last resort.

Plant diseases are among the most intimidating and insidious garden problems. You can't see what causes the symptoms, so you don't really know they are there until your plant is affected. The fact that cultural problems, like nutrient deficiencies, frost, and air pollution, can cause disease-like symptoms further complicates the issue. "Identifying Plant Diseases," starting on page 44, guides you through understanding what a disease actually is and shows you how to figure out which—if any—diseases are actually affecting your plants.

Like controlling pests, controlling disease problems starts with prevention. "Managing Plant Diseases," starting on page 54, shows you the steps to keeping plants naturally disease-resistant. If problems do occur, you'll find out how to stop the spread of a disease and how to keep it from happening again.

Insects and diseases tend to get more press, but animals can actually be the most destructive pests any gardener can face. Beetles may chew a few holes, mildew may cause a few spots, but a single deer or woodchuck can decimate a garden or girdle a fruit tree in just minutes. "Identifying and Managing Animal Pests," starting on page 64, is full of hints and tips for keeping a wide range of pest animals away from your precious plants. You'll also learn how beneficial creatures—like birds, bats, and toads—help you keep garden pest problems under control.

Insect and Disease Guide

Use these pages to look up specific problems or as a field guide to identify the insects and diseases you encounter in the garden. For easy access, the guide is separated into three parts. "Pests," starting on page 78, is where you'll turn to find plant-feeding insects and their relatives, like slugs and mites. "Beneficials," starting on page 117, is where you'll look for the good guys: insects and related creatures that eat the plant-feeding pests. "Diseases," starting on page 130, is a visual guide to common plant diseases and disorders that you might run across.

Within each of these sections, the entries are arranged in alphabetical order by common name. Each entry includes at least one color photo and a description for easy identification. For pests and diseases, you'll also find descriptions of the damage they cause and specific tips for problem prevention and control. Entries on beneficials offer information on attracting and protecting these helpful creatures.

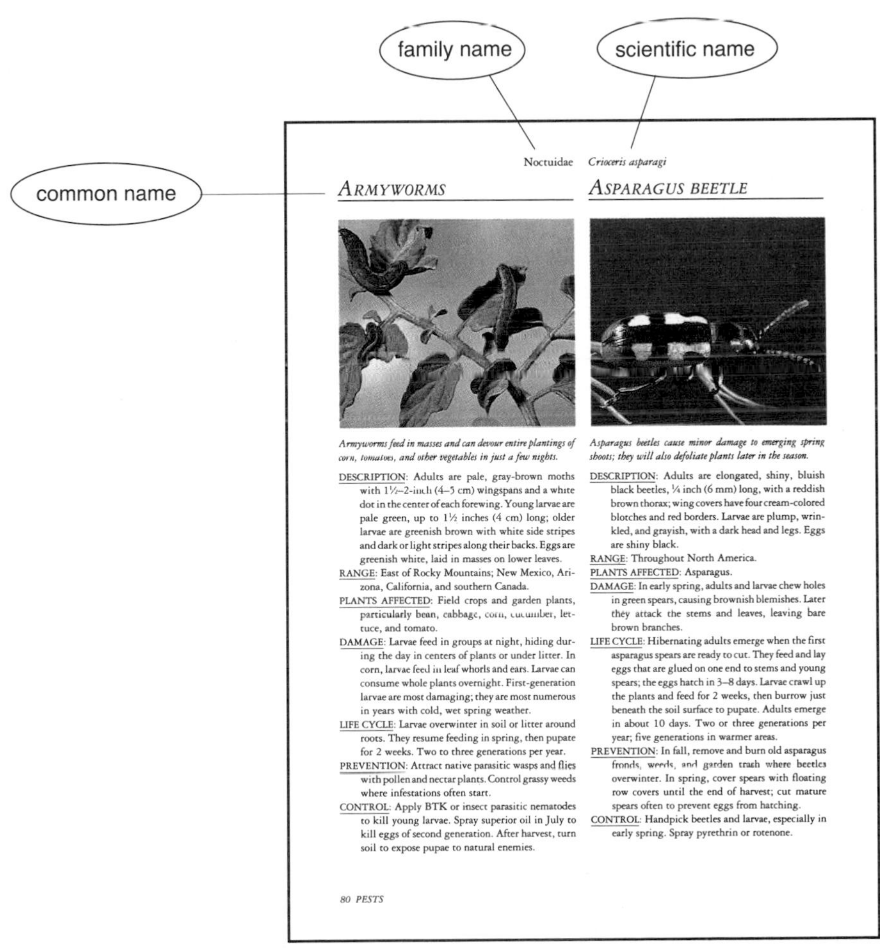

Noctuidae

ARMYWORMS

Armyworms feed in masses and can devour entire plantings of corn, tomatoes, and other vegetables in just a few nights.

DESCRIPTION: Adults are pale, gray-brown moths with 1½–2-inch (4–5 cm) wingspans and a white dot in the center of each forewing. Young larvae are pale green, up to 1½ inches (4 cm) long; older larvae are greenish brown with white side stripes and dark or light stripes along their backs. Eggs are greenish white, laid in masses on lower leaves.

RANGE: East of Rocky Mountains; New Mexico, Arizona, California, and southern Canada.

PLANTS AFFECTED: Field crops and garden plants, particularly bean, cabbage, corn, cucumber, lettuce, and tomato.

DAMAGE: Larvae feed in groups at night, hiding during the day in centers of plants or under litter. In corn, larvae feed in leaf whorls and ears. Larvae can consume whole plants overnight. First-generation larvae are most damaging; they are most numerous in years with cold, wet spring weather.

LIFE CYCLE: Larvae overwinter in soil or litter around roots. They resume feeding in spring, then pupate for 2 weeks. Two to three generations per year.

PREVENTION: Attract native parasitic wasps and flies with pollen and nectar plants. Control grassy weeds where infestations often start.

CONTROL: Apply BTK or insect parasitic nematodes to kill young larvae. Spray superior oil in July to kill eggs of second generation. After harvest, turn soil to expose pupae to natural enemies.

Crioceris asparagi

ASPARAGUS BEETLE

Asparagus beetles cause minor damage to emerging spring shoots; they will also defoliate plants later in the season.

DESCRIPTION: Adults are elongated, shiny, bluish black beetles, ¼ inch (6 mm) long, with a reddish brown thorax; wing covers have four cream-colored blotches and red borders. Larvae are plump, wrinkled, and grayish, with a dark head and legs. Eggs are shiny black.

RANGE: Throughout North America.

PLANTS AFFECTED: Asparagus.

DAMAGE: In early spring, adults and larvae chew holes in green spears, causing brownish blemishes. Later they attack the stems and leaves, leaving bare brown branches.

LIFE CYCLE: Hibernating adults emerge when the first asparagus spears are ready to cut. They feed and lay eggs that are glued on one end to stems and young spears; the eggs hatch in 3–8 days. Larvae crawl up the plants and feed for 2 weeks, then burrow just beneath the soil surface to pupate. Adults emerge in about 10 days. Two or three generations per year; five generations in warmer areas.

PREVENTION: In fall, remove and burn old asparagus fronds, weeds, and garden trash where beetles overwinter. In spring, cover spears with floating row covers until the end of harvest; cut mature spears often to prevent eggs from hatching.

CONTROL: Handpick beetles and larvae, especially in early spring. Spray pyrethrin or rotenone.

80 PESTS

Sample page from the "Insect and Disease Guide."

Preventing Plant Pests and Diseases

There are many different kinds of gardeners—beginners and experts, flower fanciers and vegetable growers—but they all share a common goal: vigorous, beautiful, productive plants. Whether you realize it or not, the steps you take to grow good plants also go a long way in preventing pest and disease problems. When your plants are growing strongly, they are inherently more resistant to attack by pest insects and disease-causing organisms. In this chapter, you'll learn how basic gardening practices can help you create and maintain a naturally healthy garden.

Preventing garden problems starts long before the first pests appear in spring. You can begin planning for pest and disease control when seed and plant catalogs arrive in winter. As you browse through books and catalogs for new plants to try, look for species and cultivars that are adapted to the conditions you have available. If you have shade, for example, you probably won't be able to grow sun-loving vegetables, like corn and tomatoes. Instead, investigate the variety of plants that will grow and thrive with less sunshine.

Once you know if a particular plant can grow in your conditions, do a little research on its common problems. You may learn that the plant is particularly prone to certain pests or diseases, like webworms or fire blight, or you may find that it is relatively trouble-free. If it is pest- or disease-susceptible but you really want to grow it, look for cultivars that are naturally more resistant. Squash, for example, is normally prone to a fungal disease called powdery mildew, which produces a dusty white coating on leaves. To avoid this problem, try cultivars that are resistant to mildew, like 'Multipik' and 'Zucchini Select'.

To stay healthy, your plants will need good soil to grow in. A soil rich with organic matter and alive with beneficial organisms requires nurturing and time. If you're starting a new garden, you may have to purchase and add organic fertilizers. All gardens benefit from regular and liberal additions of organic matter, in the form of materials like compost, grass clippings, or leaves. Besides providing an excellent, balanced source of nutrients and organic matter, composting is a great way to recycle garden and kitchen wastes you might otherwise put into a landfill.

How you water also affects the susceptibility of your plants to problems. Giving plants a steady supply of water throughout the season is important in keeping them strong and vigorous. Some watering techniques are better than others, though. Disease-causing organisms can spread quickly when plant leaves are covered in a film of water. For this reason, you'll probably want to avoid using overhead sprinklers, which wet the foliage as much as the soil. Instead, choose some kind of drip irrigation system, which delivers water directly to the soil and keeps plants dry.

Using a combination of these and other good gardening practices will soon become second nature to you. Your plants will benefit from ideal growing conditions. And you'll benefit, too, as you enjoy the beauty and bounty of your garden.

Opposite: You don't need a green thumb to have a beautiful, healthy garden: It just takes careful planning, good soil preparation, and routine scouting to catch problems before they get out of control.

Your Healthy Garden

Creating and maintaining a naturally healthy garden isn't a simple one- or two-step process. Every decision you make (or don't make) plays a part in the results you get throughout the season. And every year you're faced with new conditions, new questions, and different results. That's what makes gardening such a challenging but rewarding hobby.

Fortunately, there are some simple but effective steps you can follow each year to help promote the health of your garden. The basic thing to remember is this: Vigorous plants grown in fertile soil attract fewer pests and are less susceptible to infection by plant pathogens than plants grown in poor soil. Start with a variety of healthy plants, give them the right growing conditions, and keep an eye out for potential problems. These simple steps will go a long way toward producing a successful garden.

Including a diversity of flowering plants helps attract beneficial insects and makes your garden beautiful as well.

Create Diversity

Diversity is a key part of growing a healthy garden. Nature creates diversity by mixing many kinds of plants together. Think of a forest, with a mixture of trees, shrubs, vines, and wildflowers, or maybe a meadow, with a variety of flowers and grasses. These ecosystems provide habitats for a wide range of insects and animals. Predators and parasites help to keep pest populations at a relatively constant level.

In your garden, you can promote this natural system of checks and balances by growing lots of different kinds and cultivars of vegetables, flowering plants, and fruits. Diverse plantings attract beneficial insects and may deter some garden pests. You can take this diversity a step further by practicing crop rotation and changing the location of annual plants each year. This will help to discourage the buildup of some soilborne pest insects and diseases, like potato scab and beetle grubs. To learn more about preventing pest insects and plant diseases using crop rotation, see "Planning Crop Rotations" on page 22.

Astilbes can adapt to varying garden conditions, but they really look their best in evenly moist, humus-rich soil.

Provide Good Growing Conditions

Many good garden plants are adaptable to a wide range of growing conditions. But if you want your plants to thrive, not just survive, it's worth your time to investigate their particular needs. Vegetables, for example, generally grow best on a site that has lots of air circulation and good water drainage, with 8 to 12 hours of full sunlight each day and at least 1 inch (2.5 cm) of water each week. Fruits also tend to need lots of sun and fertile soil, while ornamental plants vary widely in their sun and soil needs.

Before buying new plants, make sure you can supply the conditions they prefer. If you already have a plant that is struggling to survive in less-than ideal conditions, consider moving or replacing it before problems strike.

Provide optimal growing conditions and your plants will reward you with high yields.

Monitoring soil fertility will help ensure strong, healthy stems and leaves, vigorous roots, and beautiful flowers.

Build Soil Fertility

Healthy soil produces healthy plants. Adding lots of organic matter will improve the physical characteristics of your soil and encourage the beneficial soil microorganisms that help make nutrients available to your plants. Check "Improving Your Soil," on page 18, for ideas on building and maintaining healthy soil.

Scout for Problems

Giving all of your plants a close look at least once a week can help you spot potential problems before they get out of hand. Take this book or a field guide along to help you identify unfamiliar insects. Become familiar with both pests and beneficials so you'll know which to control and which to leave alone.

If you do spot pests, don't immediately grab a bottle of insecticide. Check again each day over the next few days to see if the beneficial insects step in to help. If the pests are multiplying rapidly, then consider taking control measures. With a little experience, you'll learn how much damage your plants can tolerate before you have to take action.

Routine scouting helps you spot problems before they damage your plants.

You'll also want to keep an eye out for signs and symptoms of plant diseases. (Check out "Diagnosing Disease Problems," starting on page 48, to learn how to spot common disease problems.) Snipping off the infected part is often enough to stop a disease before it spreads. If you're growing disease-susceptible plants like fruit trees, you should also keep track of the environmental conditions that favor disease development—like wet, warm spells —and be prepared to apply preventive measures like sulfur or copper sprays.

Know Your Options

Become familiar with the types of controls available to you before you need them so you will know when and how to use them. The best pest control strategies usually include a combination of control methods. To learn more about handling pest and disease problems, read "Managing Insect Pests," starting on page 32, and "Managing Plant Diseases," starting on page 54.

Keep Good Records

Good garden records can be one of your most valuable control tools. As you scout for and deal with problems, keep track of when and where they occurred and what you did to control them. Write down what worked and what didn't work. If you tried new cultivars for their insect or disease resistance, jot down a few sentences on how they performed during the season. In future years, you can review your notes and be prepared for problems before they happen.

Before spraying for pests, look around for beneficial insects, like lady beetles. They may control the problem for you.

You can buy lacewings to help control pests.

Smart shoppers buy from reputable nurseries that take good care of their stock. Unhealthy plants are no bargain!

Buying Healthy Plants

One of the most basic steps in preventing pest and disease problems is starting with healthy, pest-free plants. They'll become established in their new home quickly, and you'll avoid importing pests and plant pathogens that could spread to other plants.

Start with a Strategy

Problem prevention begins long before the growing season starts. Winter is the best time to study seed catalogs and garden books, searching for plants and cultivars that are adapted to your climate. Of these, look for plants with resistance to the pests and diseases that visit your garden frequently.

Prepare a list of the plants you want, then take your business to garden suppliers you can trust. Ask friends and neighbors where they buy their plants and if they are happy with the quality. Shop around for the best quality and bargains, but don't be tempted to buy just because of a low price. If you want healthy, naturally vigorous plants, it's worth paying a little extra at the beginning.

Consider the Container

Some vegetable seedlings, like zucchini and cucumbers, and herbs, like dill and parsley, don't transplant well. If you buy them as young plants, look for seedlings growing in peat pots. At planting time, you can plant the whole seedling, pot and all; that way, you'll avoid disturbing the root system. Otherwise, the shock of transplanting can weaken these plants and make them more susceptible to pest attack.

Plants that look strong and healthy at the nursery are likely to grow when you get them home.

Plants like dill, parsley, and burnet transplant poorly, so buy or start them in peat pots to avoid root disturbance.

Inspect the Root System

Strong, healthy roots are a vital part of determining plant health. If a plant is growing in a plastic or clay container, gently remove the container and look at the roots. Roots should penetrate the soil without circling the outside of the root ball. They should be uniformly white, moist, and without breaks, bumps, or brown spots. Several exposed roots don't indicate stress, but avoid plants with lots of matted roots or plants tightly rooted to their neighbors. Separating closely rooted plants can severely damage the individual root systems. This shocks the young plants and can set them back by several weeks as they grow new roots.

Check Plant Color

Healthy seedlings are usually deep green, although you can expect color to vary among plants and cultivars. An overall pale, washed-out appearance often indicates that a nutrient is lacking. If you're not sure what a particular plant is supposed to look like, compare it with a photo from a book or catalog. This will help you determine if those stripes, spots, or colors are normal or if they indicate a problem.

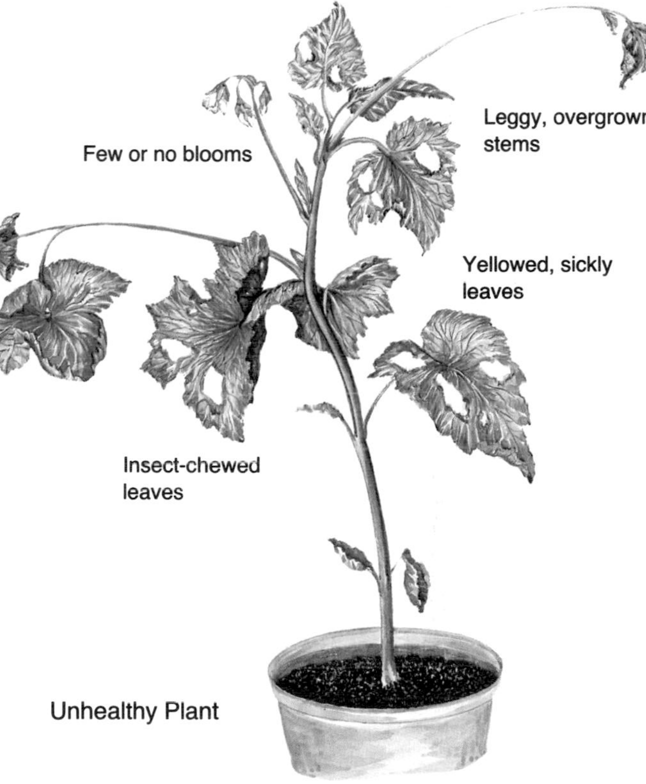

Weak, sickly plants may be cheaper to buy, but they can bring pests and diseases into your garden.

Probe for Problems

Examine plants carefully before you buy them and reject any with signs of pests or their damage. As you inspect the foliage, make sure you turn the leaves over and check their undersides as well as the tops; lower leaf surfaces are favorite pest hideouts. Common signs of insect and other pest damage include:

- Leaves with chewed holes or edges
- Shiny slime trails
- Webs on leaves or stems

If possible, remove the plant from its pot. Look for healthy roots; avoid plants with massed, circling roots.

- Tiny eggs on leaves or stems
- Brown or greenish droppings
- Wilted, curled, or discolored leaves.

Don't forget to look for signs of diseases during your inspection. Also look at other plants growing in the same area—if they are showing signs of disease, another plant that looks healthy may already be infected. Common symptoms of disease or environmental damage include:

- Spotty, discolored, or wilted leaves
- Dead areas in leaves or stems
- Fuzzy patches of fungal spores
- Leaves, roots, or stems with a soggy appearance.

Ask about Organics

If you want your garden to be completely organic, don't forget to ask your plant suppliers how they raise their stock. Many conventional growers use synthetic fertilizers and pesticides. Organic growers use starting and growing mediums that are high in organic matter and free of pesticides or synthetic nutrients. If you can't find a supplier of organically grown plants, you may decide to start them yourself.

Improving Your Soil

Pest and disease control is just one of many benefits of improving your garden soil. Your plants will grow best when all the components of the soil system—organic matter, water, and plant nutrients—are present in the right amounts, leading to more flowers and higher yields. When plants are vigorous, they're less susceptible to attack by insect pests and diseases. Adding compost is one of the best ways to improve soil and fight pests at the same time.

Create Great Compost

Composting is the best way to dispose of garden and kitchen wastes, and it provides you with a free supply of organic fertilizer and soil conditioner at the same time. In addition, beneficial organisms present in finished compost may help to prevent some plant pathogens from infecting your plants in the garden.

Composting can be fast and labor-intensive or slow and simple, depending on your needs and energy. You don't need any fancy materials to start composting—just a level, well-drained site. If you have lots of room and don't mind the appearance, you can have an uncontained heap. If you like things to be tidy, you can build a bin or pen out of wood, cement blocks, or woven wire fencing, or you can buy an already-made bin. Besides keeping the compost materials in one neat pile, a container will help keep pets and wildlife out.

Ingredients Good compost ingredients include most organic garden and kitchen wastes. Avoid oils, fats, and bones—all of which break down slowly and attract scavengers—and human and pet wastes, which can carry diseases. Also avoid adding infested or diseased material unless you are making a hot compost pile. Even then, the temperatures will not get high enough to kill some plant viruses. If you have virus-infected plants, bury them or place them in sealed containers for disposal with household trash.

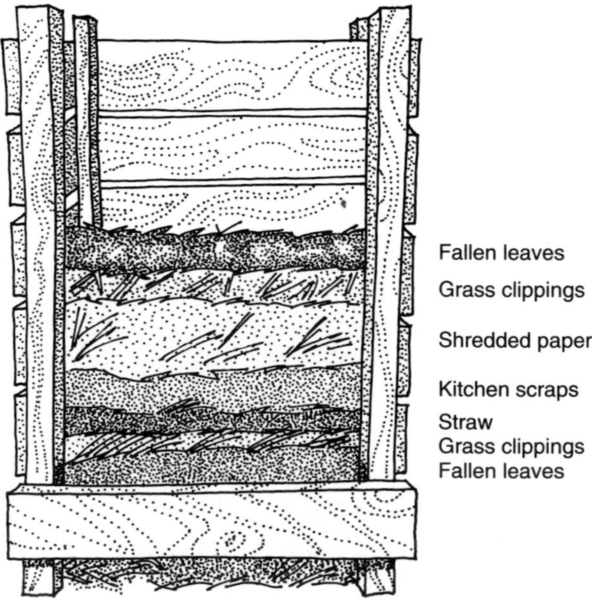

To make sure you get a balance of high-carbon and high-nitrogen materials, it's often easiest to add them in layers.

Any kind of organic material will break down more quickly when it's already in small pieces. Use a leaf shredder or lawn mower to chop materials like leaves, hard stems, bark, and twigs.

Hot, Fast Compost Hot composting takes some work, but you'll get results quickly—sometimes as fast as 2 weeks. Plus, composting at high temperatures can kill pests, some plant pathogens, and weed seeds that find their way into the pile.

Kitchen scraps—vegetable peelings, eggshells, apple cores—are great for composting. You can even add paper!

The key to hot composting is getting a balance between high-carbon and high-nitrogen ingredients. High-nitrogen ingredients are green, sloppy materials like fresh grass clippings, kitchen scraps, and manure. High-carbon ingredients include brown, woody materials like fallen leaves, straw, and newspaper.

Build the pile by alternating layers of high-nitrogen materials with high-carbon materials. Use approximately equal volumes of each. If you are adding plants infested with pests or pathogens, place them in the middle where temperatures will get the hottest.

If your ingredients are fairly dry, sprinkle each layer with water as you work. The materials should be spongy moist, but not soggy. Make sure the finished pile is at least 3 feet (1 m) on each side—a smaller pile won't heat up as well and will take longer to break down.

A properly built hot compost pile will be warm to the touch in a day or two. Use a compost thermometer to monitor your pile's progress. The temperature inside the pile should stay near but below 160°F (71°C), since

Start with the Soil

Taking good care of your soil is an important part of preventing garden problems. Here are some tips you can use to develop healthy soil and healthy plants.

- Keep the soil covered. Use organic mulches like compost and grass clippings around plants to help prevent soil erosion, retain soil moisture, keep the soil cool, add organic matter and nutrients, and provide safe hiding places for beneficial insects like ground beetles. Mulches also serve as a barrier between plants and pathogens.
- Grow a flowering, living mulch. Sow cover crops like buckwheat or clover in any vacant garden spot. The living mulch will protect the soil as it provides nectar and shelter for beneficial insects.
- Keep tillage to a minimum, especially when soil is wet or dusty dry. Soil is too wet to work if it sticks to your shoes or easily holds its shape when formed into a ball. Tillage destroys some insect pests, but kills beneficial insects and animals as well.

higher temperatures kill important decomposer organisms. When the pile cools off (in a few days), turning it should raise the temperature. Using a garden fork, invert the pile one forkful at a time just next to the original pile, fluffing it as you work. The more frequently you turn the pile, the more quickly it will break down. If the pile gets too hot, let it sit for a few days or add water to it.

Using this technique, you can have finished hot compost within 2 to 6 weeks. You'll know it's finished when the temperature stabilizes and the individual materials are no longer recognizable.

Cold, Slow Compost If you aren't in a hurry for finished compost, cold composting may be a good option for you. The most basic method is to simply pile together all the materials you have and let them sit for a year or more. Eventually, the pile will break down into usable compost. For a slightly quicker version, build the pile following the directions for hot compost, then leave it for 6 to 12 months without turning.

A cold compost pile won't actually feel cold—it just won't get as warm as a hot pile. The temperatures in a cold pile won't be high enough to kill pests, pathogens,

Cover crops are a super way to protect bare soil. Legumes, like clover, add extra nutrients when you turn them under.

or weed seeds, so don't add these materials to a cold pile.

Using Compost Compost makes an excellent, disease-free medium for starting your own plants. Begin with compost from a hot pile, then let it rest for an additional 6 to 12 months. Shake the finished compost through 1/2-inch (12 mm) wire mesh to screen out large particles. Use the screened compost alone or mix it with vermiculite, perlite, or other potting ingredients.

In the garden, compost helps to improve soil structure and increases the soil's water-holding capacity. Spread 1 to 2 inches (2.5 to 5 cm) of finished compost over the surface of your garden each year. You can work the compost in or leave it on top as a mulch. Mixing compost into the soil distributes beneficial micro-organisms that help to control soilborne pests and diseases. As a fertilizer, homemade compost contains between 1 and 2 percent each of nitrogen, phosphate, and potash, plus small quantities of trace elements.

You can make compost with a loose pile in the corner of the garden, or you can enclose it in a more formal-looking bin.

Fight Fungus with Compost

You can make disease-fighting compost tea to control some soilborne pathogens indoors and outdoors. Mix together 1 part finished compost with 6 parts water. Let the mix rest for 1 week, then strain it through burlap or cheesecloth, collecting the liquid. Spray the undiluted solution on plants, or use it to water soil around plants in the garden or in pots. Recent research suggests that the compost tea helps to control fungal diseases.

Balance Soil Nutrients

For your plants to grow to their potential, they need access to the right nutrients in the right balance. When nutrients are in short supply, plants weaken and are more susceptible to pests. Nutrient-deficient plants tend to exhibit symptoms—such as yellowing leaves or deformed fruit—that are easy to mistake for insect or disease damage. Consult "Disease Look-alikes" on page 52 or the "Insect and Disease Guide," starting on page 76, to learn more about nutrient-deficiency symptoms.

Excessive nutrients can be as much of a problem as deficiencies. For example, high levels of soil nitrogen can promote succulent, leafy growth that is more susceptible to pest insects and pathogens. In pears and apples, excessive applications of nitrogen fertilizer makes plants prone to the disease known as fire blight.

If you suspect a nutrient imbalance, have a sample of your soil tested. (In fact, it's a good idea to take a soil test every time you start a new garden, and every 3 to 5 years after that, so you can correct minor imbalances before they turn into major problems.) Your local Cooperative Extension Service can tell you where to buy soil test kits, which have instructions for collecting and mailing your soil sample. Ask for organic fertilizer recommendations for maintaining the right pH, nitrogen, phosphorus, potassium, and organic matter levels for the plants you grow.

Home pH tests are fairly accurate; just follow the instructions enclosed in the kit.

Know Your Soil's pH

The measure of your soil's acidity or alkalinity is its pH. It can range from 1.0 (most acid) to 14.0 (most alkaline or basic). The pH has a great effect on which nutrients are available to your plants and in what balance. Most plants grow best when the pH is near neutral—around 7.0—although some, like blueberries and rhododendrons, prefer more acid conditions.

Soil pH doesn't have much effect on insect pests, except that plants growing in soil with a very high or low pH may be weak and more pest-susceptible. However, some diseases that reside in garden soil, like club root, can be controlled by adjusting pH.

Look for a soil pH value among your soil test results. Soil testing laboratories will supply you with instructions for adjusting pH based on the kind of crops that you plan to grow.

Azaleas and rhododendrons grow best when the soil is acid. In high pH soils, the leaves will turn yellow.

Testing Your Soil

It's easy to collect a soil sample with a trowel. First, brush any debris from the surface.

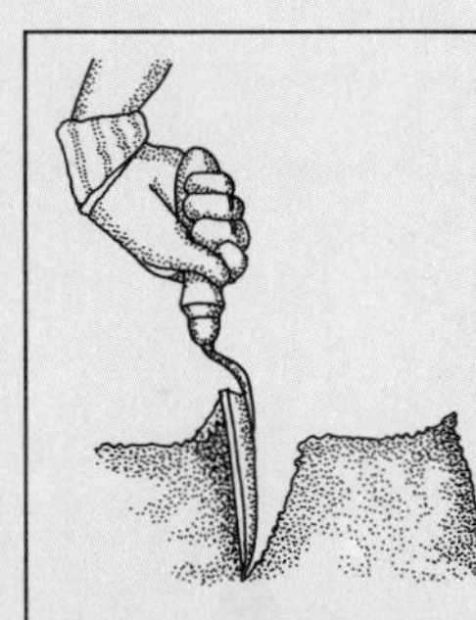

Insert the trowel and push it forward.

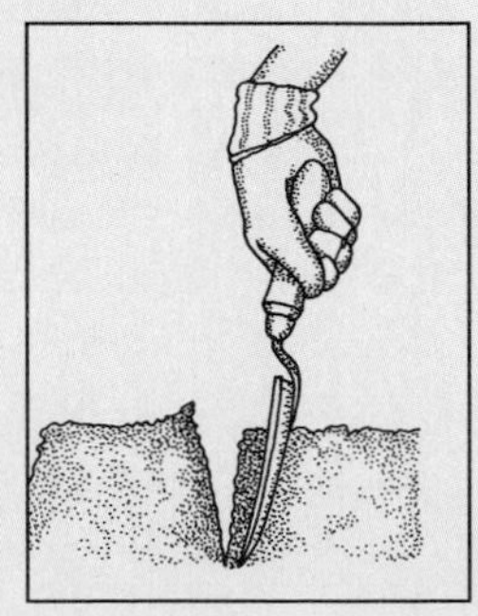

Make another cut behind; remove the slice.

Watering Wisely

When and how you water your plants can have a great effect on the development of plant diseases. Water is the vehicle that helps plant pathogens spread quickly throughout your garden. Pathogens move from infected to healthy plants by traveling in run-off water, splashing rain drops, and wind-blown rain. (They also travel in the soil that clings to tools, boots, and the hands and clothing of gardeners.)

Most pathogens can remain dormant in the soil for several years, then become activated when water films form on plant surfaces. That's why you'll find more symptoms of plant disease after periods of high humidity or rainfall. Some diseases, like apple scab and late blight of potatoes, require a moist period of the right length and temperature in order to infect healthy plants. Some pathogens, like downy mildew, stop developing when conditions dry out. But once they're established on a host, many fungal pathogens continue to develop and cause damage even in dry weather.

Keep your plants healthy by giving them a steady supply of water throughout the season. Buy a rain gauge at your local hardware store and use it to monitor weekly rainfall. Most flowers and vegetable plants need about 1 inch (2.5 cm) of water per week; woody plants like trees and shrubs can often get by on half that amount. In hot, dry climates, plants will require more water; in cool climates, plants need less. To be sure your plants are getting the moisture they need, check the soil in the root zone. Use a trowel to dig a small hole 4 to 6 inches (10 to 15 cm) deep. If the soil at that level is dry, it's time to water.

Overhead irrigation can wet flowers and foliage, providing ideal conditions for diseases to develop.

Collect rain water for garden use in large wooden or plastic barrels, and use it to douse thirsty plants nearby.

How to Water

You can catch rainwater in barrels placed under rain spouts, then use a watering can to replenish soil moisture in small gardens. In larger gardens, you can use drip irrigation or overhead sprinklers. Drip systems may have individual emitters, which direct water to the base of each plant, or soaker hoses, which ooze water evenly along their length.

A drip system initially costs more than a sprinkler, but it also offers several advantages. It's low maintenance, since you don't have to stand there and hold the hose or run around to move the sprinkler. Drip irrigation systems are water-efficient, as virtually all of the water that is released goes into the soil. (Overhead systems are notorious water-wasters, since part of the water they spray in the air is lost to evaporation and some of it is lost to runoff.) And drip-irrigated crops are much less disease-prone than overhead-watered crops, since the foliage stays dry.

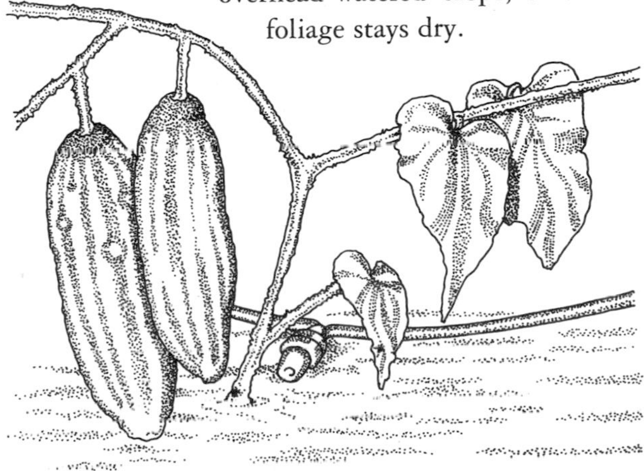

Drip irrigation systems with individual emitters deliver a supply of water directly to the base of each plant.

Planning Crop Rotations

Crop rotation involves planting your annual crops in different areas of the garden each year. This is an easy and effective way to avoid the buildup of some soil-dwelling pests and pathogens, like pest nematodes and potato scab. Since different plants grow on the same site each year, pests and diseases won't always have the host that they prefer, so their populations won't be able to build up to damaging levels.

Get Organized

On the most basic level, you can simply remember where you planted a particular crop one year and put it in another spot the following year. This will be even easier if you kept notes of where each crop was planted.

If you're willing to spend a few more minutes, you can create a simple rotation system. One easy approach is to separate your crops into three types—root, leafy, and fruit crops. Or to get the greatest level of protection against pest and disease buildup, arrange your crops in groups by their botanical family (such as Solanaceae for tomatoes and peppers and Leguminosae for peas and beans). Check "Rotation Guidelines" to see which families your crops belong to.

Put It on Paper

The more complex your rotation plan, the more important it is to jot it down on paper. To create your plan, draw the borders of your garden on a piece of graph paper, then divide the space into the same number of areas as you have crop categories. If you've decided to go with the root, leafy, and fruit crop system, for example, you'd divide your gardening space into three areas.

Now write the crop categories on index cards or slips of paper, one category per card. Deal the cards out onto your garden plan, one card for each growing area. Make a note of where each card falls. This will give you the plan for the first year.

While you're at it, figure out the next few years as well. For a basic rotation, it may be as simple as shifting each card to the next bed in sequence. Or you may want to take advantage of the fact that some crops grow better after other crops. "Rotation Guidelines" tells you the relative nutrient needs of the basic vegetable groups and their suggested place in a rotation.

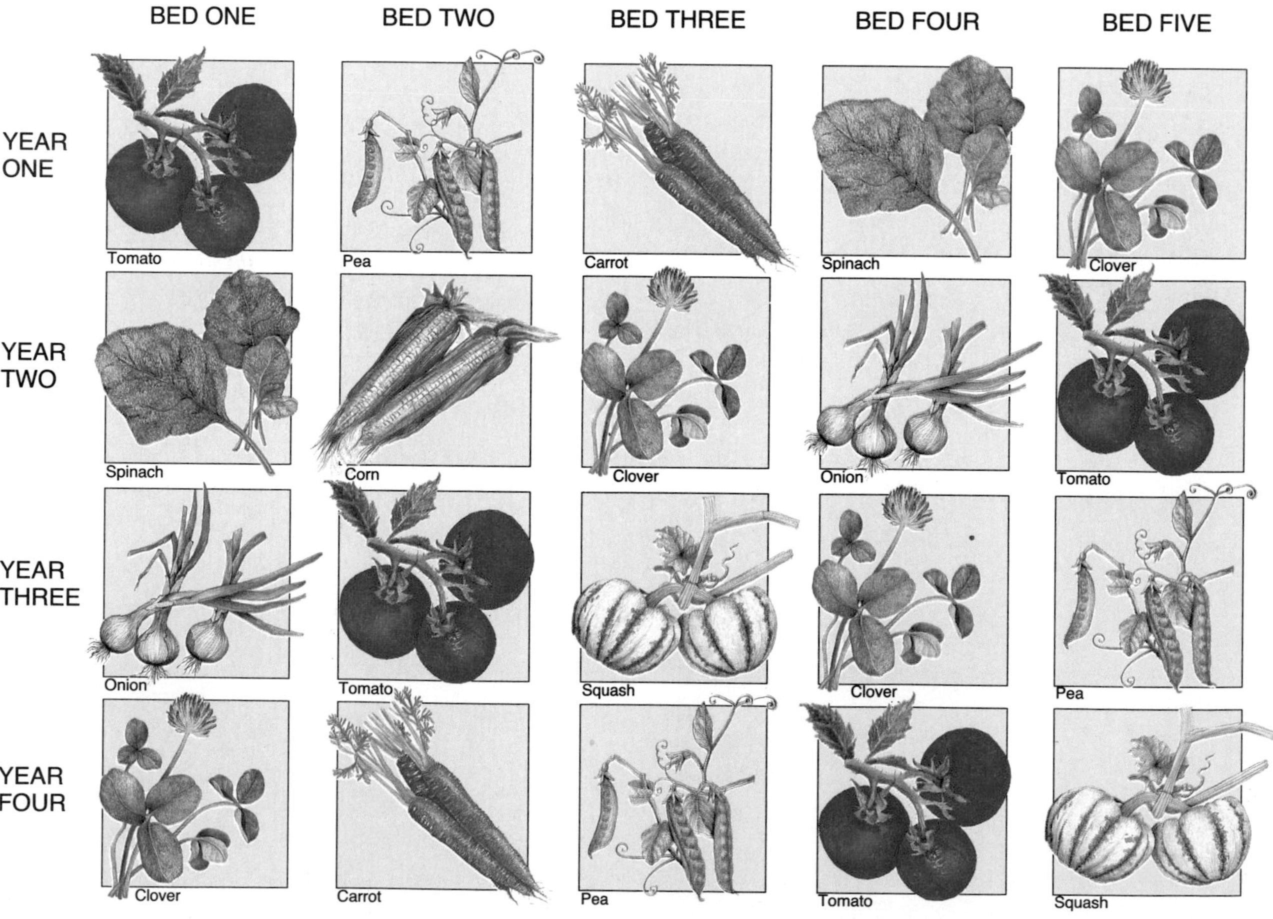

This sample rotation was worked out by a gardener for the next four growing seasons. Each year includes tomatoes (a family favorite) and a soil-improving crop. Other crops are included as space permits.

Rotation Guidelines

Crop Group	Members	Nutrient Demands	Rotation Sequence
Beet family (Chenopodiaceae)	Beets, spinach, Swiss chard	Light feeders	After other light feeders; before soil-improving crops
Cabbage family (Cruciferae)	Broccoli, cabbages, kale, rutabagas, radishes, turnips	Heavy feeders	After pea family or onion family members; before root crops family members
Carrot family (Umbelliferae)	Carrots, celery, parsnips, parsley	Light feeders	After most crops; before soil-improving crops
Grass family (Gramineae)	Sweet corn, cover crops like rye, oats, wheat	Heavy feeders	After pea family or cabbage family members; before potatoes, fruit crops, or squash family members
Onion family (Liliaceae)	Garlic, leeks, onions, shallots	Light feeders	After most heavy feeders; before soil-improving crops
Pea family (Leguminosae)	Beans, lentils, peas, alfalfa, clovers, vetches	Light feeders	After other light feeders; before most crops
Squash family (Cucurbitaceae)	Cucumbers, gourds, melons, pumpkins, squashes	Heavy feeders	After soil-improving crops; before pea family members
Tomato family (Solanaceae)	Eggplants, ground cherries, peppers, potatoes, tomatoes	Heavy feeders	After grass family crops; before pea family members or leafy crops
Fruit crops	Tomatoes, peppers, melons	Heavy feeders	After pea family members; before light feeders
Leafy crops	Arugula, chard, endive, kale, lettuce, mizuna, spinach	Moderate feeders	After heavy feeders; before onion family members or root crops
Root and bulb crops	Beets, carrots, radishes onions, parsnips, potatoes, rutabagas	Light feeders	After heavy feeders; before soil-improving crops
Soil-improving crops	Buckwheat, clovers, oats, rye, vetches, wheat	Light feeders	After other light feeders; before most crops

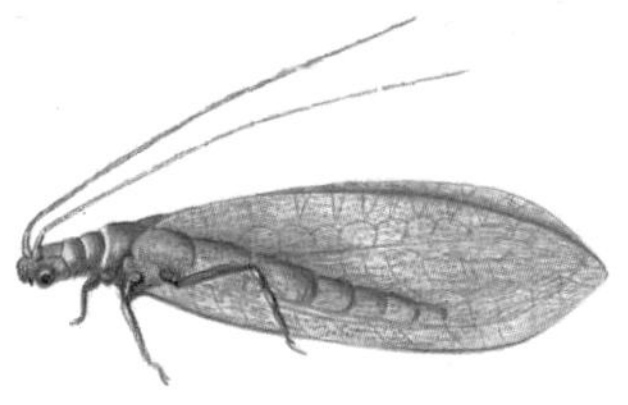

IDENTIFYING GARDEN INSECTS

Whether we like it or not, insects are here to stay. They can survive in almost every environment—from hot, dry deserts to lakes and ponds, within and on people, animals, and plants. In this chapter, you'll learn more about the wide diversity of insects that live in your garden.

Understanding a bit about how insects are put together and how they live will help you identify the ones you come across in your plantings. While we've tried to keep jargon to a minimum, there are some basic terms—like "metamorphosis" and "thorax"—that come up over and over in insect descriptions. "What Is an Insect?" on page 26 gives you the information you need to decipher some of these common insect-related terms.

As you read about the different kinds of insect feeding habits, you may be surprised to learn that not all insects feed on plants—some eat decaying materials or even other insects. Insects and their relatives that prey on pests are called beneficials. In nature, and in organic gardens, beneficials play a major role in keeping pest populations in check. Provide beneficials with their basic needs—food, water, and shelter—and they'll repay you with free and effective natural pest control.

Becoming familiar with the creatures that live on and around your plants is a key part of creating a healthy, successful garden. As you work in or walk through the garden, take time to really look at your plants and the insects that are present. Flip through the photographs in the "Insect and Disease Guide," starting on page 76, and in insect field guides. Eventually, you'll begin to recognize some of the most common pest and beneficial insects. By knowing which are harmful and which are helpful, you'll know which ones to control and which ones to protect.

Regularly scouting for plant damage will help you catch problems before they get out of hand. If you need to plan a pest control strategy, see "Managing Insect Pests," starting on page 32. If you suspect that diseases or animals are causing the damage, see "Identifying Plant Diseases" on page 44, "Managing Plant Diseases" on page 54, and "Identifying and Managing Animal Pests" on page 64.

Opposite: Before you grab the sprayer, make sure you know what insect you're looking at. These creatures, for instance, may look like pests, but they are actually beneficial rove beetles poking around for prey.

Aphids aren't fussy feeders. These pernicious pests will attack a wide range of plants, from tulips to turnips.

What Is a Pest?

You probably think of insects as pests—and sometimes they are! But the term "pest" isn't reserved exclusively for insects. A pest can be any organism that damages our plants and reduces our harvest. By this definition, common garden pests can include insects, other arthropods (like mites), snails and slugs, birds, mammals, nematodes, weeds, and plant pathogens. In this book, though, we'll use the term "pest" to mean insects and their relatives—like mites, slugs, and snails—unless specified otherwise.

What Is an Insect?

Before you can decide how to deal with the insects in your garden, you need to know some basic things about how they are put together and how they survive. By taking a few minutes to review the bit of insect biology discussed here, you'll have the basic knowledge you need to understand and cope with these creatures.

Insects 101

Insects are an extremely complex group of organisms. They can be smaller than the head of a pin or as wide as your hand, as brightly colored as a swallowtail butterfly or as camouflaged as a cabbageworm. Regardless of their size, shape, or color, insects share a number of characteristics that set them apart from other organisms. True insects have three distinct body divisions: the head, the thorax (where legs and wings are attached), and the abdomen. They also have three pairs of legs (unlike spiders and mites, which have four pairs), one pair of antennae, and at least one pair of large, compound eyes. All of the creatures with these traits are grouped into the class Insecta.

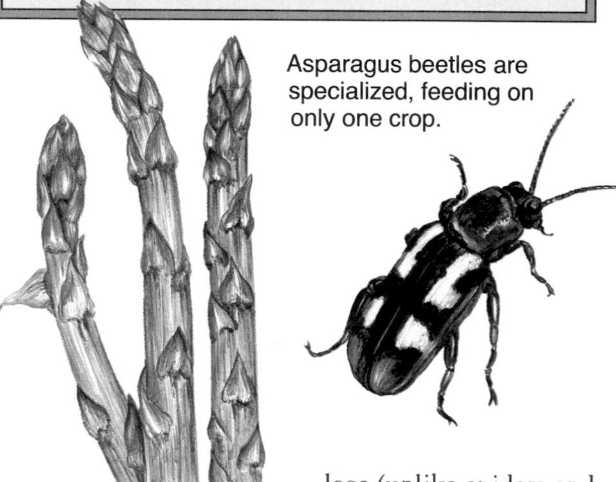

Asparagus beetles are specialized, feeding on only one crop.

Insects are particularly well adapted to be successful pests. A hard external skeleton protects them from the environment, from predation by other insects or animals, and from some of the control strategies of gardeners. They reproduce quickly and exhibit a wide array of protective coloring and camouflage that helps to keep them hidden. Considering their small size, insects are incredibly fast and strong. They are the only group of organisms besides birds and bats that are capable of flight. This gives them the ability to spread quickly and travel long distances to your garden.

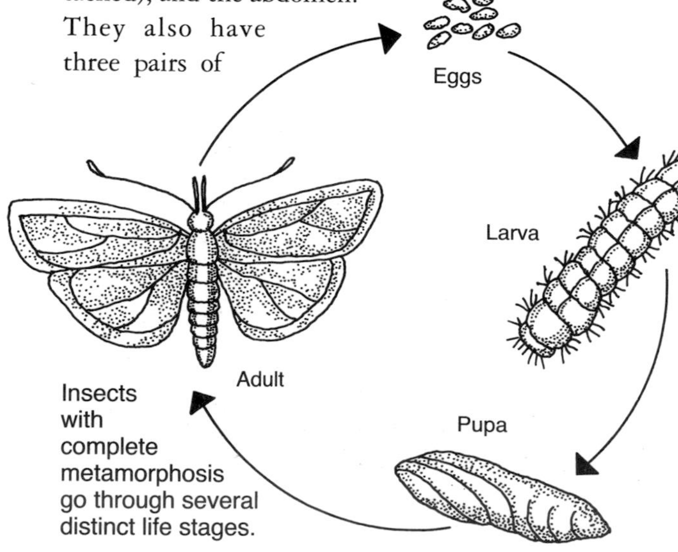

Insects with complete metamorphosis go through several distinct life stages.

Life Cycles

The series of changes that occur during an insect's growth and life stages are called metamorphosis. Most of the insects you'll encounter in your garden follow one of two patterns of metamorphosis: complete or incomplete.

Complete Metamorphosis Bees, beetles, butterflies, true flies, moths, and wasps exhibit complete metamorphosis. These insects pass through four life stages: the egg, a worm-like larval stage, the pupa, and the adult. Larvae, with their typically voracious appetites, are commonly known as caterpillars, grubs, or maggots. Larvae molt (shed their skin) several times, then enter a pupal or "cocoon" stage, from which they later emerge as an adult. Larvae that undergo complete metamorphosis usually eat different food and live in different habitats than the adults.

Incomplete Metamorphosis Insects with incomplete metamorphosis—like aphids, crickets, grasshoppers, and plant bugs—hatch from eggs into nymphs that closely resemble the adult stage. Nymphs undergo a period of growth and molting, gradually maturing to adults. Adults and nymphs of insects that undergo incomplete metamorphosis eat the same kind of food and share the same types of habitat.

Feeding Habits

Insects are also categorized by the food they eat. Most insects fall within one of four dining categories: herbivores, carnivores, scavengers, or omnivores.

Herbivores Insects that feed on plant parts are called herbivores. Some insects, including many common garden pests, are highly specific and feed only upon a certain plant species or its close relatives. For example, the asparagus beetle (*Crioceris* spp.) only feeds on asparagus. The cabbage maggot (*Delia radicum*) relishes the roots of most cabbage family members. The herbivore group contains the insects that you'll need to keep under control in the garden.

Carnivores Many mosquitoes, flies, midges, lice, and fleas depend on a meal of blood to complete their life cycle. Other carnivorous insects feast upon insects or other garden critters like slugs and worms. These are the beneficial insects that will help keep pest species

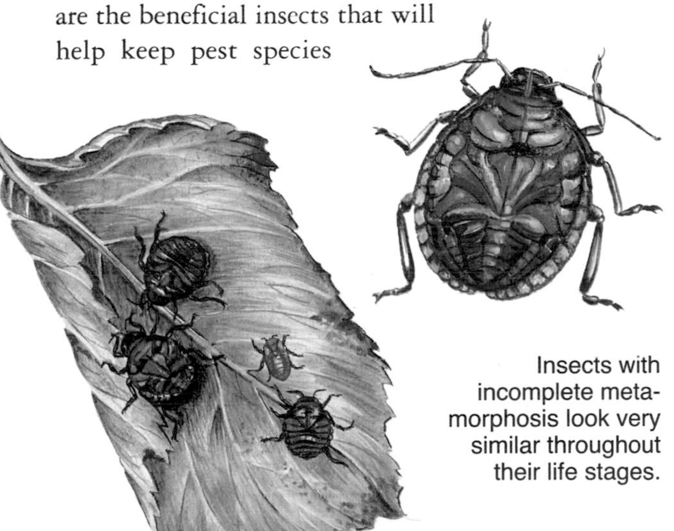

Insects with incomplete metamorphosis look very similar throughout their life stages.

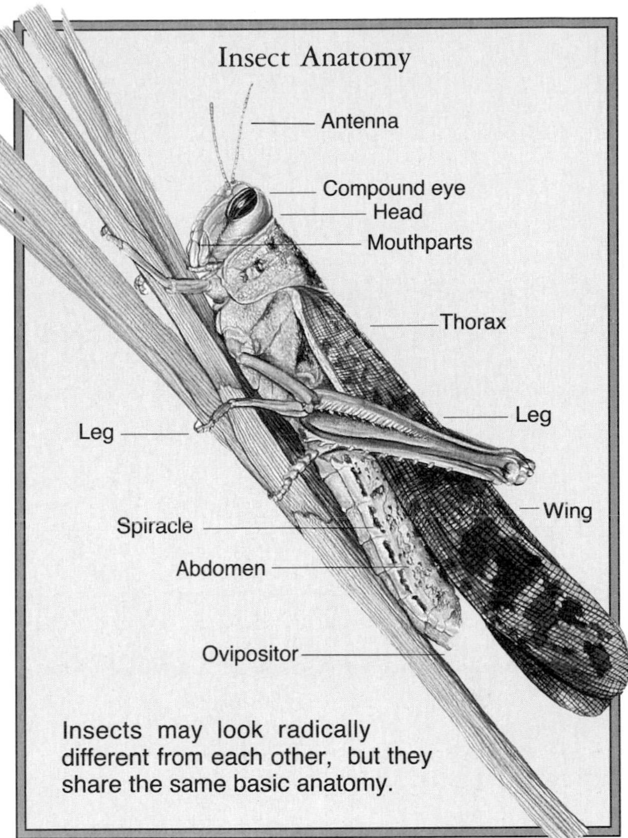

Insects may look radically different from each other, but they share the same basic anatomy.

from getting out of hand. To learn more about carnivorous insects that help to control pests, read "Beneficial Insects" on page 28.

Scavengers These insects are the recyclers of the insect world. They perform an important service by feeding and breaking down decaying plants and animals. Included are dung beetles, carrion beetles, housefly larvae, carpenter ants, termites, and many others.

Omnivores Some insects are able to eat almost anything they can get their claws on, including soap, starch, and glue. These insects, including earwigs, silverfish, and cockroaches, are common indoor pests.

Not all insects have wings, but the ones that do—like this hawk moth—can travel great distances in search of food.

Beneficial Insects

Almost none of the insects that you'll come across in the garden are harmful to you or your plants. Some insects feed primarily on wild plants and leave your garden plants alone. Other insect species directly benefit the garden. Wild and domestic bees, for example, perform vital functions like pollination. And some species survive by preying (feeding) on or parasitizing (living within) other insects.

The species that attack other insects are especially significant, since they're one of the tools you can rely on for pest control. In this section, you'll learn about the different types of beneficial insects and how to attract them to your garden. For photographs and descriptions of particular species, see the "Beneficials" section of the "Insect and Disease Guide," starting on page 76.

Praying mantids aren't picky—they'll eat any insects that cross their path, pest and beneficial species alike.

Bees are a vital part of a healthy garden. Without their pollination efforts, many plants could not set fruit or seed.

Other Beneficial Critters

Insects aren't the only beneficial creatures in your garden. Lizards and toads consume their share of pest insects, and snakes help to keep rodent populations in control. Bats consume thousands of mosquitoes each night, while barn swallows, purple martins, woodpeckers, and other birds control flying insects by day. To learn more about these and other helpful garden denizens, see "Beneficial Animals" on page 66.

Predators

Some species of lady beetles feed only on aphids.

Predators eat other organisms. Most insect predators, like ground beetles or rove beetles, aren't fussy eaters. They're called generalists, and they'll eat pest insects as well as fellow predators that are small enough to catch. Other predaceous insects are prey-specific. For example, some lady beetle species prefer spider mites, some consume only mealybugs, and others restrict their diet to aphids. Not all predators are insects. Insect predators like spiders, centipedes, and several species of mites are also important pest controllers.

Parasites

Parasites are among the most important biological pest controls. They live on or in other organisms. Parasites steal nutrients from their host but usually don't kill it.

Parasitoids are a special kind of parasite. They make ideal biological pest controllers because they kill their host. Most parasitoids are tiny, aggressive wasps or bees that lay their eggs within the living host. Parasitoid larvae hatch and consume their host, then form a cocoon before emerging as adults that are eager to find more pests. Most parasitoids are species- and host-specific. One kind may attack only a pest's larval stage, for example, while another kind will parasitize the adult form of the same pest.

Attracting Beneficials

You can entice beneficials to frequent your yard and garden by providing them with the three basic necessities: water, food, and shelter.

Water A water source will attract most kinds of beneficials (as well as insect-eating birds and toads), especially during dry spells. Fill shallow pans with water and set them in protected nooks and corners of your garden. Set rocks in the pans to serve as insect perches.

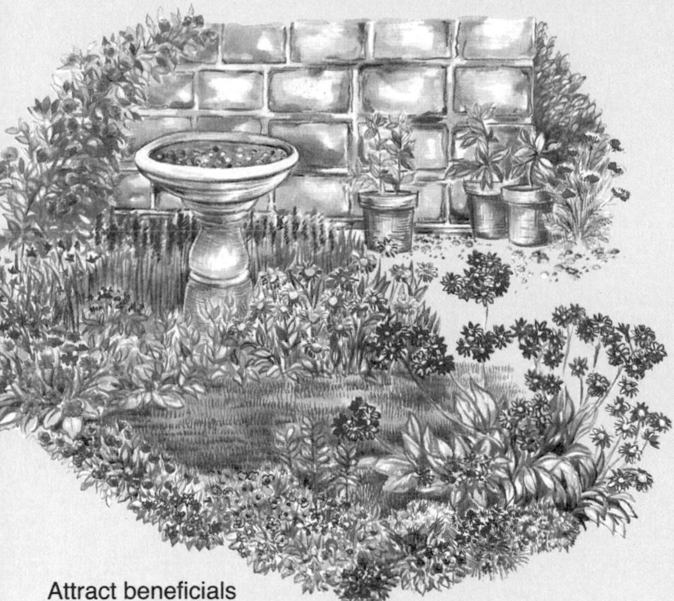

Attract beneficials to your garden with diverse plantings and a water source.

Food Access to suitable food is vital for beneficials. During various stages of their life, beneficials may need different types of food. Larvae, for instance, often prey on pests, while adults feed on pollen and nectar.

Small-flowered plants are ideal food sources for beneficials. Particularly good choices include members of the plant families Umbelliferae (such as dill, lovage, parsley, and fennel) and Labiatae (including mint, hyssop, catnip, and lemon balm). You may already have many of these growing in your herb garden or flower border. Plant them among vegetables as well to attract beneficials where pests are particularly a problem.

Spiders can play an important role in controlling garden pests.

Weeds and flowering cover crops like buckwheat, clover, and alfalfa are also good food sources. Garden-supply companies even sell special bug attractants to encourage creatures like lacewings and lady beetles to stay in your garden.

Shelter Once they have food and water, beneficials will look for a safe place to live and to lay their eggs. Provide shelter by adding organic mulches like straw, leaves, or compost to the soil surface around plants and along paths. Beneficials also appreciate the protection of trees, perennial plantings, and cover crops that aren't frequently disturbed by harvest and tillage.

You can maintain a friendly environment for beneficials by avoiding broad-spectrum pesticides (those that kill a wide range of insects). Even organically acceptable chemicals like rotenone will wipe out beneficials as readily as pests. Often, pest populations recover more quickly than the beneficials and multiply unchecked. This leads to a vicious circle—since you'll need to apply stronger control measures more frequently, the beneficials will not get a chance to recover.

Adults lacewings feed mostly on nectar and honeydew, but their larvae are voracious predators of many pest insects.

Yarrow is an excellent source of both pollen and nectar for beneficials. Daisies and coneflowers are also good sources.

Diagnosing Insect Damage

If pests stood up to be counted, gardeners would find pest identification and control an easier task. Unfortunately, pests often remain undetected until the harm is done. Even if you do spot damage, you may have difficulty identifying the culprit. Insects, diseases, and even environmental problems like nutrient deficiencies or air pollution can cause similar symptoms. But getting an accurate diagnosis is the only way to choose an appropriate and effective control measure.

Follow the Signs

Fortunately, there are clues you can look for to help pin down plant problems. Follow the steps below to spot developing damage and to identify the causes.

1. Give plantsr a thorough inspection at least once a week. Look at both sides of the leaves, around buds and flowers, and along the stems.

2. If you find damage, jot down a few notes: the identity of the affected plant, the plant parts that are affected, and the kind of damage (such as "large holes in leaves" or "distorted fruit").

Check the undersides of plant leaves, and shallowly scratch the soil or mulch, looking for likely culprits. Also search for clusters of eggs, webs, or pellet- or sawdust-like insect droppings. See if neighboring plants show similar symptoms.

3. If you actually find insects, examine them with a 10X magnifying lens (available through garden suppliers or at college bookstores). Look through the photos in the "Insect and Disease Guide," starting on page 76, to see if you can identify the insects. You can also buy insect field guides with keys for identifying unknown insects. Don't assume that the insects must be pests—they could just as easily be beneficials that stopped by to help or simply innocent bystanders!

4. If you can't find any suspects, or can't identify the ones you have, try matching the damage symptoms with those in "Signs of Damage" on page 31. This approach may help you close in on a possible cause.

5. If you still aren't sure of the cause, consider other possible sources, like wind damage, nutrient deficiency, or animal pests. You'll find information on these kinds of damage in "Disease Look-alikes" on page 52 and "Identifying and Managing Animal Pests," starting on page 64.

6. If all else fails, you may want to take your notes and perhaps a piece of the affected plant to your local Cooperative Extension Service or garden center for help in making an accurate diagnosis.

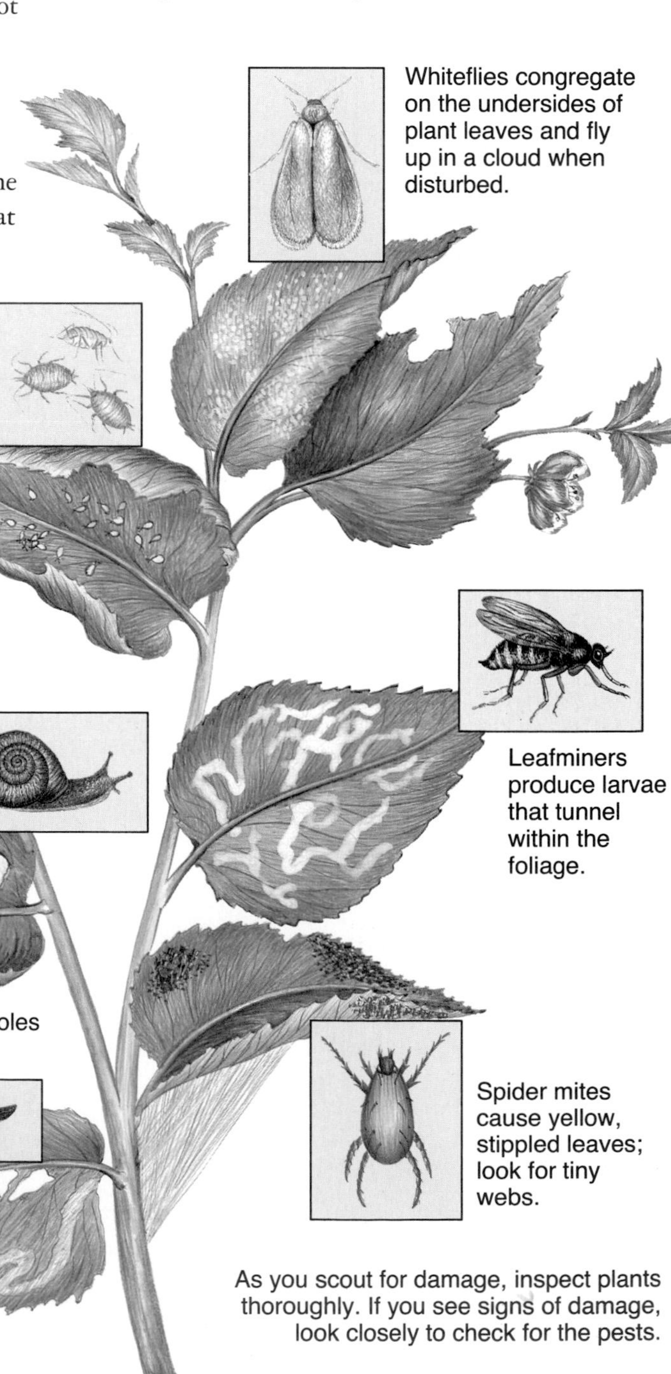

As you scout for damage, inspect plants thoroughly. If you see signs of damage, look closely to check for the pests.

Signs of Damage

When you find signs of damage, look for a description of the damage in the column on the left, then check the possible causes in the column on the right. Look up possible insect pests in the "Insect and Disease Guide," starting on page 76, for photographs, descriptions, and control information. To learn more about plant diseases and nutrient deficiencies, see "Diagnosing Disease Problems" on page 48 and " Disease Look-alikes" on page 52.

Damage	Possible Causes
Leaves with large, ragged holes	Adult or larval stages of beetles like Japanese beetles, Mexican bean beetles, and others; grasshoppers; moth larvae like armyworms or hornworms; slugs or snails; animal pests
Leaves curled, twisted, puckered, or distorted	Aphids; leafhoppers; tarnished plant bugs; nutrient deficiency
Leaves curled, webs present	Webworms; obliquebanded leafrollers
Leaves with numerous, small holes	Adult flea beetles; plant diseases
Leaves spotted	Tarnished plant bugs; spider mites; thrips; lace bugs; plant diseases
Leaves or stems speckled or silvery	Thrips
Leaves and stems with hardened bumps, scales, or cottony growths	Scales; mealybugs; plant diseases
Leaves with shallow tunnels under leaf surface	Larval leafminers; sawflies
Leaves with shiny, slimy, frothy, or sticky coating	Aphids; mealybugs; slugs and snails; pear psyllas; scales; spittlebugs; whiteflies; plant diseases
Fruit with tunnels throughout	Apple maggots; moth larvae like codling moths or European corn borers
Fruit distorted, twisted	European corn borers; tarnished plant bugs
Fruit spotted, sticky	Aphids; leafhoppers; spittlebugs; plant diseases
Roots or bulbs with signs of feeding or dead spots	Wireworms; many kinds of beetle grubs; weevils (black vine, carrot, or strawberry root weevils)
Roots or stems with galls, swellings	Gall wasps; nematodes; plant diseases
Roots or stems with excessive branching	Nematodes
Stems hollowed, with larvae inside and leaves wilted	Borers (European corn, flatheaded appletree, fruit, peachtree, roundheaded appletree, and squash vine borers)
Flowers eaten	Japanese beetles; rose chafers
Flowers fall before opening	Tarnished plant bugs
Seedlings chewed off at soil level	Cutworms; animal pests

Managing Insect Pests

Keeping garden pests under control doesn't have to require unpronounceable synthetic chemicals and fancy spray equipment. In this chapter, you'll learn how to use simple growing methods and common household items like petroleum jelly, dish soap, and portable vacuum cleaners to control many of the pests that attack your garden plants.

Effective management begins with regular pest patrols. Each week, carefully check plants for signs of damage and pests. Routinely scouting for pests will help you spot problems before they do serious damage to your crops. If you do spot damage, you need to identify the cause properly. If you don't know what's causing the problems, chances are that you won't pick an effective control measure. Review the information in "Diagnosing Insect Damage" on page 30 to help you find and identify the culprit.

When you have identified the pest, look it up in the "Insect and Disease Guide," starting on page 76. There you'll find photos of the pest, along with information on its life cycle, favorite food sources, common damage symptoms, and suggested control measures. Then come back to this chapter to learn the details on how these control measures work.

If you've had problems in previous years or if you want to stop pests before they get out of control, try a combination of preventive measures. Choosing well-adapted plants, putting them in the right place, and meeting their growth needs will go a long way toward making plants naturally healthy. You can also look for species and cultivars that have been noted for their pest resistance. Keeping the garden free of debris will remove pest hiding places. Gardening techniques like crop rotation, timed plantings, companion planting, and trap crops are other ways to keep pests from running rampant through your plants.

Protecting plants with covers and other barriers is a more active type of control measure. Row covers and plant screens keep flying insects away from your plants. Block crawling pests with sticky trunk bands, copper strips, cutworm collars, and other barrier strips.

If pests do appear on your plants, it's time to look to tougher measures. Handpicking pests is a simple but effective control. Various kinds of traps will lure pests away from your plants, thereby reducing damage. Encouraging native beneficial insects and supplementing them with purchased species are other ways to let nature help control the problem for you. You can even take advantage of the microorganisms that cause insect diseases, like bacteria and nematodes.

When prevention and other controls don't work, it's time to use serious measures. Insecticidal soaps, botanical insecticides, and other sprays are generally considered the tools of last resort, since they can kill beneficial organisms as well as the pests. But if your plants or crops are threatened, choosing appropriate sprays and using them carefully may be your only option. Once you have the problem under control, take some time to figure out how it happened and to plan suitable preventive measures to keep the problem from recurring.

Opposite: Many of the insects that you'll see in the garden aren't pests at all! Some insects help you by feeding on pest species; others, like bees, ensure good yields by pollinating flowers.

Preventing Pest Problems

Effective pest management begins with cultural controls. Cultural controls include all the techniques you use to grow healthy plants and to make your garden less desirable to pests. Providing good growing conditions, keeping the garden clean, and using methods like companion planting all help make plants less prone to problems. Cultural controls may not help once a specific problem occurs, but they will go a long way toward preventing plant damage.

Create a Good Growing Environment

When plants have all the things they need for good growth—like adequate light, moisture, and nutrients—they'll be vigorous and naturally pest-resistant. For the basics on creating the best garden environment, see "Your Healthy Garden" on page 14.

Crop rotation can reduce the buildup of some garden pests.

Choose Resistant Cultivars

As you choose new plants, select species and cultivars that are easy to grow and quick to mature so they'll have the best chance to beat the pests. Try new cultivars each season, and compare their durability and pest resistance with that of your favorites. Watch seed catalogs for new developments in insect-resistant vegetables, like sweet corn with tight ear tips that keep out corn earworms or green beans with hairy pods and leaves that deter leafhoppers and beetle larvae. If you save seed from your crops, collect it only from the healthiest plants that were least attacked by pests. You'll gradually develop your own strains of pest-resistant plants.

Keeping your garden neat and free of debris helps remove overwintering sites for pests and disease spores.

For the best yields, look for cultivars that are resistant to the common pests found in your area.

Keep the Garden Clean

To avoid importing insects and other problems, inspect new plants for signs of insects, like damage, droppings, or webs. The garden debris that can build up over the season—like dropped leaves, dead stems, and overripe fruit—is an ideal hiding place for pests and disease organisms, so remove it regularly and put it in a hot compost pile. (See "Improving Your Soil" on page 18 for instructions on creating a hot compost pile.) If soilborne pests like grubs and wireworms were a real problem last season, consider heat-treating your soil with solar energy; see "Solarize Your Soil" on page 60 for complete instructions.

Check plants regularly to catch pests before they cause serious damage.

Adjust Planting Patterns

In the vegetable garden, you have the freedom to adapt your planting techniques to help prevent problems. You may consider changing planting areas, with crop

The colorful blooms of zinnias and other daisy-like flowers attract beneficial insects that help control pests.

Some gardeners claim that nasturtiums can repel a variety of garden pests from cabbage seedlings.

Interplanted radishes may help protect squash and cucumber plants from cucumber beetles and squash bugs.

rotation, or sowing dates, with timed plantings. Other tricks involve combining compatible plants to benefit your crops (companion planting) or concentrating pests in one area (trap crops).

Crop Rotation Changing the place you plant your crops each year is a good way to prevent the buildup of soilborne pests and diseases. For complete details on using crop rotation for pest control, see "Planning Crop Rotations" on page 22.

Timed Planting If you know that the damaging stage of a particular pest is only at a certain time of year, you can plant your crops earlier or later than normal to avoid the pest. An extra-early planting of radishes, for instance, will be much less prone to damage by cabbage maggots. If timed planting is a viable solution to a particular pest, you'll find timing hints in the "Insect and Disease Guide," starting on page 76.

Companion Planting Growing a planned diversity of vegetables, herbs, and ornamentals in a given area is a technique some gardeners use to confuse or repel pests. Mixing herbs and flowers with vegetables and fruit plantings is also a good way to attract beneficial insects. (To learn more about encouraging these helpful creatures, see "Beneficial Insects" on page 28.)

Trap Crops It may seem like a strange idea, but some gardeners deliberately include insect-prone plants in their garden. This method is known as trap cropping. Once pests are concentrated on the trap crop, you can spray or destroy it and thereby remove the pests. Trap crops also help by luring pests away from your good crops. For instance, an early crop of mustard will lure flea beetles away from your cabbage seedlings; then, you can sacrifice the mustard crop.

Plant trap crops around the border of your garden or between crop rows. Early in the season, consider starting trap crops indoors in pots and then moving the pots outdoors near rows of tender seedlings. To protect your onion crops, for example, start onion sets indoors, then move the pots outdoors next to rows of onion seedlings. Onion maggot flies will be attracted to the older plants. Wait several weeks, then pull and destroy the potted onions, along with the pests.

Lovage lures hornworms from your tomato plants.

Keeping Pests Off Plants

If pests can't reach your plants, they can't cause damage. This is why physical barriers are so effective in keeping your garden plants problem-free. Obviously, they won't help if pests are already on the plants, so these measures need to be in place before pests appear.

Plant and Row Covers

Physically covering or screening your plants works to control pest insects that crawl or fly into your garden. It's also useful for preventing damage from animal pests like groundhogs, rabbits, and birds. Covering plants won't control pests already waiting in garden soil, like Colorado potato beetles or corn rootworms.

You can purchase row cover fabric made from several lightweight synthetic materials in various thicknesses, widths, and lengths. These fabrics are often called floating row covers since they are light enough to rest directly on your plants without causing damage. They allow air, water, and light to pass through while keeping out most pests. Cover rows, beds, or fruit-bearing shrubs and trees with the fabric. Bury the edges with soil, stones, or bricks, leaving enough slack to allow small plants to grow upward. You can make or buy hoop supports to keep the fabric off very tender crops like lettuce. You will have to lift the fabric to weed or harvest. Since it also traps heat, you may want to remove the fabric from heat-sensitive crops, like kale, during hot spells.

If you're the do-it-yourself type, build screened cages for plants, rows, or beds. Construct a wooden frame, then staple screening or fabric to the outside.

Remove covers permanently when plants are large enough to withstand some damage, when pests are no longer a threat, or after you've harvested the crop. If you use covers on insect-pollinated crops like squash, remove the covers when flowers appear—otherwise, you'll have to hand-pollinate the flowers to get fruit.

Homemade paper or cardboard collars will protect seedlings from cutworm damage.

If slugs or earwigs have damaged your plants in the past, try trapping them in inverted pots. Check traps daily.

Sticky Trunk Bands

Create a barrier around tree trunks to stop crawling pests like ants, codling moth and gypsy moth caterpillars, leaf beetles, and snails and slugs. Wrap a 3- to 5-inch (7.5 to 12.5 cm) wide band of heavy fabric, paper, or corrugated cardboard around the trunk; fasten the ends with duct tape. Coat the band with a commercial sticky coating, like Tanglefoot, or make your own sticky stuff by mixing equal parts of petroleum jelly or mineral oil with liquid dish soap. Pests on their way up or down the tree will get stuck.

Fasten sticky bands to tree trunks to trap pests like caterpillars and some beetles as they climb.

When the bands are filled with pests, discard them and replace with fresh materials.

Copper Strips

If slugs and snails are a real problem in your garden or greenhouse, try using copper barriers to protect your plants. The pests get an electric shock when they touch the copper and will look elsewhere for food.

Place a continuous edge of copper-backed paper, or strips of copper sheeting, around the plants or beds you want to protect. Staple the materials to raised bed frames, garden fences, or greenhouse bench legs; use duct tape to fasten copper bands around tree trunks. To form an extra barrier, fold down the top ½ inch (12 mm) of the strips at a right angle (like an upside-down L). Copper strips won't affect any slugs or snails that are already within the protected area. You may have to trap or handpick those pests before the copper strips will provide control.

Try a two-part approach against gypsy moths: destroy the fuzzy yellow egg masses produced by the female moth, and use trunk bands to trap the larvae.

Plant Collars and Barriers

You can protect individual seedlings from crawling pests like cutworms by placing collars, made from recycled cardboard tubes, around plant stems. Use scissors or a sharp knife to cut the tubes into 2- to 3-inch (5 to 7.5 cm) lengths, then slide them over plant stems while transplanting. Push the tubes partly into the soil to settle them. By the time the cardboard breaks down, your plants will be past the susceptible stage. Rings of heavy paper will also work.

Poorly applied trunk wraps can actually encourage pests. Wrap only the base of the trunk, and ensure the layers overlap.

Squares or circles of heavy paper, cut to fit around the base of your plants, will prevent root maggot flies from laying eggs at the base of susceptible seedlings, like broccoli, cabbage, and onions.

An alternative barrier for crawling pests is a 2- to 3-inch (5 to 7.5 cm) strip of abrasive material on soil around plants, beds, or trees. Scratchy dusts and powders like diatomaceous earth, wood ashes, crushed eggshells, or seashells pierce the insect pest's waxy coating, causing dehydration and death. They also deter slugs and snails. Diatomaceous earth and ashes are most effective when kept dry; replace them after rain. Diatomaceous earth also controls pests when used as a dust on foliage.

Mulch Matters

Mulching is a routine part of conserving soil moisture and preventing weeds, but it's also effective in controlling some pests and diseases. Materials like newspaper, biodegradable paper mulch, and black plastic mulch help to control thrips, leafminers, and other pests that must reach the soil to complete their life cycle. Strips of aluminum foil repel aphids, leafhoppers, and thrips on garden and greenhouse crops. (Leave the foil in place only as long as pests are a threat, to avoid leaf damage from reflected heat.) Mulches also prevent raindrops from splashing soilborne disease spores onto plant leaves.

To keep slugs from attacking your beautiful berries, grow plants in raised beds surrounded by copper strips.

If pests start damaging your plants, consider more active control measures, like handpicking or trapping.

What to Do If Pests Appear

If pests arrive and begin damaging plants, it's time to consider tougher control measures. Unlike barriers, these types of physical controls involve actually removing pests from plants, either by handpicking or by luring them away with a variety of traps. You can also supplement native populations of beneficial insects by purchasing and releasing biological controls like insect parasites and predators. If pests persist, see "If All Else Fails" on page 41.

Manual Controls

For the brave gardener, handpicking is often an effective and viable pest control option. This method works best on slow-moving pests, like caterpillars, slugs, and scales. It's also handy for destroying the egg masses of gypsy moths and Colorado potato beetles.

As you look over each plant, squash any pests you find or drop them into a container of soapy water. You can also kill pests by putting them in a sealed container in the freezer overnight.

Use pruning shears to cut away infestations of tent caterpillars, pest egg masses, or other pest infestations limited to one part of the plant. Compost these pests in the center of a hot pile, squash them, or put them in sealed containers for disposal with household trash.

Pruning off infested stems and leaves is a quick and effective control measure.

A forceful spray of water is an effective way to knock soft-bodied pests—like aphids, leafhoppers, and spider mites—from plants. Keep the spray moving to avoid damaging foliage.

Colored Sticky Traps

Flying insects generally move too quickly for manual controls, but you can catch them with sticky traps. Use sticky traps as part of your overall control program to monitor pest populations so you'll know if pests are getting out of hand. In some cases, sticky traps catch enough pests to provide sufficient control.

You can buy sticky traps or make your own from pieces of scrap wood, cardboard, or stiff plastic. Fasten them to stakes or put a hole in one corner to hang them. Paint traps white to attract tarnished plant bugs and flea beetles; yellow to attract aphids, whiteflies, and leafhoppers; or bright blue to attract thrips. Coat the trap with a commercial insect glue like Tanglefoot or with a homemade mixture of equal parts of petroleum jelly or mineral oil and liquid dish soap.

Handpicking large, slow-moving pests like snails is an easy way to control damage. Drop pests into a bucket of soapy water.

If slugs are causing serious damage, lure them to their doom with beer traps or capture them under fruit rinds.

Sticky red traps can help control apple maggots.

Start by placing one trap near each group of several plants. If damage continues, add more traps or switch to more aggressive controls like soap sprays or botanical pesticides. To clean traps, remove debris with a paint scraper; renew the glue every 1 to 2 weeks.

A modified sticky trap—actually a sticky red sphere that resembles an apple—is often an effective measure for controlling apple maggots in the home garden. Starting in mid-June, hang one red sticky ball in each dwarf tree or up to six traps in full-sized trees. Clean and maintain them like regular sticky traps.

Pheromone Traps

Insects produce chemicals called pheromones to help them communicate with other insects and find suitable mates. You can use traps baited with synthetic pheromones to monitor or control pest insects, including codling moths, apple maggots, and cherry fruit flies. (Japanese beetle traps are also available, but they can lure pests from your neighbors' yards as well as your own. Control these pests with other methods, like handpicking and applying milky disease spores.)

Sticky traps with pheromone lures are useful for monitoring and controlling some pests.

Purchase pest-specific pheromone lures and traps from garden suppliers. Follow manufacturers' directions for using lures to monitor or control pest insects.

Slug and Snail Traps

Capture these nocturnal plant destroyers in homemade traps or in purchased commercial versions, available from garden suppliers. You can make traps from plastic cups or shallow pie pans. Sink the containers to the brim in garden soil near damaged plants, then fill with beer or a mixture of yeast, molasses, and water. Use one trap for every 10 square feet (0.9 sq m) of garden space. Remove pests and replenish the bait daily.

Cabbage leaves or grapefruit or melon rinds also make easy, effective traps. Place the materials upside down on the soil surface. Check traps in the early morning and destroy any pests lurking underneath.

Sawfly larvae may rear up when disturbed, making them quite easy to spot.

Prune off and destroy any galls or unusual growths as soon as you spot them to prevent larvae from emerging.

Beneficial Insects

Natural populations of beneficial insects often provide good control of pest insects. For details on attracting beneficials to your garden, see "Beneficial Insects" on page 28. You can also supplement native populations by purchasing beneficials from mail-order suppliers that specialize in biological pest controls.

Deciding which beneficials and how many to buy requires accurate identification of the pest and an estimate of the size of the pest population. Consult with your supplier to be sure you're buying the best beneficial to control the pest. Follow the supplier's instructions for storing and releasing beneficials when they arrive. Monitor their progress by

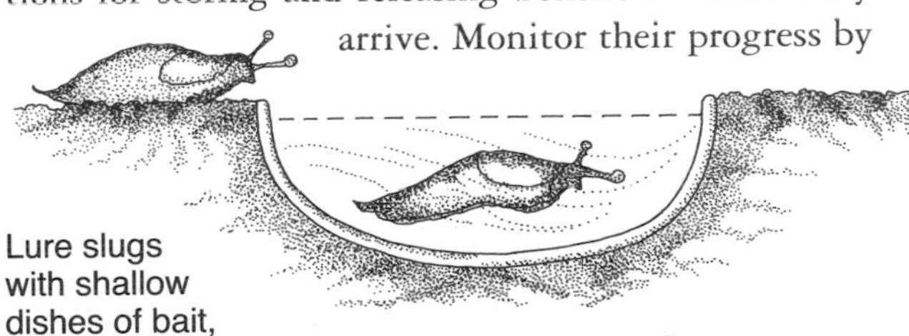

Lure slugs with shallow dishes of bait, sunken so the tops are even with the soil surface.

Provide shelter and a water source for hoverflies and other beneficials, and they'll control pests in return.

watching for dead or immobilized pests and a decrease in damage. You may need several releases for control.

Beneficial Microorganisms

Like other creatures, insects are susceptible to various disease-causing organisms, including bacteria and nematodes. Because these organisms are host-specific (meaning they only attack one host), you can use them to treat specific problems with few hazards to the environment, beneficial organisms, people, or pets. Most microbials attack pest insects at only one of their life stages, so pest identification and timing are crucial for successful control.

Control Colorado potato beetles by handpicking, or you could try BTSD.

BT BT (*Bacillus thuringiensis*) was the first bacterial insecticide. It is usually sprayed or dusted onto leaves where insects feed. When ingested, the bacteria produce toxins that paralyze and kill susceptible insects.

You can purchase varieties of BT in liquid, dust, or bait form. Use *B.t.* var. *kurstaki* (BTK) to control caterpillar pests like imported cabbageworms, codling moth larvae, and tomato hornworms. *B.t.* var. *israelensis* (BTI) controls fly and mosquito larvae in standing water, where they breed. *B.t.* var. *san diego* (BTSD) controls leaf-feed-ing beetles like boll weevils, elm leaf beetles, and Colorado potato beetles.

Scientists are finding that some of these insects are developing resistance to the BT toxin. For this reason, don't rely on BT as a cure-all—use it only when prevention and milder control measures don't work. Also be aware that BTK will kill butterfly larvae as well as pest caterpillars. Only apply this material to plants that you know are infested with pests.

Milky Disease Milky disease, caused by *Bacillus popilliae* and *B. lentimorbus*, affects the grubs of Japanese beetles and several other related beetles. Apply the spore dust to your lawn anytime the ground is not frozen. As the grubs feed in the soil, they ingest and are infected by the disease spores. When the grubs die, they release more spores into the soil. The spores usually live from year to year, but they may not survive very cold winters, so Northern gardeners may want to reapply them each year.

Parasitic nematodes can help to control codling moth larvae.

Beneficial Nematodes Nematodes are tiny worm-like creatures. Some species are harmful—feeding on and damaging plants—but many are helpful. Beneficial parasitic nematodes invade host insects and release a bacterium that kills the host. You can purchase beneficial nematodes to control pest insects found in or on soil, including onion maggots, codling moth larvae, and Colorado potato beetle larvae.

Several types of nematodes are available, so check with your mail-order supplier to know which you need. Follow the supplier's instructions for applying.

High-tech Handpicking

Hand-held, rechargeable vacuum cleaners are handy for removing some pests from your plants. Try them for whiteflies, cucumber beetles, and Japanese beetles. Skim only the plant tops to catch pests and avoid beneficials. Remove and destroy captured pests.

If All Else Fails

If pest populations spread out of control, you may decide to spray with some type of organically acceptable insecticide. These materials are nonselective, which means they kill beneficial insects along with the pests. For that reason, use these controls only as a last resort when trying to control pests and their damage.

Insecticidal Soap and Oils

Insecticidal soaps are effective controls for aphids, plant bugs, leafhoppers, thrips, scales, mealybugs, whiteflies, and other common garden and greenhouse pests. Soaps are nontoxic to people and pets, but they will kill beneficial insects, so use them only on pest-plagued plants.

You can buy commercial soaps or prepare your own solution by mixing 1 to 3 teaspoons of liquid dish soap in 1 gallon (4 l) of water. Insecticidal soaps can harm some plants, like beans, cucumbers, and ferns. Before treating a whole plant, test the spray on a few leaves and wait a few days to see if damage appears. Repeated sprays can also harm plants, so use the sprays only when really necessary.

Pyrethrum daisies are the source of pyrethrin, a potent botanical insecticide.

Refined petroleum oils are also effective for control measures. They work by smothering and killing pests

Know your pest before you spray! Snails, for instance, may not be affected by materials that control insects.

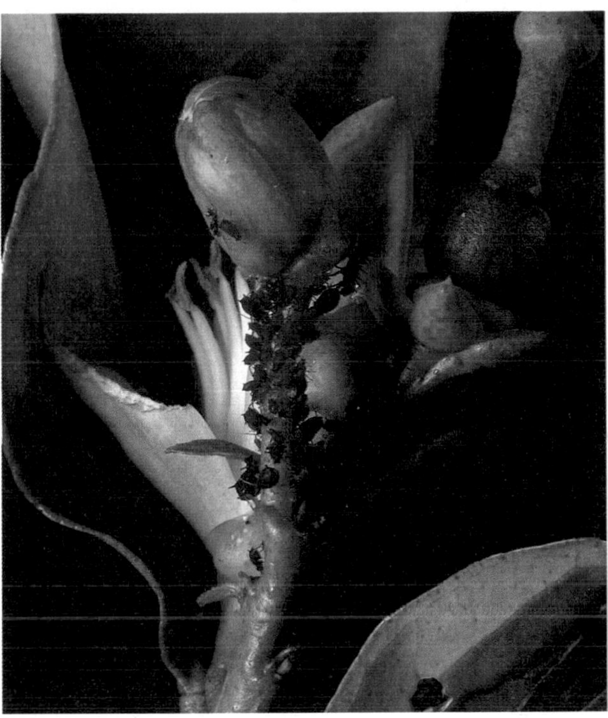

If aphids are out of control and pruning is not an option, try a homemade or commercial soap spray.

Before You Spray

Follow these guidelines when using any pest control sprays or dusts.

- Before buying, be sure to read the label on the package to determine which pests the product controls, if there are specific precautions, the recommended rate of application, and if you need to buy any special equipment to apply it.
- Spray or dust on calm, dry days, early in the morning or in the evening when beneficials are relatively inactive.
- Wear protective clothing, including a dust mask or respirator, plastic gloves, long-sleeved shirt and long pants, and goggles.
- Follow the label instructions for mixing and applying the product. Prepare only as much as you expect to use immediately.
- Dispose of any leftover solutions by diluting with water and pouring in a bucket. Leave the bucket in direct sunlight for 1 to 2 days (out of reach of children and animals) to let the pesticide break down. Then dump the solution away from water sources like ponds, lakes, and wells.

and their eggs. "Dormant" oils are only applied during winter, when trees are not growing. The highly refined "superior" or "summer" oils can be applied to most growing plants. A few plants are sensitive to oil sprays; always follow label directions and precautions before applying.

Botanical Pesticides

This group includes some of the oldest pest control remedies. Botanical pesticides are derived from raw plant materials like flowers, roots, stems, or seeds. Some are extracted using specialized equipment, then refined and purified. Use the information in "Choosing and Using Botanical Pesticides" on page 43 to learn more about the kinds that are available.

Botanicals tend to be broad-spectrum insecticides, meaning they kill a wide variety of both pest and beneficial insects. Although most botanicals tend to break down quickly when exposed to the environment, they are toxic to people, pets, and wildlife when first applied. Always read and follow label directions to apply these materials as safely as possible.

Pest Controls from Your Kitchen

Before you reach for commercially available botanical insecticides, try these homemade pest control remedies. These formulations are fairly safe to you, but be careful when mixing and using them, since ingredients like hot peppers and garlic can burn sensitive skin and eyes. These controls may also harm beneficials along with pest insects.

You'll have to experiment to be sure your homemade sprays control pests and don't damage plants. Make test applications by treating a few leaves, then waiting a few days. If leaves are damaged—spotted, discolored, or distorted—dilute the mix with water or refrain from using it on sensitive plants.

Garlic Oil Soak 3 ounces (85 g) of minced garlic in 2 teaspoons of mineral oil for 24 hours. Strain out the garlic and add 1 pint (600 ml) water and 1 teaspoon liquid dish soap to the remaining liquid. Mix thoroughly. Spray plants with a solution of 1 to 2 tablespoons of soap mixture and 1 pint (600 ml) water. This mixture will control a wide range of insects and even some fungal diseases.

Oils extracted from citrus peels will control many pests, including aphids and spider mites.

Your kitchen can provide the makings for many pest control sprays, including dish soap, hot pepper, and garlic.

Soap and Oil Add 1 tablespoon liquid dish soap to 1 cup (8 fl oz/250 ml) oil (peanut, safflower, corn, soybean, or sunflower). Mix 1 to 2½ teaspoons of the prepared soap-and-oil base to 1 cup (8 fl oz/250 ml) water; spray plants to control a variety of insect pests.

Hot Dusts To protect vegetable seedlings from root maggots, sprinkle seasonings like black pepper, chili pepper, dill, ginger, paprika, and red pepper over soil in a band on each side of the row after sowing. Make the bands several inches wide. Renew the application after irrigation or heavy rain.

Regular scouting can help you spot damage before it gets this serious, reducing the need for strong sprays.

Choosing and Using Botanical Pesticides

If pest problems are severe, you may decide to spray with a botanical pesticide. Use this chart to check out the products that are available, what pests they control, and what precautions you need to consider.

Product	Source/Active Ingredient	Target Pests	Precautions	Formulations
Citrus Oils	Linalool and d-limonene are extracted from citrus peels	Aphids, Colorado potato beetles, leaf-eating caterpillars, spider mites, fire ants, flies, wasps, fleas	Considered non-hazardous with normal use; some dogs or cats experience tremors and salivation on exposure	Liquid spray concentrate
Neem	Seeds of the neem (*Azadirachta indica*) tree	Wide range of pests including aphids, mealybugs, leaf-eating caterpillars and beetles, leafminers, plant bugs, weevils, whiteflies	Not yet approved for edible crops; may damage hibiscus flowers	Liquid spray concentrate
Nicotine	Leaves of the tobacco plant	Most garden pests	Highly toxic to people and pets; remains toxic on leaf surfaces for several weeks; toxic to beneficials	Dust; liquid spray concentrate
Pyrethrin	Extracted from pyrethrum daisies (*Chrysanthemum cinerariifolium* and *C. coccineum*)	Most garden pests	Moderately toxic to mammals; harmful to some beneficials	Dust; dried pyrethrum flower heads; liquid spray concentrate
Rotenone	Found naturally in many tropical plants	A wide range of garden pests (particularly those with chewing mouthparts, like beetles)	Moderately toxic to people and pets; may persist on plants well after harvest and cooking; very toxic to most beneficials, birds, and fish	Dust; wettable powder
Sabadilla	Extracted from seeds of *Schoenocaulon officinale*	Aphids, caterpillars, cucumber beetles, flea beetles, squash bugs, thrips, and others	Moderately toxic to people and pets; toxic to honeybees; strength increases with age	Dust; wettable powder

IDENTIFYING PLANT DISEASES

To just about any gardener, plant diseases are among the most intimidating plant problems. The microorganisms that cause plant disease are difficult to monitor since they are so small. And the same microorganism may attack many different plants, producing different symptoms on each one. Fortunately, there are a limited number of diseases that you'll actually need to deal with in the garden, depending on the plants and the growing conditions you have.

In this chapter, you'll learn about the different microorganisms that share your garden, including fungi, bacteria, viruses, and nematodes. Just like insects, the millions of microorganisms in your garden can be beneficial or harmful to your plants. Beneficial microorganisms help to break down organic matter in soil and compost, making the nutrients available to plants. Some microorganisms even help to control insects and plant diseases. Others, known as plant pathogens, are the ones that can infect your garden plantings.

As with insects, a key part of coping with plant diseases is figuring out the cause of the problem. "Diagnosing Disease Problems" on page 48 gives you an easy step-by-step approach to interpreting what you see. Then refer to "Common Signs and Symptoms" on page 50 for an overview of the most common disease indications, as well as their possible causes.

When you come across a sickly plant in your garden, remember that it may not be suffering from either insects or microorganism attack. The environment and your gardening practices also have a great impact on the overall health of your plants. You may not be able to avoid conditions like frost, wind, or air pollution, but you can take steps to minimize their effects. You can also change your gardening habits to avoid problems like too much or too little fertilizer or water. "Disease Look-alikes" on page 52 tells about some of the most common plant disorders and their symptoms. Use this information to diagnose problems you may already have (and to avoid making the same mistakes in next year's garden!).

Opposite: Just as with pests, dealing with diseases effectively means that you have to identify the problem first. These leaf spots are common symptoms of rust, a fungal disease that attacks a wide range of plants.

What Is a Disease?

Before you can cope with diseases, you need to understand what they actually are. Unfortunately, diseases are more difficult to define than insects. After all, insects are actual organisms with specific traits and characteristics. Plant diseases, on the other hand, can be anything that interferes with normal growth functions (like water uptake and photosynthesis).

To make this definition a little more useful, it's helpful to divide plant disease into two categories. Infectious diseases can spread from one plant to another. They're the problems we usually think of as plant diseases—like rust, fire blight, powdery mildew. Noninfectious diseases—commonly known as disorders—cannot be transmitted from one plant to another. Nutrient imbalances, air pollution, and waterlogged soil are a few causes of noninfectious diseases.

Powdery mildew is a common fungal disease that attacks many plants, including lupines.

Infectious Diseases

Infectious plant diseases are caused by microscopic living organisms called pathogens. Pathogens are commonly broken down into four groups: fungi, bacteria, viruses, and nematodes.

Desirable Diseases

Strange as it may sound, there are some diseases that are actually beneficial to plants or their growers. For instance, plants like clover and peas host specialized nitrogen-fixing bacteria on their roots. These bacteria take some nutrients from the plants, but they also trap nitrogen gas and release it as a form that the plants can use. The roots of many plants are infected with mycorrhizal fungi, which help the roots absorb more nutrients. Even viruses can be useful by causing attractive spots or markings on leaves or flowers.

Viruses are often spread by insects as they feed. The only effective control is destroying infected plants.

Fungi Many kinds of molds, mildews, and mushrooms play an important part in breaking down organic matter in soil and compost. There are, however, a number of fungi that also attack living plants. These plant pathogenic fungi are the most common causes of garden diseases. Powdery mildew, damping-off, anthracnose, apple scab, club root, late blight, and black spot are all caused by fungi.

Some pathogenic fungi are host-specific, but most will attack a variety of garden plants. Fungi produce spores that move with wind, soil, water, and animals to plant surfaces. Given the right environmental conditions and the right host plant, spores of plant pathogenic fungi will germinate and infect plants.

Bacteria Like fungi, bacteria are specialized organisms with both beneficial and pathogenic species. Beneficial bacteria recycle soil organic matter and nutrients, and they can even help control insect pests, like caterpillars and beetles. Plant pathogenic bacteria, however, can infect plants and cause diseases like crown gall, bacterial wilt, and fire blight.

Bacterial cells travel to plants the same way as fungal spores. Once they reach a susceptible plant, bacteria move into and infect plants through wounds and natural openings in leaves, stems, and roots.

Viruses Viruses are the smallest disease agents. Once inside a living cell, they multiply by making their host plant produce even more virus particles, upsetting the plant's normal metabolism and

Blossom blights are common problems on many kinds of flowers during cool, humid weather.

causing disease symptoms. Virus particles are carried to healthy plants by pests like insects, mites, and nematodes. They're also spread by taking cuttings, grafts, layers, or divisions from infected plants.

Viral diseases can be the most difficult to diagnose. Some common indications of viral attack include mottled or discolored leaves. Symptoms can vary from one plant to the next; infected plants may not even show symptoms. If your plants have suffered from viral infection in the past, your best course is to become familiar with the common viruses in your area and the symptoms they cause so that you'll know when to take control measures.

Nematodes Nematodes are microscopic roundworms, which are found free-living in soil and as parasites on plants and animals. Beneficial nematodes are important members of the soil community, since they feed on decaying material and pests like cutworms and grubs. Pest nematodes damage plants by puncturing cell walls with their needle-like mouthparts and drawing out the cell contents. This causes disease-like symptoms—including yellowing, wilting, stunting, and reduced yields—that are difficult to distinguish from other causes.

Plant parasitic nematodes travel to healthy plants in water and in infested soil carried on tools, boots, and animals. If you suspect your plants suffer from nematode damage, you may want to submit root and soil samples to a diagnostic laboratory or your Cooperative Extension Service for positive identification.

Brown rot is a common fungal disease on plums, peaches, and cherries.

Plant Disorders

Changes in the environment and in your gardening techniques can also interfere with normal plant functions, so technically they are considered diseases. Unlike infectious diseases, though, disorders cannot be transmitted from plant to plant. Disorders can still be very serious once they occur, but they're often easy to prevent and remedy with good gardening practices, like regular soil improvement.

Symptoms of disorders vary widely, depending on the cause and the plant. It's important to recognize the symptoms of common disorders so you'll be able to treat the problem effectively, instead of mistaking it for an infectious disease. You'll find more about identifying disorders under "Disease Lookalikes" on page 52.

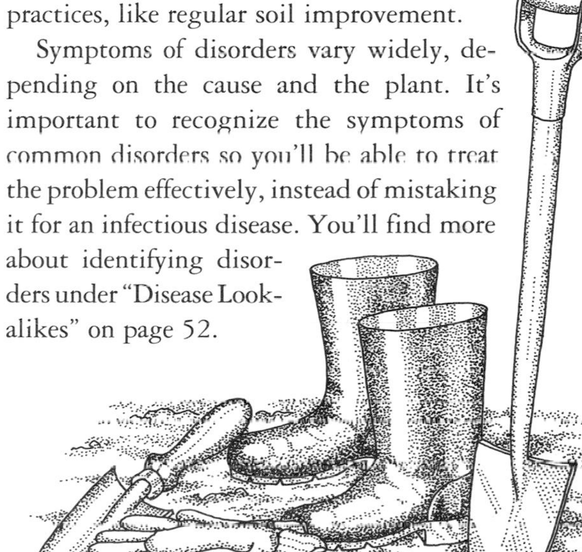

Disease-causing fungi, bacteria, and nematodes can be carried by soil clinging to dirty tools, boots, and gloves.

Fungal diseases often produce a fuzzy or powdery appearance on plants as the spores develop.

Diagnosing Disease Problems

Like most garden problems, plant diseases are easiest to control if you catch them early. But unlike insect pests, pathogens are generally too small to see without magnification. In most cases, you won't know they've struck until your plants begin to suffer and display symptoms. Environmental and cultural problems, like frost injury, air pollution, or nutrient imbalances, can also be tricky to diagnose, since the conditions that cause them are seldom visible.

Fortunately, there is a limited number of diseases or disorders likely to harm your plants. As you become familiar with the common problems that happen in your garden, you'll be able to make early and accurate diagnoses. And once you know the cause of the problem, you're well on the way to selecting the most appropriate controls and taking the right steps to prevent the problem in the future.

Sooty mold grows on the sticky honeydew produced by aphids and other pests. It is easy to wipe off.

Step-by-step Disease Diagnosis

Plant pathologists (scientists who study plant diseases) can go through a series of procedures to examine affected plants and isolate the pathogen before coming up with a diagnosis. But if you, like most of us, don't have access to microscopes and other fancy lab equipment, just grab a notebook and a pencil and follow these steps to help pin down plant diseases.

1. Identify the plant. Although it sounds obvious, this one simple step can put you surprisingly close to an accurate diagnosis in just a few minutes. Many popular garden plants are commonly attacked by easy-to-identify diseases and disorders, like black spot on roses, powdery mildew on lilacs, smut on corn, or blossom end rot on tomatoes.

If you're not sure what the plant is, ask a fellow gardener, a local nursery or botanical garden, or your local Cooperative Extension Service for help. Even if identifying the plant doesn't help you diagnose the disease, it can be important later on when you are deciding on a control measure. Some plants, for instance, are sensitive to soap- or oil-based sprays, so you'd want to use a different type of control on these plants to avoid causing more damage.

2. Take a good look. Jot down anything that you notice about the affected plant. What parts seem to be most affected: the leaves, stems, flowers, or fruits? If the plant parts are spotted or discolored, note the color, size, and general shape of the patches. If leaves are affected, is it the old or new leaves? Is the plant shorter than similar plants around it? Was it recently planted, or has it been in your landscape for many years? Anything you know or notice about the affected plant—no matter how minor—may help you or your consultant make or confirm a diagnosis.

3. Consider the environment. Extreme weather conditions, like strong wind, hail, and waterlogged or dry soils, can give plants an unhealthy appearance that resembles symptoms of plant disease. Make a

Weather extremes and nutrient imbalances can cause disease-like damage, such as blossom end rot on tomatoes.

Use the News

Watch for garden pest and disease alerts provided by garden clubs, your Cooperative Extension Service, and other gardening experts. In some communities, newspapers and other media offer weekly advice from the experts. Their predictions let you know when to begin watching for signs of certain pathogens in your area, so you can begin preventive measures or make early diagnoses.

If the leaves of your roses have dark, circular spots, you can be fairly sure that black spot fungi are at work.

note of any unusual weather conditions that you can remember. (Actually, it's smart to jot down weather occurrences, like frosts, heavy rains, or dry spells, as they happen so you'll have those notes to refer back to when a problem strikes.) Also consider whether your plants have been exposed to pollutants like acid rain, herbicide drift, or road salt.

4. Rule out insect pests. Some insects cause damage that resembles plant disease symptoms. When in doubt, use a magnifying lens to check for insect signs like webbing or droppings. Symptoms that are particularly unusual might mean that damage is the result of two or more pathogens or pests; open wounds from insects or other damage make convenient entrances for plant pathogens. "Signs of Damage" on page 31 lists many of the common types of insect damage.

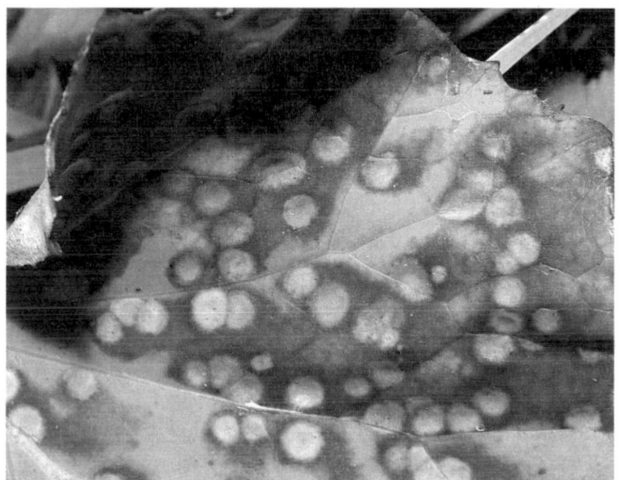

If a plant's symptoms leave you stumped, ask for diagnostic help at your local Cooperative Extension Service.

Off-color or mottled leaves can indicate several different problems, including viruses and air pollution damage.

5. Do some research. Once you've ruled out the possibility of insects, it's time to narrow down your disease diagnosis. Compare your notes to those given in "Plant Disease Symptoms and Causes" on page 51. You'll also want to flip through the "Insect and Disease Guide," starting on page 76. There you'll find entries on many common plant diseases, with a photo and detailed symptom description for each (as well as suggested prevention and control measures). "Disease Look-alikes" on page 52 will also give you clues for identifying plant disorders.

A rain gauge and weather notes can help you diagnose environment-related problems, like drought stress.

6. Consult the experts. If a particular problem has you stumped, submit samples to your local or state plant disease diagnostic laboratory. Personnel at Cooperative Extension Service offices can provide you with the right forms, mailing supplies, and instructions for sending plant samples by mail. Local botanical gardens and arboreta may also be willing to help you identify plant problems. All of the information you gathered about the plant and the symptoms will be useful to the professional making the diagnosis.

Bacterial fire blight attacks pyracantha and other rose family members.

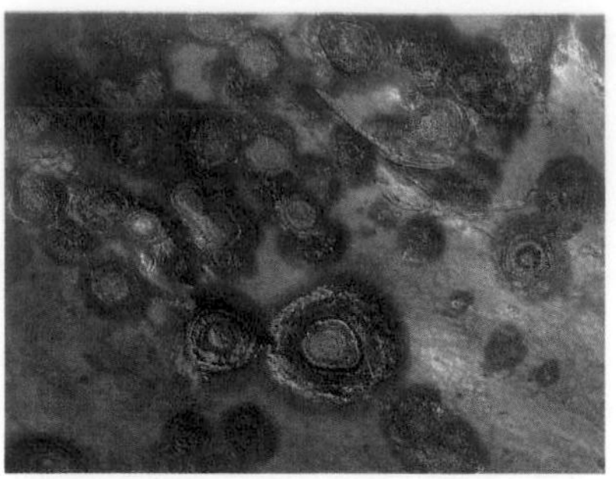

Anthracnose is common on cucumbers, causing sunken spots on fruit.

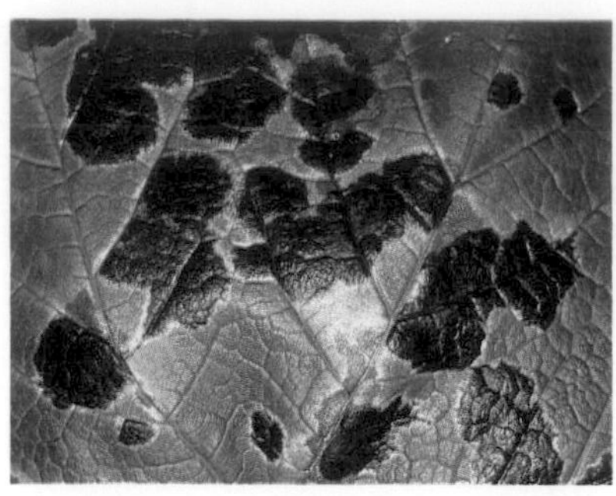

Tar spot is one of the many kinds of leaf spots you may see in the garden.

Common Signs and Symptoms

Unhealthy plants have special distress signals that let you know when pathogens have attacked. Plants will respond to the stress of infection with a wide range of symptoms, from leaf spots and damaged fruit to wilting and even death. Different diseases and disorders tend to affect different plant parts and produce different symptoms. In order to identify and control these problems, it's helpful to be aware of the common signs and symptoms you may encounter.

Powdery mildew often appears on the buds, leaves, and shoots of roses.

Follow the Signs

Infectious diseases are often grouped according to the symptoms they produce. To help narrow down your diagnosis, see if any of the descriptions below match the affected parts of your plant.

Blights Leaves, flowers, stems, and branches that suddenly wilt, wither, and die are common indications of blight. Common garden blights include Botrytis, early and late blight (caused by fungi), and fire blight (produced by bacteria).

Cankers Affected woody plants produce dead, and often sunken, patches in stems and branches. These cankers may ooze a sticky or foul-smelling material and can spread to kill whole trunks or shoots. The fungal Cytospora canker is a common orchard problem; bacterial fire blight is another canker-causer.

Galls Swellings or overgrown patches of leaf or stem tissue are commonly known as galls. They may be caused by fungi (like leaf gall), bacteria (such as crown gall), or even insects (such as gall wasps).

Leaf Curl Deformed and discolored leaves suffer from leaf curl. Peach leaf curl is caused by a fungus; viruses may also produce these symptoms.

Leaf Spots Rounded or irregular areas in various colors are common leaf symptoms. They are produced by a wide variety of pathogens.

Mildews Dusty white, gray, or purplish patches on the surfaces or undersides of leaves are an easy clue to the fungal powdery and downy mildews.

Rots Soft or discolored and dying plant tissue generally indicate some kind of rot. Fungi and bacteria can cause rot on fruit, stems, flowers, or roots.

Rusts Orange or yellowish spots, galls, or coatings are caused by rust fungi. Rusts may affect leaves, stems, flowers, or fruits.

Wilts Drooping leaves and stems indicate that the plant isn't getting enough water. This may be caused by improper watering or by fungi and bacteria that can clog the plant's water conducting system. Fungi cause Fusarium and Verticillium wilt; bacterial wilt is a problem in cucumbers and related crops.

Brown corky patches or cracks on the fruit are a symptom of apple scab.

Cankers are problems on woody plants and can damage whole trunks.

Late blight on celery causes spots on leaves and may spread to stems.

Plant Disease Symptoms and Causes

When you find signs of disease among your plants, look for a description of the damage in the column on the left, then check the possible causes in the column on the right. Next, look for photographs and information on specific problems in the "Insect and Disease Guide," starting on page 76.

What You See	Possible Causes
Leaves mottled or discolored	Mosaic; nutrient deficiency; ozone, PAN, or sulfur dioxide injury; sooty mold; sunscald; yellows; insect pests
Leaves with yellow or brown spots	Anthracnose; apple scab; bacterial spot; Botrytis blight; cedar-apple rust; downy mildew; Septoria leaf spot
Leaves with black or brown spots surrounded by yellow	Bacterial spot; black spot; cherry leaf spot; late blight
Leaves curled, cupped, or blistered	Leaf gall; mosaic or other viral diseases; peach leaf curl; herbicide drift; insect pests
Leaves, shoots, or fruit with white spots or patches	Downy mildew; powdery mildew; salt injury
Leaves and stems wilted and dying	Bacterial wilt; Dutch elm disease; Fusarium wilt; oak wilt; Verticillium wilt; waterlogged soil; lack of water
Leaves or stems with orange spots	Rust
Stems with irregular swellings	Black knot; cedar-apple rust; crown gall
Stems with oozing slimy or gummy substance	Cytospora canker; slime flux
Stems condensed into short, bushy "rosettes"; plant stunted	Peach rosette; nematodes
Stems of seedlings rotted at the soil line; infected seedlings collapsed	Damping-off
Flowers or fruit with brown spots	Brown rot; Botrytis blight or fruit rot; fire blight; frost damage
Fruit with small, dark sunken spots	Anthracnose
Apple fruit with green or velvety brown spots that turn into raised, dark, corky areas	Apple scab
Fruit with water-soaked spots that turn brown and leathery at the blossom end	Blossom end rot
Roots of young and old plants rotted; plants stunted or wilted	Root rot
Roots with irregular swellings	Club root; crown gall; nematodes

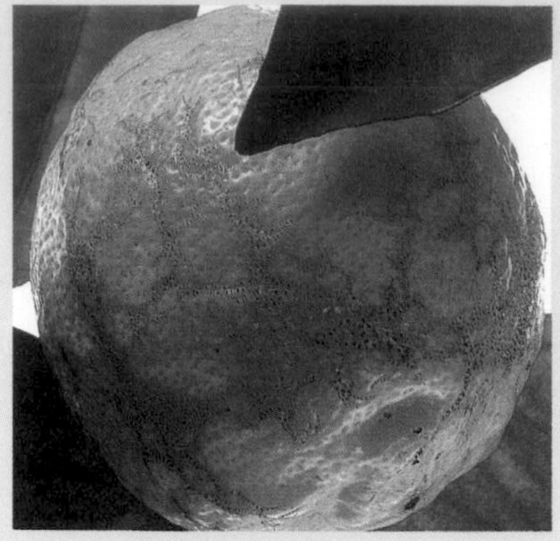

Strong winds may lead to russeting on developing citrus fruit.

High levels of sulfur dioxide can cause spotted or discolored leaves.

A purplish cast to leaves often indicates a phosphorus deficiency.

Disease Look-alikes

Although plants can adapt to many different environments, they all have certain conditions that they need to grow their best. Factors like air pollution or widely fluctuating temperatures can upset a plant's normal functions, causing symptoms that resemble plant disease. Since such problems aren't transmitted from plant to plant, they are called noninfectious diseases or physiological disorders.

Common Symptoms of Disorders

As you plan your garden, it's helpful to consider the many factors that affect plant growth so you can choose the plants that will be best adapted to your conditions and site them in the most appropriate spots. Good gardening practices, like proper watering and fertilizing, will also go a long way toward preventing many of these problems. But it's a good idea to be aware of the symptoms produced by common disorders so you can deal with them effectively when they do occur instead of mistaking them for an infectious disease.

Excessive Water Too much water means that most or all of the tiny soil pores, which normally hold some oxygen, are filled with water. When roots don't get the oxygen they need, they can't function properly and are more prone to infectious diseases, like root rot. Affected plants lack vigor and may wilt; leaves become a greenish yellow color. Raised beds can help improve drainage on naturally waterlogged sites.

Drought A shortage of soil water can stunt plant growth and slow flower and fruit production. Leaves either turn pale and wilt or develop brown, scorched areas. Shallow-rooted annual plants are often most affected. Regular deep irrigation can help mildly affected plants recover and prevent future problems.

Cold Stress Sudden cold snaps can kill tender buds, growing tips, and other woody plant parts. Leaves turn yellow or drop, buds may drop, stems can crack, and bark may split. Unseasonably low temperatures during the growing season can damage warm-weather vegetables like corn, beans, and tomatoes. Protect actively growing plants with floating row covers or other frost shields. Avoid fertilizing after midsummer; later fertilizing promotes soft growth that is more frost-prone.

When the ground is frozen, dry winter winds can pull moisture out of buds and evergreen leaves, causing browning and tip dieback. Protect dormant plants with windbreaks or spray with an anti-transpirant to block moisture loss.

Heat Stress Young plants exposed to high temperatures often wilt and may die. Cold-weather vegetables like lettuce and spinach stop producing new leaves and will bolt (go to seed). Shade and water may help plants recover; shade can also help prevent damage. Avoid planting cool-weather crops that will mature in midsummer. Pull out and compost plants that bolt.

Insufficient Light Plants become spindly and are more susceptible to lodging (falling over) when light is inadequate. Green leaves become pale, and variegated

The foliage of some golden-leaved plants will scorch (turn brown) when exposed to strong sunlight.

or colored leaves may turn evenly green if they don't get enough light. If plants show these symptoms, try moving them to a sunnier spot.

Manganese deficiency causes leaf tissue to turn yellow between the veins.

High levels of salt in the soil may produce browned leaf tips and dead buds.

Excessive Light When exposed to direct sunlight, some fruits and leaves develop sunscald, discoloration, or blisters. Too much light can burn the foliage of shade-loving plants, causing brown patches or dead leaves. Plants with purple or yellow leaves often fade or burn in direct sunlight. If you're not sure how much light a plant needs, see how it grows in partial shade; if it turns pale or spindly, gradually move it into more sunlight. Provide temporary shade when setting out seedlings or young plants.

Strong Wind Leaves develop a silvery discoloration and tattered leaf edges when exposed to prolonged high winds. Windblown plants may lose large amounts of water through their foliage, causing leaves to appear wilted. Walls and windbreaks may be the solution.

Deficient Nutrients When nutrients are lacking, plants are less vigorous and yield poorly. Common deficiency symptoms are abnormal leaf color, curled or stunted leaves, and dead growing tips. Regular soil tests can alert you to developing deficiency problems.

Excessive Nutrients High concentrations of nutrients may cause the same symptoms as nutrient deficiencies. In some cases, the effects of excess nutrients are indirect. Too much nitrogen, for example, often produces lush plants with few flowers or fruit. Soil tests can show you if an imbalance is developing. Follow package directions for fertilizer application rates.

Ozone Pollution Ozone pollution, from automobile exhaust and other internal combustion engines, causes stippling or yellowing of leaves. Damage is especially severe on the upper leaf surfaces and on leaves that have just matured. See the Ozone damage entry on page 147 for prevention and control suggestions.

Peroxyacetyl Nitrate (PAN) Pollution Exposure to PAN pollution, from automobile exhaust and other internal combustion engines, shows as silvery white or brown patches on the undersides of leaves. See the PAN damage entry on page 147 for prevention and control.

Sulfur Dioxide Pollution Sulfur dioxide, from burning sulfur-containing fuels (like coal), causes leaves to turn yellow or brown between veins. Sulfur dioxide also combines with moisture in the air to form acid rain, which lowers soil pH and can cause nutrient-imbalance symptoms. See the Sulfur dioxide injury entry on page 153 for prevention and control advice.

Herbicide Drift Under windy conditions, herbicides applied along roadways, in farm fields, or in neighboring yards may drift over to your property and injure your plants. Depending on the product used, leaves may appear burned, bronzed, distorted, or discolored, or plants may die. Protect your plantings with walls, windbreaks, or other barriers.

Early fall frosts often damage ripening vegetables. Protect crops with floating row covers or other shields.

Late cold snaps can injure flowers and reduce crop yields.

Managing Plant Diseases

The real key to controlling plant diseases is to stop them from occurring in the first place. To do that, you need to understand a bit about how diseases actually occur.

Before you see signs of disease on your plants, there are three conditions that have to be met. First, the disease-causing organism (the pathogen) has to be present. Second, a plant that is susceptible to that pathogen must be present. And third, the environmental conditions (such as temperature and humidity) must be just right for the pathogen to attack and cause disease. As the gardener, you have the ability to control these factors. If you prevent any one of the conditions, you can break the disease cycle.

Let's look at an example. Black spot, for instance, is a common problem on roses, but it doesn't attack other garden plants. If you are lucky enough to always buy healthy roses and none of your neighbors' roses has black spot, you may never have black spot problems. Why? Because the pathogen isn't present. Unfortunately, since you can't see pathogens, you can't know for sure whether they're around or not. But there are steps you can take—like careful garden cleanup and smart shopping—that will reduce the chances of you bringing in or harboring pathogens.

Your second line of defense rests with the plant itself. Some kinds of roses, for example, are much more prone to black spot than others. Hybrid tea roses have a good chance of getting this fungal disease. Many species and shrub roses, on the other hand, are much more resistant; even if the pathogen is present and conditions are right, the plant can fight back and resist infection. If you're buying new plants, look for ones that are resistant to diseases that are common in your area. If you already have plants that are disease-prone and don't feel they're worth the trouble, you may want to remove them or replace them with naturally disease-resistant species or cultivars.

The third step to preventing disease outbreaks is controlling the environment. To go back to our example, a crowded bed of hybrid tea roses is much more likely to have black spot problems than an airy, well-pruned bed of the same roses. Many diseases, including black spot, thrive in moist conditions and can spread rapidly when plant leaves are wet. Siting plants carefully and pruning for good air circulation help keep leaves dry. You can't stop rain from wetting the leaves, but you can avoid wetting them yourself by using drip irrigation (or some other method of watering that won't wet the foliage).

In this chapter, you'll learn many techniques for keeping diseases from happening in the first place, as well as steps for dealing with them when they do occur. "Planning for Disease Prevention" on page 56 tells how you can use good garden planning and smart shopping to get a jump on the disease season. Once your garden is up and growing, "Minimizing Disease Development" on page 58 offers tips for keeping your plants strong and healthy. If problems appear, the simple recommendations in "What to Do If Disease Appears" on page 60 can stop pathogens in their tracks. When disease damage threatens the life of your plants, see "If All Else Fails" on page 62 for information on commonly used organic disease-control methods.

Opposite: Plant diseases may not destroy your crops, but they can reduce yields considerably. Once you've identified the disease affecting your plant, you can decide what sort of control measure to take, if any.

Planning for Disease Prevention

Like insect control, disease prevention begins long before the growing season starts. And, fortunately, many of the techniques that help you prevent insect damage also make your plants much less susceptible to disease problems. Make these factors a routine part of your garden planning, and you'll greatly reduce the chances of having diseases damage or destroy your plants.

To keep fruit trees healthy, start with disease-resistant cultivars, give them lots of room, and clean up dropped fruit.

Pick Your Plants Carefully

Whenever you choose new plants for your garden, you have a real opportunity to prevent disease problems in your low-maintenance landscape. Before you buy, follow the guidelines below so you can make informed decisions about your purchases.

Consider Your Climate The first part of picking the right plants involves choosing plants that are adapted to your climate. In hot-summer areas, you'll need plants that can take the heat; in cold-winter areas, look for plants that are adapted to the chill. Plants that prefer cooler temperatures (like delphiniums, lilacs, and lettuce) will languish in hot Southern sites; heat-lovers like crape myrtles (*Lagerstroemia* spp.) and verbenas (*Verbena* spp.) may barely survive from year to year in a cool Northern garden. Plants in the wrong place are prime targets for insect and disease attack. If you give plants the conditions they prefer, they'll produce strong, healthy growth that is naturally less susceptible to infection by disease organisms.

How do you know if a plant is adapted to your climate? Look around you, and see what's growing well for your neighbors. Check out local botanical gardens and arboreta. Your local Cooperative Extension Service may also be able to recommend landscape plants that are proven performers in your climate.

Research for Resistance Let's face it, some plants are just plain disease-prone. Plant garden phlox (*Phlox paniculata*), and chances are that it will get powdery mildew. Plant a bed of hybrid tea roses, and black spot is almost sure to follow. This doesn't mean that you can't enjoy these plants in your landscape. It does mean, though, that you should do some research before you

Neglected, debris-filled gardens provide ample over-wintering sites for disease-causing organisms.

Don't Buy Diseases

Sounds obvious, but plants that are diseased are no bargain at any price. Inspect potential purchases for spots or discolorations on leaves, flowers, fruit, and stems; make sure you check the undersides of leaves, too. If you buy bareroot plants, reject those with dark or cracked roots or wart-like swellings. Select bulbs that are firm and healthy looking, and pass by those that are soft, moldy, or bruised. If you have any doubts about a plant you've already purchased, isolate it from related plants in your garden for a few weeks until you're sure it's healthy. If the plant shows symptoms, try the appropriate controls.

buy so you know if the plant you want will be disease-prone or fairly trouble-free.

For a great-looking, healthy, low-maintenance landscape, concentrate on growing plants that are naturally problem-free. If you really want to grow a plant that is a prime target for particular diseases, look around for cultivars or similar species that tend to be disease-resistant or disease-tolerant. (Resistant means that plants will resist infection when exposed to certain pathogens. Tolerant plants may get the disease, but they usually won't be severely damaged by it.)

If you can't live without phlox, for instance, you could try the cultivar 'David' or perhaps the closely related species *Phlox maculata.* If you've always dreamed of having your own apple trees but hate to spray, consider planting cultivars like 'Freedom' and 'Liberty', which tend to be much more disease-resistant than other apples. Many disease-resistant cultivars are also available for popular vegetable crops. Every year, breeders and nurseries are developing and selecting new disease-resistant choices for a wide range of edible and ornamental plants.

Select the Right Site

Be fussy about garden location, since plants will be most vigorous and productive and able to fend off attack by pathogens—when they are provided with the right amount of light, water, and nutrients. If you are buying new plants, find out what conditions they need, and make sure you can supply those conditions. If you have existing plants that aren't thriving, do a little research to find out what growing conditions they prefer. If the plant is in the wrong place, move it if you can, or consider digging it out and replacing it with a better-adapted plant.

Coordinate Crop Rotations

Control soilborne diseases, like corn smut and potato scab, by growing different crops in different parts of the garden each year. Crop rotation helps break the life cycle of pathogens, since you've planted the preferred host plant out of reach. Learn more about using crop rotation to control pests and pathogens in "Planning Crop Rotations" on page 22.

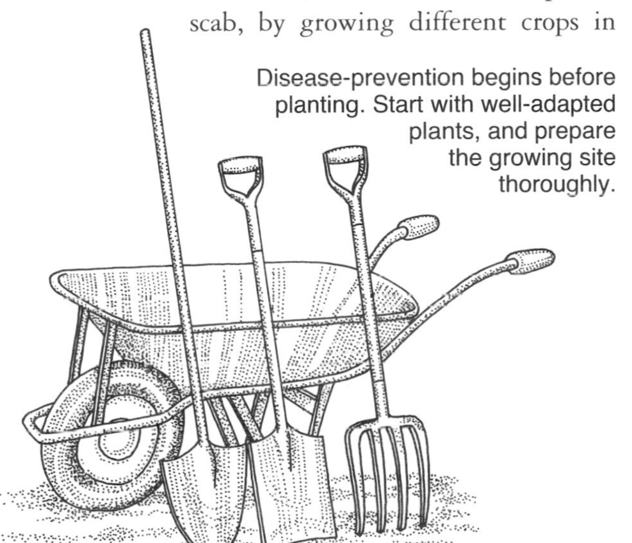

Disease-prevention begins before planting. Start with well-adapted plants, and prepare the growing site thoroughly.

Picking plants that are adapted to your yard's growing conditions will lead to a healthy, beautiful landscape.

Strive for Diversity

Besides controlling some insect pests, companion planting also works to reduce the spread of plant disease. Pathogens spread quickly among related plants that are grouped together in solid clumps. This is mostly a concern in the vegetable garden, where crops are planted closely in rows or beds.

At the least, you could try mixing a few herbs and flowers into the vegetable garden to separate disease-susceptible crops. For even more diversity, create an edible landscape throughout your yard by mixing your vegetables and fruit-bearing plants with herbs and ornamentals. That way, even if disease strikes some of your plants, there's a chance that related plants growing elsewhere in the landscape won't be affected.

Delphiniums are garden stars in cool climates, but they tend to be weak and problem-prone in hot, dry areas.

Good garden care—including proper planting, careful watering, and mulching—will help your plants thrive.

Minimizing Disease Development

Throughout the season—from seed starting to harvesting—a combination of good gardening practices can keep your plants healthy and disease-free. These simple principles may just seem like common sense, but they're a vital part of any disease-control program.

Water Wisely

Providing an even supply of moisture to your plants is vital for healthy growth, especially with high-yielding, shallow-rooted crops like vegetables. Drought-stressed plants are less vigorous and more prone to disease problems. Plants in waterlogged soil are highly susceptible to root rot.

Before you water, see how wet the soil is. If the surface looks dry, dig down about 3 inches (7.5 cm): If the soil is moist there, wait a day or two and check again; if it's dry, you may want to water. If possible, use drip irrigation or some other system that wets the soil

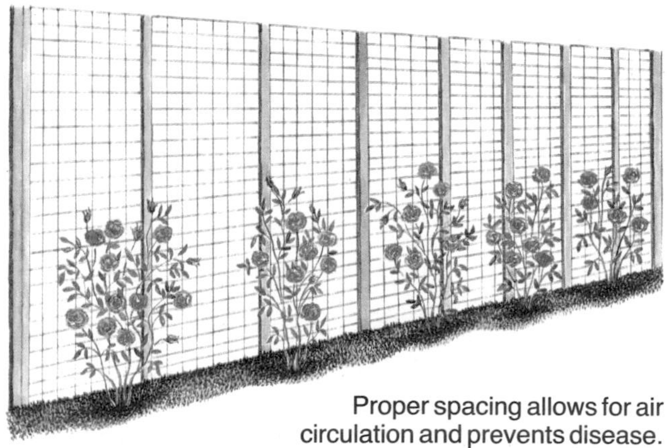

Proper spacing allows for air circulation and prevents disease.

A layer of compost mulch provides a small but steady supply of nutrients for strong, healthy growth.

without wetting the foliage; diseases can spread quickly when leaves are coated with a film of water. If you must use a sprinkler, try to water early in the day, so leaves will dry more quickly.

Spread on the Mulch

Control pathogens at the soil surface by mulching with compost. Apply a layer of compost 2 to 4 inches (5 to 10 cm) thick over the soil surface around and between plants. For one thing, the compost layer acts as a barrier between soilborne pathogens and plant leaves by preventing rain or irrigation water from splashing soil onto the foliage. (Actually, any organic mulch can serve this function.) But besides just serving as a barrier,

Mulch prevents soil from splashing onto plants, keeping flowers clean and minimizing the spread of diseases.

Tips for Smart Seed Starting

Don't let diseases destroy your crops before they even get growing. Here are some handy hints for getting seeds off to a good start:

- Use a clean growing medium for indoor seed starting. Materials like vermiculite or packaged "sterile" potting soil are usually a good bet. Don't use plain garden soil, which could harbor pathogens.
- Before planting seeds in pots or trays, surface-sterilize the growing medium by pouring boiling water over the top. Let it drain before sowing.
- Avoid sowing seeds too thickly, and provide good air circulation around germinating seedlings.
- Sprinkle a thin layer of sand or perlite over germinating seedlings to keep the stems dry at the soil level (where damping-off often strikes). Or use fine sphagnum moss, which can keep the surface dry and repress fungal growth.

compost contains beneficial microorganisms that can compete with or consume many plant pathogens.

Allow for Air Circulation

Good air circulation helps eliminate the moist, humid conditions that encourage many fungal diseases. Prune and thin perennial plants each year. In beds and rows, space plants at the recommended intervals to avoid cramped growing conditions and poor air circulation. Grow bushy crops, like tomatoes or peppers, inside wire cages to keep fruit and foliage off the soil and away from pathogens, and to promote air movement around stems and leaves.

Keep Things Clean

Throughout the season, regularly pick up any dropped or damaged fruit or flowers. And at the end of the season, conduct an annual fall cleanup to prevent pathogen inoculum from over-wintering in your garden. Gather up stalks, stems, leaves, and dropped fruits and place them in the middle of a hot compost pile. (See "Create Great Compost" on page 18 to learn how to compost garden and household wastes.)

Thin crowded stems by snipping a few at the base.

Clean up seed heads, dead flower stalks, and other plant debris in the fall to destroy pathogen overwintering sites.

To avoid spreading diseases from plot to plot or season to season, it's important to keep gardening equipment clean. Disinfect reusable plastic mulches, floating row covers, garden stakes, and tools between uses by dipping them in a 10 percent bleach solution (1 part bleach to 9 parts water), then allowing them to air dry. Before storage, give tools a light coat of oil.

Apply Protective Sprays

Materials known as antitranspirants are typically used to protect trees and shrubs from winter damage. Antitranspirants are not registered for use as fungicides, but gardeners have found that these materials can help to prevent infection by some diseases like powdery mildew.

Thin stems of bushy perennials—such as common sneezeweed (*Helenium autumnale*)—to promote air circulation.

Removing and destroying rust-infected leaves can be an effective control for this fungal disease.

Clean up damaged or diseased fruits as soon as you spot them to keep pathogens from infecting more of your crop.

What to Do If Disease Appears

If disease does strike, don't despair! Try the techniques discussed below to stop diseases before they can spread out of control.

Prune Off Infected Parts

Inspect your plants periodically throughout the gardening season, keeping watch for signs of disease. If you catch a disease early, you can prune away infected leaves and branches and possibly avoid any further problems. Get rid of infected material by any one of the methods discussed below.

Compost Them Use a hot compost pile—keep it at about 160°F (70°C)—to kill most fungi, bacteria, and pathogenic nematodes. Add infected plants to the center of your pile, where the temperature is hottest.

Toss Them If your compost pile doesn't get hot enough to destroy pathogens, add infected plants to your household trash.

Bury Them Dig a hole in an out-of-the-way spot in your yard, then bury whole plants or plant parts. This is a good technique for materials infected with hard-to-kill viruses.

Burn Them Burning is a good way to destroy persistent pathogens like viruses, but first check for local burning regulations.

The first step toward effective control is making the right diagnosis.

Solarize Your Soil

If you suspect that soilborne diseases are damaging your crops, try a simple technique called soil solarization. This process uses the sun's energy to heat the soil and kill off many pathogens, as well as most insects and weed seeds. Soil solarization works best in midsummer, just before fall crops are planted, or during any long stretch of clear, hot weather.

You'll need a sheet of 1- to 4-mil clear plastic large enough to cover the treatment area. Remove existing plants and prepare the site for replanting. Water the area thoroughly, and dig a small trench several inches deep around the border. Cover the area with the plastic, and bury the edges in the trench to hold them down and "seal" the site.

Leave the plastic in place for 3 to 4 weeks. During that time, the soil temperature should rise high enough to destroy most soil pests and weed seeds in the top few inches of soil. Then remove the plastic and plant your crops as usual. Avoid deep digging or soil turning, or you may bring up infested soil from below.

Keep in mind that solarization can kill beneficial soil organisms too, so only use it if you have a serious disease problem.

Sooty mold grows on the honeydew that is excreted by aphids and similar pests.

Fight Fungus with Compost

Compost tea can help stop the spread of some diseases, like powdery mildew, before they get out of control. It can also give your plants a nutrient boost. To make the tea, mix 1 part finished compost with 6 parts water in a large bucket. Set it in a warm place for 1 week. Before using, filter the mixture through several layers of burlap or cheesecloth, then pour the liquid into a spray bottle. (You can toss the solids into your next compost pile.)

As soon as you spot disease, pinch off any heavily damaged leaves, then spray infected plants, saturating the leaf surfaces. For best results, treat plants in the evening when they are likely to remain damp for several hours. Repeat the application in 3 or 4 days if plants still show symptoms.

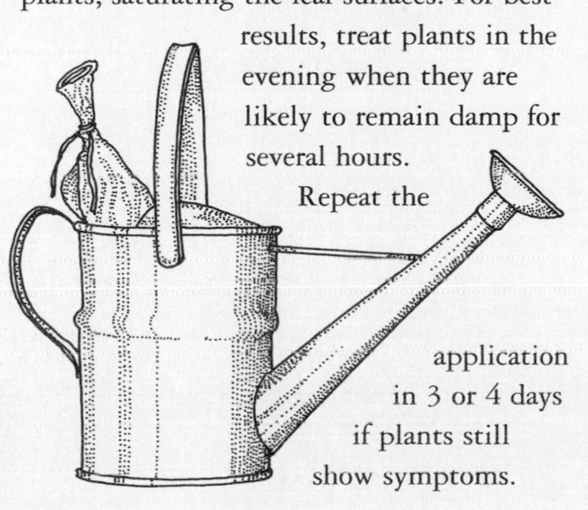

Incorporate Them Use a shovel or rotary tiller to chop and mix plants into the soil, where they are attacked by beneficial soil microorganisms. You'll be improving soil organic matter at the same time.

Control Disease Carriers

Vectors are animals that carry pathogens from one plant to the next. Vectors like insects and nematodes usually carry pathogens in their mouthparts, then inoculate new host plants when they begin feeding. That's how cucumber beetles spread bacterial wilt and aphids spread viruses. You can control the diseases they spread by controlling the pest. Barriers, like floating row covers, are an easy and effective way to keep disease-carrying pests from spreading diseases to healthy plants.

People can act as vectors when they unknowingly carry inoculum on shoes, hands, and tools after working among infected plants. And don't forget that pets are frequent vectors of plant diseases in gardens, greenhouses, and among houseplants: They often carry inoculum on their coats and paws. Whenever possible, stay out of the garden when plants are wet, and try to keep pets out of the garden then, too. After working around diseased plants, be sure to wash and dry your hands and tools thoroughly, and knock any clinging soil off your shoes.

Prune or pick off infected plant parts and dispose of them in household trash, bury them, or burn them.

If All Else Fails

Despite your best efforts, disease can occasionally get out of hand. When things get to this stage, you have several choices: mix up a home remedy, resort to an organically acceptable chemical, or remove and dispose of the infected plant.

Handy Home Remedies

Many gardeners have reported success against fungal diseases, including black spot and powdery mildew, with a baking soda (sodium bicarbonate) spray. It can help prevent problems, as well as kill some of the organisms that have already infected your plants. Make a baking soda solution by dissolving 1 teaspoon of baking soda in 1 quart (1 l) of warm water. If desired, add up to 1 teaspoon of liquid dish soap to help the solution cling to foliage. Use a spray bottle to wet both tops and bottoms of leaves thoroughly.

Garlic works against some fungi and nematodes, as well as many insect pests. "Pest Controls from Your Kitchen" on page 42 offers a recipe for preparing garlic oil spray.

A baking soda solution is an effective control for black spot and powdery mildew.

Biological Fungicides

Plant scientists are quickly developing new biological controls that halt plant diseases, just like the biological controls that work against insect pests. Several fungi and bacteria that act like pathogen predators have been isolated. *Agrobacterium radiobacter*, for instance, is a nonpathogenic bacterium (available in products like Galltrol-A and Norbac 84-C) that controls crown gall, a bacterial disease of woody plants. In the future, look for these biological fungicides at your garden center.

Wear protective clothing when applying fungicides.

Organically Acceptable Chemical Controls

Materials like lime-sulfur, Bordeaux mix, and copper are commonly known as controls, but a more correct term would be "protectants." Most of these materials can only stop diseases from spreading further by killing disease spores or preventing the spores from germinating. They generally will not "cure" a damaged plant. But they can buy you some time to improve the growing conditions around an affected plant. And they're also useful as preventive measures if you've had problems with a particular disease in the past and want to prevent it in the future. "Organically Acceptable Fungicides" summarizes the most commonly used materials for controlling garden diseases.

Destroy Infected Plants

Sometimes the most radical cure is the only way to go. A severely infected plant may be beyond saving, and keeping it around can endanger other related plants in your garden. For annual flowers and vegetables, and even most perennials, pulling out the damaged plant may be no big deal. (See "Prune Off Infected Parts" on page 60 for tips on safely disposing of diseased materials.) Chalk up the loss to experience, and take steps to avoid the same problems in the future.

More permanent plants, like shrubs and trees, represent a bigger investment in time and money. Before you decide to remove these plants, consider consulting an arborist to get a professional opinion.

If the same diseases attack year after year, consider replacing the affected plants with less-susceptible species.

Organically Acceptable Fungicides

These traditional organic fungicides act as "protectants" since they can prevent infections from spreading if you apply them early. Always follow label directions when applying these materials, and wear protective clothing like gloves, goggles, and a long-sleeve shirt.

Product	Diseases Controlled	Formulations/Precautions
Copper	Protects vegetables, fruits, ornamentals, and nuts against infection by a broad spectrum of plant pathogens.	Sold as a dust, sprayable solution, or mixable powder. Buy fixed copper or copper sulfate (bluestone); also in bordeaux mix. Toxic to people and other mammals; irritates eyes and skin. Highly toxic to fish and aquatic invertebrates. Persists indefinitely in soil.
Bordeaux Mix	Protects most garden plants against many common diseases including anthracnose, bacterial leaf spots and wilts, black spot, fire blight, peach leaf curl, powdery mildew, and rust.	Sold as a dust or mixable powder. To avoid burning plant foliage, apply just before plants leaf out in spring; injury is common when mix is applied at temperatures below 50°F (10°C) and when humidity is high.
Lime-Sulfur	Protects and eradicates anthracnose, brown rot, leaf spot, mildew, and scab on dormant perennials, roses, evergreens, and fruit crops.	Sold as a liquid concentrate. Extremely toxic to mammals. Wear rubber gloves and goggles to protect eyes and skin from irritation. To avoid burning plant foliage, don't use lime-sulfur when temperatures exceed 85°F (29°C). Lime-sulfur discolors wood and painted surfaces.
Fungicidal Soap	Controls powdery mildew, black spot, brown canker, leaf spot, and rust on food plants and ornamentals.	Sold as a liquid concentrate. Nontoxic to humans and mammals. Test plants for sensitivity by spraying a few leaves before treating the whole plant.
Sulfur	Protects against apple scab, brown rot of stone fruits, powdery mildew, black spot, rusts and other common diseases of most food crops.	Sold as a dust or mixable powder. Moderately toxic to humans and other mammals; wear protective clothing to avoid irritation to lungs, skin, and eyes. Do not apply within 1 month of using an oil spray; use a copper fungicide instead. Avoid using when temperatures exceed 80°F (27°C).

Identifying and Managing Animal Pests

While most discussions of pest control deal primarily with insect pests, gardeners know that animals can cause equally as much, and often more, damage than any insect. Whether you live in the country or the city, preventing and controlling animal pests can be a real concern. In this chapter, you'll find lots of suggestions for controls that have worked for other gardeners to keep damage to a minimum.

Basically, dealing with animal damage involves the same plan of attack you use against insect and disease pests. The best control is prevention. Start by modifying the habitat—eliminating or reducing the amount of food or shelter pests will find in the garden. Designing your yard with suitable fences so animal pests stay out is another effective way to prevent damage.

If you don't take steps to prevent animal pests, or if the preventive measures don't work, you may suddenly be facing a lot of damage. Most animal pests are secretive and nocturnal, causing damage when you're least likely to be a witness. And larger pests, like deer and woodchucks, can decimate a planting in a few hours.

Once you discover the damage, look for clues like tracks or droppings to help you identify the pest. To get tracks for identification, sprinkle dry soil in the area with flour (or lay down plastic sheets dusted with flour), and check the next morning. Study field guides on the identification of mammals and birds to learn more about the culprit and for clues about its habits.

Only you can decide whether the amount of damage caused warrants taking control measures. If only a small portion of your harvest is spoiled or stolen, you may decide to tolerate the pest. If more serious damage is being done to permanent plantings or whole crops, you may want to take action.

If damage from animal pests is heavy, use barriers like fences, row and plant coverings, or netting for the most successful control. Find fencing specifications for animal pests in the sections that follow. See "Keeping Pests Off Plants" on page 36 for detailed instructions on using plant and row covers.

Animal repellents and scare tactics are less dependable control methods and are most likely to be effective when used in combination with other methods. You can buy a variety of commercial repellents, or experiment with your own recipes. Animal pests quickly learn to tolerate both repellents and scare tactics. If repellents seem effective in your situation, try rotating their use for the best results.

When working to control animal pests, take precautions to guard against animal bites and infectious disease. Use live traps instead of attempting to transport pests by hand. Some animal pests may carry the rabies virus. Lyme disease is transmitted by ticks that hitch a ride on deer and mice. Be safe, and apply an insect repellent to clothing and exposed skin when working in areas frequently traveled by these pests.

Opposite: To most people, wild animals are a beautiful sight; to besieged gardeners, these creatures are mortal enemies. Only you can decide how much damage you can tolerate and what controls you're willing to use.

Beneficial Animals

If you've had animals attack your garden in the past, you may find yourself thinking of all four-legged critters as pests. Actually, though, there are a wide range of animals—from bats and birds to snakes and toads—that are on your side. These creatures can play a large role in keeping pest problems to a minimum.

Make your yard an attractive refuge for beneficial animals by offering plenty of fresh water and a diversity of plants to provide protective cover and food, including berries, nuts, and seeds. Before tilling or mowing, check the area for toads and snakes, then shoo them away temporarily. Put up bird- and bat houses to attract these insect-eating animals. Most important, if you spot insects feeding on your plants, give the natural controls (beneficial animals and insects) a few days to work before resorting to stronger measures.

Keep in mind that many of the steps you take to attract beneficial animals—like providing water and shelter—can also produce ideal conditions for pest animals. As a compromise, you may want to allow animals access to some parts of the garden but protect crops and special plants with fences or barriers.

Toads

If you're looking for an efficient and effective pest controller, make a place for toads in your garden. Almost 90 percent of a toad's diet consists of insects and slugs, making this creature the ideal garden partner. Toads spend most of their lives on dry land but require an aquatic habitat to reproduce. Encourage them to visit by installing shallow pools of water among your garden plants. Sink pans or birdbaths partially filled with rocks and water into garden soil in shady corners, to serve as sources of drinking water in summer months. Change the water frequently, especially during hot, dry spells.

Toads prefer a cool, shady hideaway—like the space under large cabbage leaves or nestled within a cool, moist organic mulch—

Insects make up three-quarters of a bluebird's diet.

Foxes are usually too shy to build a home in your backyard, but they may travel through in their hunt for prey.

during the day, when they're inactive. Leave overturned clay flowerpots (with a chipped edge to serve as an entrance) in shaded areas as daytime toad hotels. You can also buy terra cotta toad houses designed for the garden from specialty garden suppliers.

Upended, broken pots provide shelter for toads.

Snakes

Snakes are important yard and garden predators, since their diet includes pests like insects, mice, and baby rabbits. These reptiles hibernate underground or in rock dens during cold weather. Snakes are most likely to show up in country gardens that border woods, meadows, or farm fields.

You can encourage their presence in your garden by setting out boards and other debris for them to hide under. They'll appreciate a source of water, too. Unless you are familiar with snakes, avoid handling them, since bites by poisonous species can be fatal. Learn to recognize the snake species that are common in your area, so you won't be intimidated by them.

Bats

Bats are among the most beneficial and misunderstood of garden inhabitants. These pest predators consume

Birdhouses provide welcome nesting areas for garden birds. Clean out the houses after each nesting season.

thousands of flying insects each night. During the day, they rest in shady, protected nooks and crevices within caves, hollowed trees, or accessible attics and barns. You can provide extra housing for local bats by installing bat nesting boxes within your landscape. Bats prefer a location near a body of water.

Birds

Birds can be friends or foes in the garden. While some birds seem to be one step ahead of you in the race to the fruit harvest, most are a source of beauty and a means of garden insect control during the summer when pests are at their peak. Pest-eating birds include chickadees, titmice, swallows, bluebirds, phoebes, native sparrows, nighthawks, nuthatches, vireos, wrens, and woodpeckers. Food preference varies with species, but many of these birds

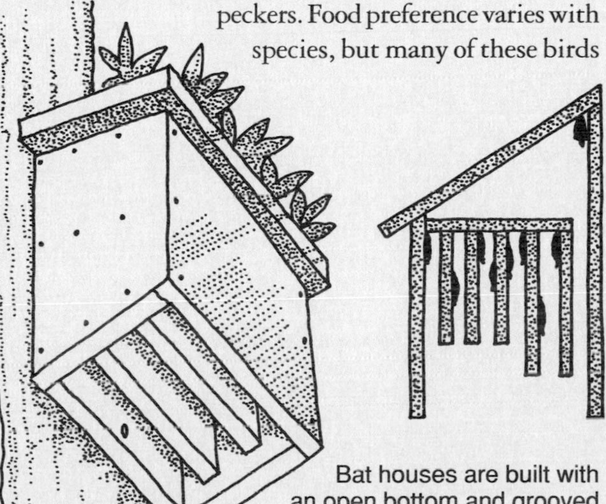

Bat houses are built with an open bottom and grooved walls for the bats to hang from.

Chickadees feed on the larvae and eggs of many garden insects, including aphids.

can be counted on to include insects as 90 percent or more of their daily diet.

You can attract birds to your yard by including flowering, fruit-bearing shrubs and trees—like Virginia creeper (*Parthenocissus quinquefolia*), serviceberry (*Amelanchier* spp.), and native cherry (*Prunus* spp.)—in your landscape as sources of shelter and food. Supplement their food during cold seasons, and provide a year-round source of fresh water. Include nesting boxes in your landscape to encourage birds to take up residence.

Other Animals

Foxes, weasels, skunks, hawks, and owls are important predators of common garden pests like rabbits and mice. There isn't much you can do to attract them, but it's helpful to understand that they work to keep natural pest populations in check. You may want to avoid setting traps for garden pest animals, which can lure these predators as well.

Owls help to control rodents like rats and mice; some species also feed on insects, including moths and cutworms.

Deer

Deer are common pests in gardens and landscapes located near wooded areas. Besides feeding on the leaves and stems of a wide range of plants, deer also cause damage by rubbing their antlers on the stems of woody plants, injuring the bark.

You can expect the most damage to your cultivated plants—like vegetable seedlings, fruits, and trees and shrubs—when natural food sources are scarce and when deer populations are high. That's also when deer are most difficult to control. To confirm the presence of deer, look for their distinctive tracks and their ¾-inch (18 mm), hard, dark pellet-like droppings.

Habitat Modification

Gardens and orchards located near the edges of wood lots that offer deer cover are invitations for deer damage. Under low to medium population pressure, deer are less likely to damage plants that are surrounded by plenty of open space.

Some gardeners report success by restricting their landscape plantings to species that deer find least palatable. Some plants that may deter deer include flowering herbs (like mint, lavender, borage, fennel, yarrow, and sage), spruces (*Picea* spp.), rugosa rose (*Rosa rugosa*), and other plants with thorns and spines that discourage feeding. Ask around or experiment to discover the food preferences of deer in your area.

Deer will nibble off the plump buds and soft bark of many landscape plants.

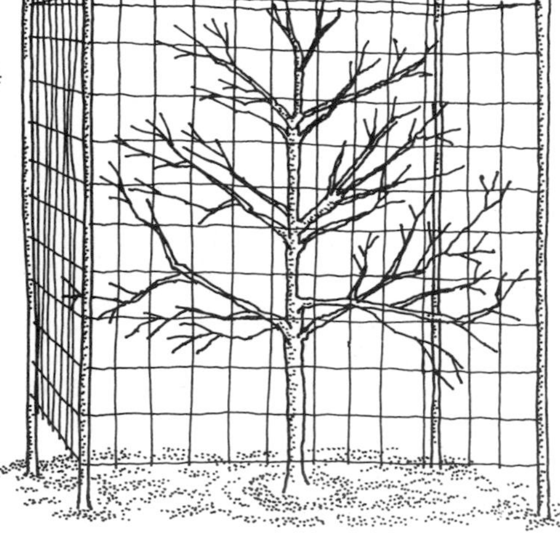

Protect individual plants with a wire-mesh cage.

Deer are becoming increasingly troublesome in suburban gardens. Tall fences are the best way to avoid damage.

Barriers

To protect individual plants from deer, surround the plants with homemade cylindrical cages made from galvanized hardware cloth, chicken wire, or snow fencing. Encircle the plants with 6-foot (1.8 m) tall cages that extend several feet beyond the farthest branch tips. To hold the cages in place, drive wooden stakes or fence posts into the soil and attach the stakes to cages using twist-ties or twine.

Deer Deterrent Sprays

When deer problems aren't too severe, sprays may help prevent some damage. If you purchase a commercial repellent, check the ingredients to be certain it's organic. Organic sprays usually include materials like hot peppers or putrefied eggs. Mix up a home version of commercial egg-based repellents by blending one dozen eggs with 5 quarts (5 l) of water. (This will make enough solution to treat ¼ acre [0.1 ha].) The deer will be able to smell the decaying eggs, but you won't.

Use a sprayer to coat soil and plant cover thoroughly or a brush to apply repellent to individual plants. Repeat the application after rain. To prolong the period of effectiveness, try mixing liquid repellents with an anti-transpirant, like Wilt-Pruf, before spraying.

As they feed from their lowest to highest reach, deer often give a strange "skirted" appearance to plants.

Many gardeners report success with deodorant soap as a repellent.

The most effective way to protect large plantings, like orchards or landscaped areas, is by erecting a fence that completely encloses the area. Deer aren't likely to jump a high, solid fence they can't see through. Fences that deer can see through, like wire or chain link, should be 8 feet (2.4 m) high to be successful.

Electric fencing is an expensive but effective option. To get good control, install a six- or seven-wire fence, with the lowest wire 10 inches (25 cm) above the ground and the other wires spaced 8 to 10 inches (20 to 25 cm) apart. (A similar fence structure, with three wires spaced 3 to 4 inches [7.5 to 10 cm] apart and off the ground, may help foil racoons and smaller pests.) Angling the supports so the fence slopes away from the garden at the top will create an even more imposing deer barrier.

Repellents

Repellents are most successful when deer populations are low. It's best to begin using these materials before any damage occurs or when it is minimal. Once deer develop a taste for your plants, they're less likely to be deterred.

Researchers and gardeners report good results using ordinary bath soap (with the wrappers left on) as a repellent. Drill a hole through each of the soap bars, then use string or twine to hang them from branches or stakes 4 to 6 feet (1.2 to 1.8 m) high and 3 feet (90 cm) apart. Rain renews the repellent effect. Replace the bars when they are too small to stay attached.

Some gardeners control deer using human hair as a repellent. Place handfuls of hair inside small bags made from nylon netting or cheesecloth, then hang the bags as you would soap bars. Ask your hairdresser to save hair for you. Renew the hair every 3 months or when it seems to lose effectiveness.

Custom-blend other homemade repellents using ingredients like hot sauce, garlic, bonemeal, or bloodmeal. Experiment with various rates and combinations of repellent materials to find a recipe that works in your situation. Fill muslin bags with the dry repellents, or soak rags, socks, or string with repellent solutions.

Finding out what deer will and won't eat is often a matter of trial and error. Lavender is usually not damaged.

Deer often pass by borage and other herbs, but they may stop to feed if more-preferred food is unavailable.

Rabbits are common and destructive garden creatures. They chew on many kinds of plants—even tree bark.

Rabbits

Fresh vegetables, new plant shoots, and the tender bark and buds of woody landscape plants are favorite year-round rabbit foods. Rabbits make their nests in soil (sometimes under the leaves of large plants), and bear up to 18 young in one season. If you suspect rabbits are damaging your plants, look for their dark, pellet-like droppings at feeding sites to confirm the identification.

Habitat Modification

Locate your garden away from shrubs and brambles that offer cover to rabbits. Keep the surrounding area mowed, and remove brush and other piles of debris.

Repellents

To repel rabbits, use a sprayer to apply repellents to a path surrounding the area to be protected or use a brush to coat individual plants. Purchase commercial repellents that mimic the scent of predators, or experiment with homemade recipes; as a guide, start with some of the suggestions in "Repellents" on page 69.

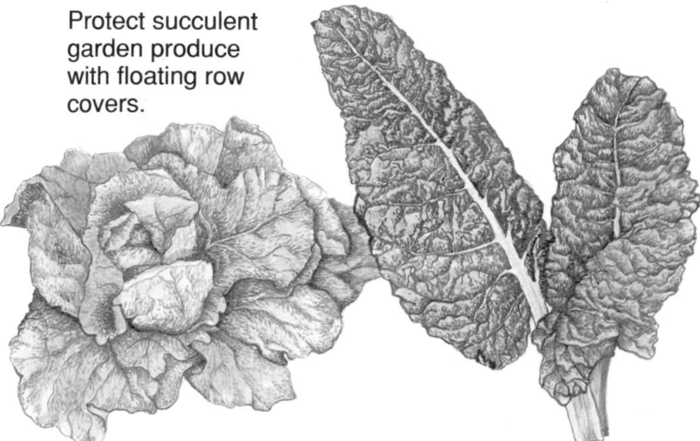

Protect succulent garden produce with floating row covers.

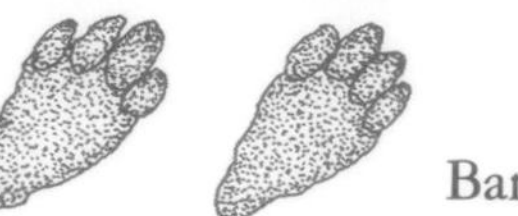

Barriers

Protect individual plants with homemade cylindrical cages of galvanized ¼-inch (6 mm) mesh hardware cloth around stems and trunks. Make the cages at least 1½ to 2 feet (45 to 60 cm) high. Position them 1 to 2 inches (2.5 to 5 cm) away from the trunk, and bury the bottom edge 2 to 3 inches (5 to 7.5 cm) below the soil surface. In areas with heavy snow, make the cages taller to compensate for deep snow cover or rabbits will just hop over the fence.

To protect larger areas, erect a 2-foot (60 cm) tall fence from chicken wire, then sink the bottom edge 2 to 3 inches (5 to 7.5 cm) into the soil. If you already have a garden fence, make it rabbit-proof by lining the bottom with chicken wire.

Keep Rabbits Running

To protect small gardens from rabbits, place inflatable snake, owl, or hawk-like images or statues around your plants. Move the scare tactics frequently to keep the pests away.

Block bunny access to individual plants with commercially available plastic tree guards. You can also use row cover fabric, or bird netting with a 1-inch (2.5 cm) or smaller mesh, to cover and protect most plants.

Fences may not be very attractive, but they are usually quite effective in preventing plant damage from rabbits.

Birds

Birds like to vary the ingredients in their diet, so don't be surprised when the same birds you enjoy watching in the wild begin stealing treats from your garden. Common culprits include the American robin, blackbird, bluejay, cedar waxwing, common starling, grackle, gray catbird, house finch, oriole, sparrow, and warbler. Most garden pest birds prefer ripe fruit; vegetables, including sweet corn, tomatoes, and cucumbers; and newly planted seeds.

Barriers

Prevent birds from reaching your crops by covering fruit trees, brambles, small fruits, and vegetables with lightweight fine-mesh netting or floating row cover fabric. If you use netting, buy the kind that is stiff, to keep birds from becoming tangled. You can purchase row cover fabric in narrow widths to cover rows or beds, or in wide pieces to cover entire trees. Use twine and clothespins attached to branches to hold the netting or covers in place. Make sure there are no gaps where birds can sneak through.

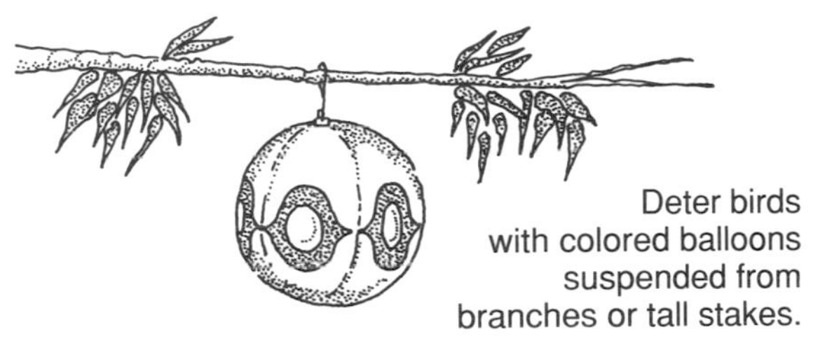

Deter birds with colored balloons suspended from branches or tall stakes.

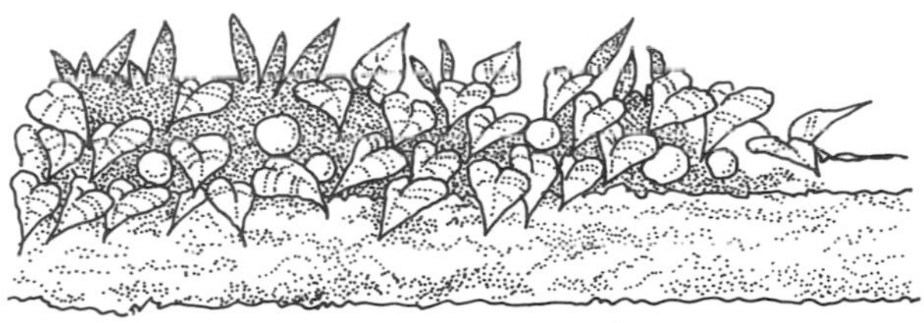

Even though real owls may not nest in your garden, you can scare some birds with inflatable or solid likenesses.

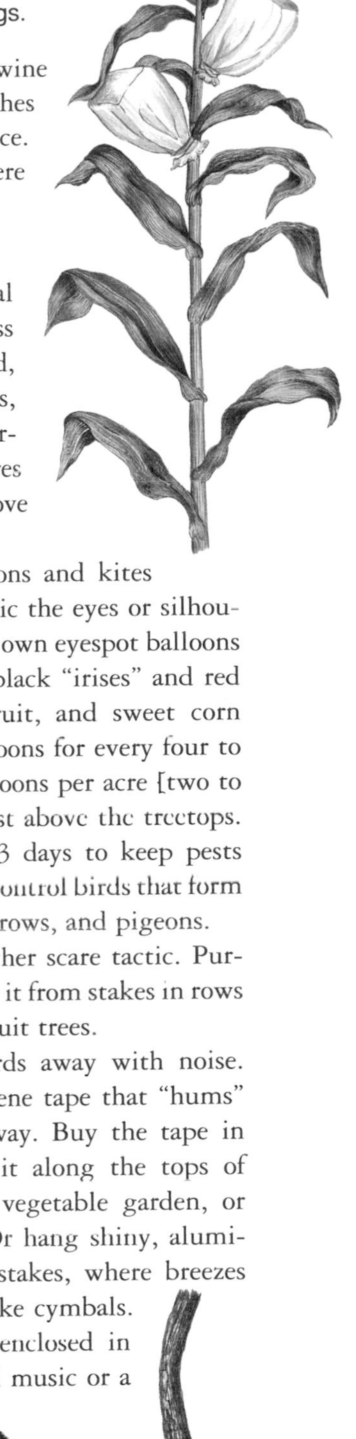

Keep birds from damaging your sweet corn by covering the ears with paper bags.

Scare Tactics

Birds are wary of their natural predators, so make your plants less inviting by posting inflatable, solid, or silhouetted likenesses of cats, snakes, and owls around your garden or orchard. The scary figures will be most effective if you move them periodically.

You can also purchase balloons and kites with colorful patterns that mimic the eyes or silhouettes of predators. Or make your own eyespot balloons from beach balls painted with black "irises" and red "pupils." In orchards, small fruit, and sweet corn plantings, hang one to two balloons for every four to eight trees (or four to eight balloons per acre [two to four per hectare]) from poles just above the treetops. Move the balloons every 2 to 3 days to keep pests guessing. Balloons work best to control birds that form flocks, like starlings, grackles, crows, and pigeons.

Reflective Mylar tape is another scare tactic. Purchase the tape in rolls, then hang it from stakes in rows of berries or from branches of fruit trees.

Some gardeners frighten birds away with noise. You can purchase a polypropylene tape that "hums" in the breeze to keep birds away. Buy the tape in rolls, then stretch and fasten it along the tops of fences, between stakes in the vegetable garden, or among branches in orchards. Or hang shiny, aluminum pie pans from fences or stakes, where breezes cause them to crash together like cymbals. Try placing a portable radio, enclosed in a plastic bag and tuned to loud music or a 24-hour talk show, among your plants. (Keep in mind that while loud noises may chase pests away, they may attract irate neighbors to your door!)

Orioles are both friends and foes. They mainly eat insects but may also feed on fruit crops.

Moles are much maligned for damaging lawns and gardens, but these creatures feed mostly on insects, not plants.

Moles can cause unsightly mounds. If this is a real problem, try to control the insects that attract the moles.

Moles and Gophers

These burrowing pests are often mistaken for each other, since their tunnels and damage to lawns and gardens look similar. Moles, however, primarily eat soil-dwelling insects, while gophers are plant pests that damage roots, bulbs, and woody plants.

Habitat Modification

Soil-dwelling insects, like beetle grubs, are the main food source for moles. You may be able to control mole problems by reducing the grub population. Dust your lawn with spores of milky disease, a beneficial bacterium that kills several kinds of beetle grubs. (For more information on milky disease, see "Beneficial Microorganisms" on page 40.) Moles feed on earthworms as well, though, so they may remain even after the grubs are gone.

Barriers

To exclude both moles and gophers, dig a trench around the perimeter of your garden or beds, and install a fence of hardware cloth or chicken wire extending 2 feet (60 cm) underground. To keep out gophers, the fence should extend 2 feet (60 cm) above ground as well.

> **Homes of Moles and Gophers**
>
> You can identify mole runs by the ridges they form in the lawn and by the volcano-like mound of excavated soil they throw out from their tunnels, with an exit hole in the center. Gophers burrow more deeply and don't tend to form ridges. Their mounds are offset, with the exit hole to one side.

Gophers feed on a variety of plant material, including bulbs, tubers, roots, and seeds.

Flooding and Trapping

If you feel that the damage caused warrants extreme measures, you can force moles and gophers out of the soil by flooding their main tunnels with water from a garden hose. Look for ridges of raised soil or sod to locate the main burrow and entrance holes. Use a shovel to make a small hole into a main tunnel, then poke the end of a garden hose into the burrow. Leave the water running for 10 to 15 minutes, or until the adults are driven to the surface, then kill them with a shovel. Trapping is another effective way to stop mole damage.

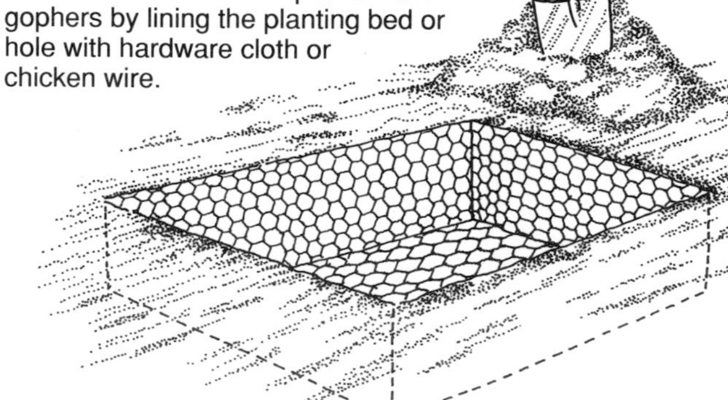

Protect bulbs and other plants from gophers by lining the planting bed or hole with hardware cloth or chicken wire.

Free-roaming dogs can trample or dig up precious plants. Some dogs even develop a taste for garden produce.

Dogs and Cats

Dogs and cats can be destructive garden pests, especially if they aren't your own pets and you can't control them. Even the most well-mannered dogs are likely to step on or knock down garden plants or dig holes in their search for rodents or buried treasure. Both dogs and cats leave behind excrement with the potential to transmit diseases.

If your pets aren't the ones causing the damage, find out who the problem animals belong to. Explain the problem to the owners and see if they're willing to control their pets. If that doesn't work, or if the animals are wild, try the options below.

Habitat Modification

Keep tall vegetation cleared away from garden areas so animals have fewer hiding places. Discourage cats by positioning a garden hose and sprinkler attachment to wet the garden for 10 to 20 minutes intermittently; cats don't like getting wet. Some gardeners report success by planting a border of prickly shrubs, like roses or blackberries, around the area to be protected. Entice cats away from your garden with plantings of catnip.

Repellents

Few odors repel dogs sufficiently. Some gardeners report that cats are repelled by strong-smelling plants like onions, garlic, and French marigolds; by citrus peels; or by the oil of wintergreen or camphor. Try planting clumps of the repellent plants throughout your garden, or soak rags or cottonballs with the aromatic oils and tuck them underneath plants; renew them after rain.

You can also buy commercial dog and cat repellents. If you plan to apply a repellent in the vegetable garden, read the label to be sure the product is safe to use on edible plants. Follow application instructions on the label.

Some gardeners claim that strong-smelling marigolds will repel cats.

Barriers

A fence is the best way to separate pets and gardens. To keep dogs and cats out, fences should be at least 6 feet (1.8 m) tall; for complete control, include a fence ceiling as well. Use a small-mesh wire to keep cats from squeezing through. To keep cats from digging in beds, lay 1-inch (2.5 cm) chicken wire flat on the soil surface where you plant annual flowers or vegetables or cut sections to fit around perennial plants.

Well-behaved cats can be pleasant garden companions, but others may dig in the soil or chew or roll on plants.

Citrus peels scattered on the soil surface may repel cats and prevent them from digging in garden beds.

Woodchucks—also known as groundhogs—are most commonly found in the northeast United States and Canada.

Woodchucks

Woodchucks, also known as groundhogs, are a common site along country roads and in farm fields during the growing season. In winter, they hibernate in extensive underground burrows. They eat a wide variety of garden, orchard, and landscape plants, preferring to feed in the early morning and evening, though they may emerge at other times.

Woodchucks are fairly large creatures and can weigh up to 10 pounds (4.5 kg) or more. Their front feet have long, curved claws that are specially adapted for digging. Of more concern to gardeners are woodchucks' sharp front teeth, which can decimate an entire planting in just a few hours.

Habitat Modification

Like other animal pests, woodchucks prefer to feed close to protective cover. Remove brush piles and other debris where these animals may take up residence. Keep an open mowed area around orchards and vegetable gardens.

Barriers

A length of floating row cover fabric on top of plants may be all that you need to prevent woodchucks from dining in your garden. If the pests are persistent, you can exclude them from the garden with a sturdy fence. First, dig a trench 1 foot (30 cm) deep and 3 feet (90 cm) wide around the area to be protected. Line the bottom and outer side with chicken wire, then extend the wire 3 feet (90 cm) above ground. Use wooden or steel fence posts spaced 6 to 8 feet (1.8 to 2.4 m) apart to support the wire above ground. Tie the fence to the posts with twine—one tie near ground level and one about a foot down from the top of the fence. When the animal tries to climb up, the top of the fence will fold down over it. This type of fence also works to keep rabbits and porcupines away from your vegetables.

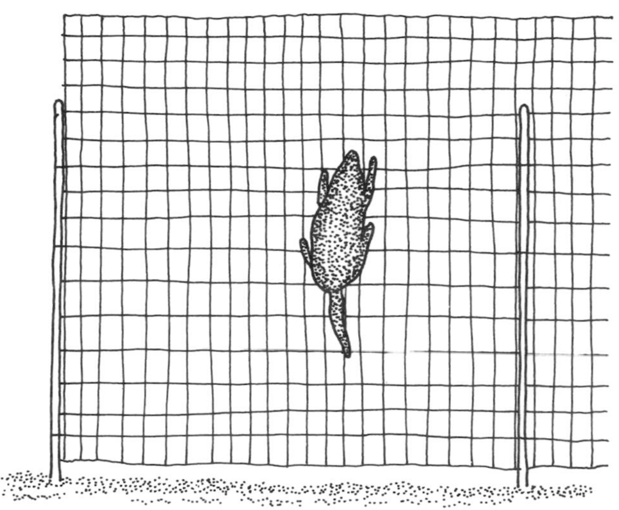

A fence can keep woodchucks out. Leave the top untied, so it will flop down as the animal tries to climb up.

Other Controls

Some gardeners claim that planting onions or garlic around the burrows will chase woodchucks away; others suggest sprinkling red pepper around the holes and the garden. Dogs may bark at and chase off woodchucks, but smart dogs won't attack: Cornered woodchucks can be fierce fighters.

Woodchucks build large underground burrows where they hibernate and raise their young.

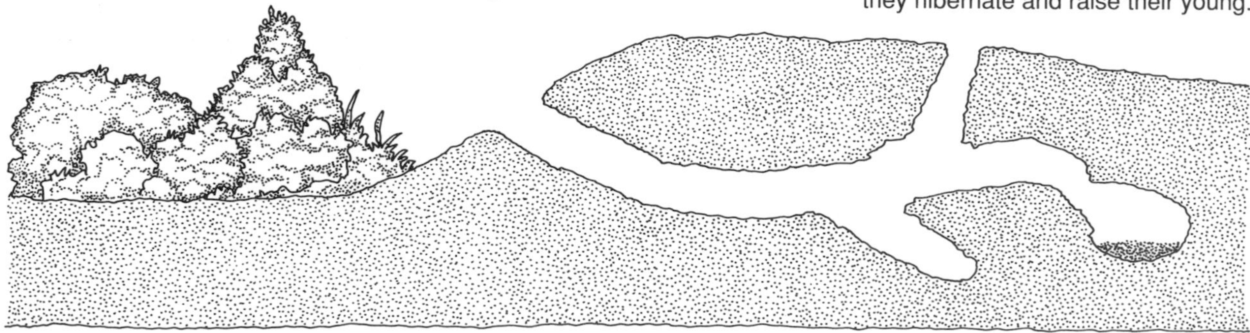

Meadow Mice

Meadow mice, also known as voles, are common vegetarian inhabitants of grassy meadows and woods that offer plentiful plants for food and cover. Sometimes they feed on lawns, gardens, and orchards. If winter food supplies grow scarce, they begin feeding on the bark and roots of fruit trees, girdling the trees and possibly killing them. Mice may even chew holes in drip irrigation tubes that are buried under mulch.

You can confirm the presence of meadow mice in winter by locating their system of runways, about 1½ inches (3.5 cm) wide, just above the ground and below snow. They may also travel in mole tunnels.

When winter food supplies dwindle, meadow mice often feed on the bark of young trees, girdling and killing plants.

Habitat Modification

Keep vegetation cleared away from the base of orchard trees. Mulch with stones to a depth of 2 to 3 inches (5 to 7.5 cm); lightweight organic materials, like bark or compost, provide more hiding places for mice. If you do use an organic mulch, keep it at least several inches away from stems. Conduct a thorough garden and orchard clean-up, removing old debris like boards or logs that mice nest underneath. Wait until the ground has frozen to mulch perennial beds; by that time, mice will probably have found other winter quarters.

Meadow mice are tiny, but they can cause significant damage to plants.

Barriers

Make 18- to 24-inch (45 to 60 cm) protective cylinder cages for trees from ¼-inch (6 mm) mesh hardware cloth. Sink the cages several inches into the soil surface. You can also purchase commercial tree guards made of plastic.

Trapping

If you feel that the wintertime damage caused to your orchard trees calls for extreme measures, you may choose to trap and kill the pests. Wear gloves to bait snap traps with peanut butter, apple slices, whole grains, bread, or other enticements, then place the traps in tunnels at right angles to the runway. You can coat traps with bacon grease to mask human odors as well as to help preserve the traps. Check traps twice daily, replacing the bait until pests are no longer captured; repeat after several weeks.

Keeping your garden free of debris can eliminate some mouse hiding places. Cats may also chase mice away, so you might consider investing in one!

Insect and Disease Guide

This "Insect and Disease Guide" is your handbook for identifying and dealing with common garden problems. Here's where you'll go to look up specific controls for particular pests and diseases. You'll also use it as a field guide to help you identify insects and diseases that are unfamiliar to you.

For easy reference, this guide is divided into three parts: "Pests," starting on page 78; "Beneficials," starting on page 117; and "Diseases," starting on page 130. These sections contain many individual entries, each with at least one color photograph.

Pests "Pests" is where you'll find the entries dealing with plant-eating garden denizens, from aphids and apple maggots to whiteflies and wireworms. The entries are arranged alphabetically by the common name of the pest. Most pests belong to the Class Insecta: the insects. If one species of insect is usually to blame for the damage, you'll find its scientific name in the upper left of the column, above the common name. If a whole family of insects causes similar damage, you'll find the family name in the upper right of the column, above the common name. A few pests—including nematodes, slugs and snails, and sowbugs—belong to completely different scientific groupings, so no species or family name is listed.

Each entry has a photograph of the pest or its damage, along with a detailed description of the pest, including its geographic range, life cycle, and favorite targets. You'll also find a description of the different types of damage it can cause on different plants or different plant parts. Each entry includes advice on organically acceptable controls to reduce pest damage on existing crops and suggestions for preventing the pest from causing damage to future crops.

Beneficials "Beneficials" is arranged much like "Pests": alphabetically by the common name, with a photo and description of each. But instead of discussing damage, the entry will tell you about the beneficial effect of each creature. And in place of control and prevention information, you'll find tips on attracting these natural pest controllers to your yard and garden.

Diseases "Diseases" is also arranged alphabetically by the common name of the problem. Where appropriate, we've included the scientific name (genus, species, or family) of the organism responsible. Some problems are caused by several different organisms; others—like nitrogen deficiency and lightning damage—aren't caused by organisms at all. For each entry, though, you'll find out where the problem most commonly occurs, what kinds of plants it affects, and what sorts of symptoms it produces. You'll also learn about suggested controls (if any), as well as tips for preventing the problem in the future.

To get the most out of this guide, refer to it regularly. Become familiar with the common pests, beneficials, and diseases so you'll recognize them when you see them on your garden plants. Then you'll know whether to cheer them on (the beneficials, of course) or start some kind of control measures (for those pesky pests and disastrous diseases).

Opposite: Many pests are easy to control without sprays of any kind. Large pests, like this caterpillar, are easy to handpick, once you see them. This one stands out against the flower but would blend in on a leaf.

P E S T S

APHIDS

Aphids attack many of our favorite garden and houseplants. Fortunately, these tiny pests aren't difficult to control.

DESCRIPTION: Adults are fragile, pear-shaped insects, 1/16–3/8 inch (2–9.5 mm) long, with two short tubes (called cornicles) projecting backward from the tip of the abdomen. They have long antennae and are variously colored green, pink, black, or dusty gray. They can be winged or wingless. Winged forms appear later in the season when there is crowding in the aphid colony or when there are changes in the host plant. Aphid wings are transparent, longer than the body, and held roof-like over the back. Nymphs are similar to adults, but smaller and wingless. Aphids are generally found in crowded colonies.

RANGE: Throughout North America; more than 1,350 species.

PLANTS AFFECTED: Most fruit and vegetable plants, flowers, ornamentals, fruit and shade trees. Some aphid species feed on only one kind of plant; some alternate between two different species of host plants; yet others attack a wide range of plants.

DAMAGE: Adults and nymphs pierce the leaf and suck huge amounts of plant sap. Feeding often causes distorted leaves, buds, and flowers; severely infested leaves and flowers may drop. As they feed, aphids excrete a sweet honeydew onto leaves, which supports growth of sooty mold. Some species spread plant viruses as they feed. In fall, late feeding by aphids helps harden off succulent new growth on fruit trees.

Masses of aphids cluster on stems, buds, and the undersides of leaves. Check these areas thoroughly when scouting for pests.

LIFE CYCLE: Eggs overwinter on woody stems or in crevices in bark. They hatch in spring into "stem" females that give birth continuously to live nymphs. Nymphs mature in 1–2 weeks and start producing offspring. Because of their swift reproductive rate, aphid colonies develop very quickly. When days become shorter in fall, males and normal females are born; these offspring mate and the females lay eggs, which are the overwintering stage of the insect. In greenhouses, some strains of aphids continue to give birth to nymphs year-round.

PREVENTION: Maintain healthy plants; do not over-fertilize with nitrogen. Large numbers of aphids are killed by native predators and parasites; attract these to the garden by planting pollen and nectar plants.

CONTROL: Spray dormant oil to control overwintering eggs on fruit trees. Spray plants frequently with a strong stream of water to knock aphids off the plants; most will be too injured to survive. Release aphid midges, lady beetles, lacewings, or parasitic wasps. Spray insecticidal soap or make homemade garlic sprays. As a last resort, spray pyrethrin or rotenone.

Rhagoletis pomonella

APPLE MAGGOT

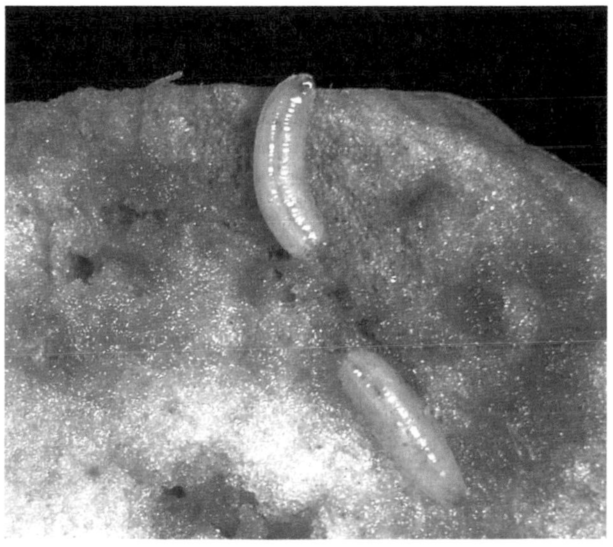

Apple maggot larvae—or "railroad worms"—tunnel into fruit, especially on thin-skinned or early-maturing cultivars.

DESCRIPTION: Adults are dark-colored flies, ¼ inch (6 mm) long, with yellow legs and transparent wings patterned with dark, crosswise bands. Larvae are white maggots that develop inside fruit.

RANGE: Eastern United States and Canada; Northern California.

PLANTS AFFECTED: Apple, crab apple, blueberry, occasionally cherry and plum.

DAMAGE: Maggots bore through fruit, leaving brown, winding tunnels in the flesh, usually causing fruit to drop early.

LIFE CYCLE: Adults emerge from overwintering pupae in the soil from mid-June to July. Female flies lay eggs in punctures in the skin of the fruit; eggs hatch in 5–7 days. The larvae tunnel inside the fruit until it drops. They leave the fruit after completing their development to pupate several inches deep in the nearby soil. One generation per year in most areas; in Southern regions, there may be a partial second generation, with adults emerging in early fall. Some pupae can stay dormant in the soil for several years.

PREVENTION: Plant late-ripening cultivars. Collect and destroy dropped fruit daily until September, then twice a month in fall. Plant clover groundcovers to attract ground beetles that prey on pupae.

CONTROL: Hang sticky red apple-maggot traps in trees from mid-June until harvest (use one trap per dwarf tree, up to six traps per full-sized tree).

Noctuidae

ARMYWORMS

Armyworms feed in masses and can devour entire plantings of corn, tomatoes, and other vegetables in just a few nights.

DESCRIPTION: Adults are pale, gray-brown moths with 1½–2-inch (4–5 cm) wingspans and a white dot in the center of each forewing. Young larvae are pale green, up to 1½ inches (4 cm) long; older larvae are greenish brown with white side stripes and dark or light stripes along their backs. Eggs are greenish white, laid in masses on lower leaves.

RANGE: East of Rocky Mountains; New Mexico, Arizona, California, and southern Canada.

PLANTS AFFECTED: Field crops and garden plants, particularly bean, cabbage, corn, cucumber, lettuce, and tomato.

DAMAGE: Larvae feed in groups at night, hiding during the day in centers of plants or under litter. In corn, larvae feed in leaf whorls and ears. Larvae can consume whole plants overnight. First-generation larvae are most damaging; they are most numerous in years with cold, wet spring weather.

LIFE CYCLE: Larvae overwinter in soil or litter around roots. They resume feeding in spring, then pupate for 2 weeks. Two to three generations per year.

PREVENTION: Attract native parasitic wasps and flies with pollen and nectar plants. Control grassy weeds where infestations often start.

CONTROL: Apply BTK or insect parasitic nematodes to kill young larvae. Spray superior oil in July to kill eggs of second generation. After harvest, turn soil to expose pupae to natural enemies.

Crioceris asparagi

ASPARAGUS BEETLE

Asparagus beetles cause minor damage to emerging spring shoots; they will also defoliate plants later in the season.

DESCRIPTION: Adults are elongated, shiny, bluish black beetles, ¼ inch (6 mm) long, with a reddish brown thorax; wing covers have four cream-colored blotches and red borders. Larvae are plump, wrinkled, and grayish, with a dark head and legs. Eggs are shiny black.

RANGE: Throughout North America.

PLANTS AFFECTED: Asparagus.

DAMAGE: In early spring, adults and larvae chew holes in green spears, causing brownish blemishes. Later they attack the stems and leaves, leaving bare brown branches.

LIFE CYCLE: Hibernating adults emerge when the first asparagus spears are ready to cut. They feed and lay eggs that are glued on one end to stems and young spears; the eggs hatch in 3–8 days. Larvae crawl up the plants and feed for 2 weeks, then burrow just beneath the soil surface to pupate. Adults emerge in about 10 days. Two or three generations per year; five generations in warmer areas.

PREVENTION: In fall, remove and burn old asparagus fronds, weeds, and garden trash where beetles overwinter. In spring, cover spears with floating row covers until the end of harvest; cut mature spears often to prevent eggs from hatching.

CONTROL: Handpick beetles and larvae, especially in early spring. Spray pyrethrin or rotenone.

Thyridopteryx ephemeraeformis

BAGWORM

Bagworms live in curious bag-like cocoons that are camouflaged with bits of foliage from the host plant.

DESCRIPTION: Adult males are black, clear-winged moths, with 1-inch (2.5 cm) wingspans; females are wingless. Larvae are shiny, dark brown, and hidden inside silken bags. Pupae are inside the finished bag, which is 2–2½ inches (5–6 cm) long and attached to the tree. Eggs are light tan, laid inside the bags.

RANGE: East of Rocky Mountains; related species in the West.

PLANTS AFFECTED: Most deciduous and evergreen trees.

DAMAGE: Larvae eat the foliage, leaving a ragged appearance; in large infestations, the foliage may be stripped or the tree defoliated. Bags attached to foliage and branches are unsightly.

LIFE CYCLE: Eggs overwinter inside the bag and hatch in late spring when trees have all their leaves. Larvae spin a silken sack covering their body, which they take with them as they feed. In September, full-grown larvae attach the bag to a twig with silk, then pupate. After several days, the males emerge and fly to females, which remain in their bags for mating. Females lay eggs, then die.

PREVENTION: Attract native parasites with pollen and nectar plants.

CONTROL: Handpick and destroy the bags during winter. Cut bags away with a knife to avoid leaving a band of silk that could girdle the twig. Spray with BTK early in the season to kill larvae.

Otiorhynchus sulcatus

BLACK VINE WEEVIL

Black vine weevils chew notches in leaves of trees and shrubs—especially yew and rhododendron. Larvae feed on roots.

DESCRIPTION: Adults are oval, brownish gray or black, "snout beetles," ⅓ inch (8 mm) long, with small yellow patches on their backs. They cannot fly; all are female (there is no male black vine weevil). Larvae are fat, white grubs up to ½ inch (1 cm) long, with yellowish brown heads.

RANGE: Northern United States and southern Canada, especially California; Pacific Coast.

PLANTS AFFECTED: Blackberry, blueberry, cranberry, strawberry, and many ornamentals, particularly azalea, rhododendron, and yew.

DAMAGE: Adults chew along leaf margins, leaving characteristic scalloped bites; they rarely cause serious damage. Larvae feed on roots and can severely stunt or kill plants. Plants may also die from diseases that enter the injured roots.

LIFE CYCLE: Larvae overwinter in the soil and resume feeding on roots the following spring. They pupate in the spring; adult weevils emerge in June. After a delay of several weeks, weevils lay eggs in the soil around host plants. Eggs hatch in about 10 days, and the larvae burrow into roots to feed for the rest of the year. One generation per year.

PREVENTION: Plant rhododendron cultivars that have leaves with rolled edges; these deter feeding.

CONTROL: At night, knock weevils off plants onto a ground sheet or into a sweep net. Spray rotenone to control adults. Drench soil with insect parasitic nematodes to control larvae.

Meloidae

BLISTER BEETLES

Blister beetles are both the gardener's friend and foe. Adult beetles feed on garden plants; larvae eat grasshopper eggs.

DESCRIPTION: Adults are metallic or iridescent blue-black or purplish brown beetles, ⅜–¾ inch (9.5–20 mm) long, with soft, elongated bodies. They have long legs and narrow "necks." Beetles cling to plants when they are disturbed. Youngest larvae are tiny, narrow, and elongated with large heads; last-stage larvae are plump with very short legs.

RANGE: Throughout North America.

PLANTS AFFECTED: Adults feed on many flowers, shrubs, and vegetables.

DAMAGE: Large numbers of adults feeding on flowers and foliage can rapidly defoliate plants. Beetles contain a compound called cantharidin, which blisters human and animal skin. Larvae of most species are predators of grasshopper eggs.

LIFE CYCLE: Overwintering larvae pupate in the soil in spring. The adults emerge and lay eggs in midsummer in grasshopper egg burrows, where larvae feed for a month. They overwinter in these burrows for up to 2 years. Most species have one generation per year, synchronized with grasshopper life cycles.

PREVENTION: Protect plants with floating row covers or screens in midsummer.

CONTROL: Except in areas where high adult populations damage crops, control is not desirable because larvae control grasshoppers. If necessary, knock adults from plants into a pail of soapy water (wear gloves to avoid contact with crushed beetles). Spray plants with pyrethrin or rotenone.

Trichoplusia ni

CABBAGE LOOPER

Cabbage loopers can be hard to spot against the green leaves of cabbage family plants, but the damage they cause is easy to see.

DESCRIPTION: Adults are gray moths with a silvery V-shaped spot in the middle of each forewing and wingspans of 1½–2 inches (4–5 cm). They fly at night, so you'll rarely notice them. Larvae are green "inchworms" (so called because they move by humping their bodies up into a loop) with a pair of white lines down their backs and one line along each side. Eggs are light green and dome-shaped.

RANGE: Throughout most of the United States; southern Canada.

PLANTS AFFECTED: Primarily cabbage and related plants; also beet, celery, lettuce, pea, spinach, and tomato; flowers including carnation, nasturtium, and mignonette.

DAMAGE: Larvae chew holes in leaves; whole plants may be ruined or destroyed in severe infestations.

LIFE CYCLE: In May, the moths emerge from overwintering pupae and lay eggs on the upper surface of leaves. The larvae feed for 2–4 weeks, then pupate for 10 days in thin silk cocoons attached to stems or leaves. Three to four generations per year in most areas.

PREVENTION: Attract native parasitic wasps with pollen and nectar plants. Till in crop residues before adults emerge in spring.

CONTROL: Handpick the larvae several times weekly. Spray with BTK to control caterpillars. Spray severe infestations with garlic oil, pyrethrin, ryania, or sabadilla.

Delia radicum (=Hylemya brassicae)

CABBAGE MAGGOT

Cabbage maggots tunnel into roots and stems, causing plants to wilt. Look for white larvae and brown pupae below soil line.

DESCRIPTION: Adults are gray flies, ¼ inch (6 mm) long, with long legs. Larvae are white, tapering maggots burrowing in roots.

RANGE: Throughout North America.

PLANTS AFFECTED: Cabbage family plants.

DAMAGE: Injury usually shows first as sickly or stunted plants that suddenly wilt in the midday heat. This is caused by maggots boring into the roots. Plants may die, often because entry wounds from maggots allow diseases to infect roots; surviving plants yield poorly.

LIFE CYCLE: Pupae overwinter in the soil. The adult flies emerge from late March (in warmer regions) onward. Females lay eggs in the soil beside the plant roots. After they hatch, the larvae tunnel in roots for 3–4 weeks, then pupate in soil for 2–3 weeks. Two to four generations per year.

PREVENTION: Plant radishes earlier and cabbages later than usual to avoid main generations. Cover seedlings with floating row covers; make sure the edges are buried in soil. Set out transplants through slits in tar-paper squares to prevent females from laying eggs. Burn or destroy roots of cabbage family plants when you harvest the tops.

CONTROL: Apply insect parasitic nematodes to soil around roots. If pest populations are moderate, repel females by mounding wood ashes, diatomaceous earth, hot pepper, or ginger powder around base of stems.

Geometridae

CANKERWORMS

Cankerworms—often known as "inchworms"—loop their bodies as they crawl. They feed ravenously on leaves and buds.

DESCRIPTION: Adult males are light gray moths, with wingspans over 1 inch (2.5 cm); they are well camouflaged. Females are wingless, with plump, furry bodies, ½ inch (1 cm) long. Larvae are slender light green, brown, or black caterpillars with white stripes. Eggs are round and grayish brown.

RANGE: Nova Scotia to North Carolina; west to Missouri, Montana, and Manitoba; also Colorado, Utah, and California.

PLANTS AFFECTED: Apple, elm, oak, linden, beech, other deciduous trees, and ornamental shrubs.

DAMAGE: Caterpillars chew on young tree leaves and buds. As the pests grow, they move to larger leaves, leaving behind only leaf midribs and large veins. Heavily damaged trees look scorched.

LIFE CYCLE: Adults emerge in November and December and lay compact masses of eggs on twigs and branches of dormant trees. Eggs hatch in the spring about the time the first leaves open on trees. Larvae feed for 3–4 weeks, then crawl into the soil to pupate until early winter. One generation per year.

PREVENTION: Attract native parasitic wasps with nectar and pollen plants.

CONTROL: Use sticky tree bands to trap females as they climb trees to lay eggs in late fall. Destroy egg masses on branches. Spray with dormant oil to kill eggs. Spray BTK to kill larvae.

Psila rosae

CARROT RUST FLY

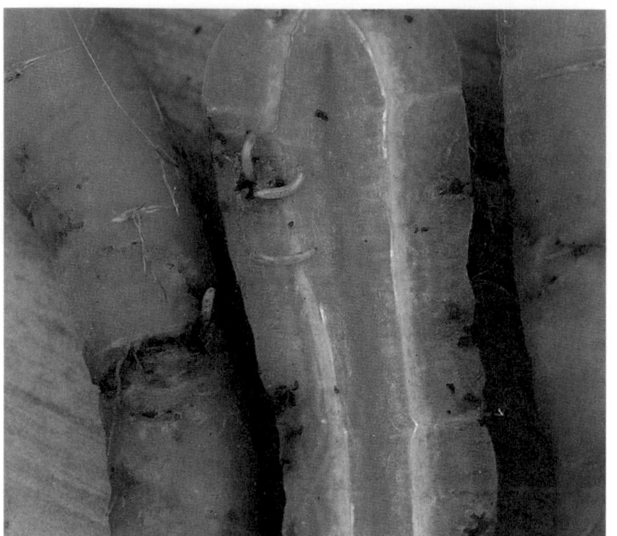

Carrot rust flies produce creamy white larvae that tunnel into the roots of susceptible plants, causing stunted growth.

DESCRIPTION: Adults are shiny, metallic, greenish black flies about 1/4 inch (6 mm) long with yellow legs and head. Larvae are creamy white, tapering maggots found in tunnels in roots.

RANGE: Throughout North America.

PLANTS AFFECTED: Carrot, celery, parsley, parsnip, and related plants.

DAMAGE: The root maggots eat fine root hairs, then tunnel through the roots. The tunnels are filled with rusty brown castings. Plants are stunted or killed and root crops are deformed and ruined. Injuries to roots allow disease organisms to enter. After harvest, maggots feed in stored roots.

LIFE CYCLE: Adults emerge in mid-April to May and begin laying eggs in the soil close to plants. Eggs hatch in 7–10 days; the tiny maggots burrow in roots for 3–4 weeks, then pupate. Two to three generations per year.

PREVENTION: Covering seedbeds with floating row covers before seedlings emerge provides excellent protection; bury edges under soil and leave crop covered until harvest. In areas with severe rust fly problems, control wild carrot and related weeds in the area. Avoid leaving carrots in the ground over winter. Sow midseason carrots after the first egg-laying period passes, and harvest roots early to avoid main generations.

CONTROL: Drenching soil with parasitic nematodes may help control larvae.

Blissus leucopterus

CHINCH BUG

Chinch bugs are fast-moving pests that most commonly attack grasses. A large infestation can quickly destroy a lawn.

DESCRIPTION: Adults are 1/6 inch (4 mm) long, with reddish legs and white forewings with a black triangular spot near the margin. The youngest nymphs are bright red with a white stripe across the back; older nymphs are black with white spots.

RANGE: Most common in eastern North America.

PLANTS AFFECTED: Sod, corn, and cereal grain crops.

DAMAGE: Adults and nymphs suck sap from roots and stems, leaving wilted and dying plants. Infested lawns show dying patches of turf.

LIFE CYCLE: Adults overwinter in clumps of grasses, especially along southern sides of fence rows and hedges. In warm spring weather, adults fly to fields and turf. Females lay eggs on grass roots or on lower leaves of grain plants. Eggs hatch in 1–3 weeks; nymphs chew on roots for 4–5 weeks, then molt to adults in late June. Two generations per year, three in Southern areas.

PREVENTION: For lawns only (not where animals will graze) plant endophyte-containing turf-grass cultivars. Encourage predators, like lady beetles and birds. Chinch bugs avoid shade, so shade bases of corn and cereal crop plants by interplanting with legumes (such as soybean and clover).

CONTROL: For small lawns, soak sod with soapy water (1 ounce/25 g liquid dish soap to 2 gallons/8 l water), then lay a flannel sheet over the grass to snare the bugs as they flee. Drown them in a bucket of soapy water, and rinse the lawn with clean water.

Cydia pomonella

CODLING MOTH

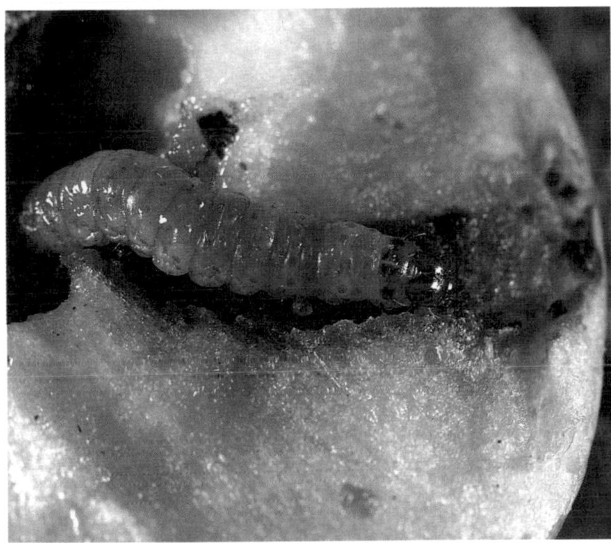

Codling moths are serious pests of apples and pears. The larvae feed within the fruit, causing unsightly tunnels.

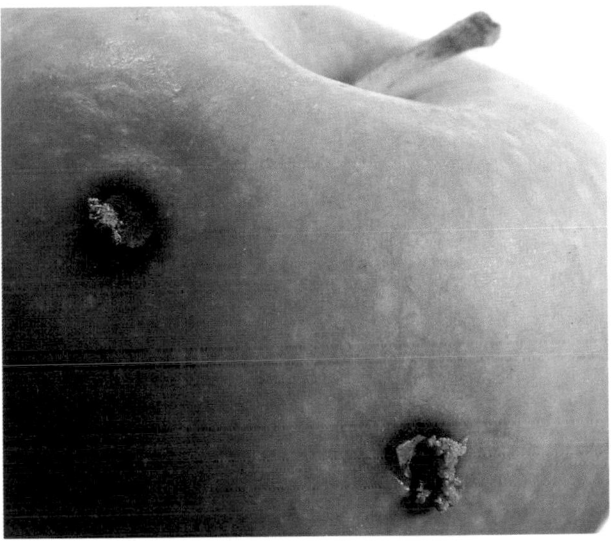

If you see surface blemishes like these, don't bite into that apple! Cut it open to check for codling moth damage first.

DESCRIPTION: Adults are gray-brown moths with wingspans of ¾ inch (2 cm); wings have a fine coppery brown, wavy pattern, and the forewings are tipped with chocolate brown. Larvae are pinkish white with brown heads, up to ¾ inch (2 cm) long. Eggs are white disks.

RANGE: Throughout North America.

PLANTS AFFECTED: Apple, crab apple, pear, occasionally other fruit. In many areas, they are the most damaging pest in apple and pear orchards.

DAMAGE: The larvae ruin fruit by tunneling to the core. An infested apple has a hole (usually near the blossom end) filled with dark masses of castings. Damage may not be obvious until you cut the fruit open.

LIFE CYCLE: Larvae overwinter in thick cocoons under bark or nearby litter. They pupate in spring, and adults emerge when apple trees bloom. Females lay eggs on foliage and fruit, usually on upper surface of leaves. Eggs hatch in 1–3 weeks, and larvae chew their way into the fruit core, usually from the blossom end. They feed for 3–5 weeks, then crawl down the tree to pupate under loose bark or under nearby plant litter. Two to three generations per year, 5–8 weeks apart.

PREVENTION: In winter, attract birds to eat overwintering cocoons. Grow cover crops to attract native parasites and predators, especially ground beetles.

CONTROL: In late winter, scrape bark to remove cocoons; apply dormant oil sprays. Use sticky tree bands or bands of corrugated cardboard to trap larvae leaving the tree to pupate; check for larvae and destroy daily. Diligent trapping of first generation will considerably reduce second generation. Apply codling moth granulosis virus sprays when and where product is available. As a last resort, spray ryania when 75 percent of petals fall, followed by three sprays at 1–2-week intervals. In larger orchards, use pheromone traps to determine the main flight periods for moths (when more than two males are caught for 2 weeks in a row); then time sprays to coincide with egg hatch or release *Trichogramma* parasitic wasps to attack eggs. Also in larger orchards, use pheromone twist-tie dispensers throughout trees to confuse males and prevent mating; if used together with tree bands, widespread control can be achieved.

Leptinotarsa decemlineata

Colorado potato beetle

Colorado potato beetles can devastate plantings of potatoes and tomatoes. Both adults and larvae chew on leaves and stems.

The brightly colored larvae are easy to spot. Handpicking the adults and larvae can be an effective control.

DESCRIPTION: Adults are yellowish orange beetles, ⅓ inch (8.5 mm) long, with ten lengthwise black stripes on the wing covers and many black spots on the midsection behind the head. Larvae are dark orange, humpbacked grubs, 1/16–½ inch (2–10 mm) long, with a row of black spots along each side. Eggs are bright yellow ovals.

RANGE: Throughout North America, except California, Nevada, and west coast of Canada.

PLANTS AFFECTED: Potato, tomato, eggplant, and related plants, including petunia.

DAMAGE: Both adults and larvae chew on leaves and stems. Younger plants may be killed and older plants severely defoliated. Although the yield of defoliated plants is reduced or destroyed, a moderate amount of feeding on leaves has little effect on potato yields.

LIFE CYCLE: Adults and sometimes pupae overwinter 2–14 inches (5–35 cm) deep in the soil (deeper in colder areas). They emerge in spring to feed on potato plants as soon as the first shoots appear. After mating, females lay eggs on end in upright clusters on the undersides of leaves; they produce up to 1,000 eggs during their life span of several months. Eggs hatch in 4–9 days, and larvae feed for 2–3 weeks. They pupate in soil for another 2–3 weeks, and adults emerge in 5–10 days. Two generations per year in most areas, a third generation in Southern states.

PREVENTION: Plant potato cultivars with some resistance, such as 'Katadin' and 'Sequoia'. Plant pollen and nectar flowers to attract native predators and parasites. Mulch plants with deep straw, which seems to impede the movement of emerging beetles in early spring before they have fed enough to be able to fly. Cover plants with floating row covers until midseason. Till the soil in fall to kill overwintering beetles.

CONTROL: Eliminate the first generation for good control through the season. Starting in early spring, inspect shoots and undersides of leaves for adults, egg masses, and larvae. Crush any egg masses. Handpick adults, or shake them from plants onto a ground sheet early in morning, then drown beetles in soapy water (this is very effective if started as soon as overwintering adults emerge). To control larvae, handpick or spray the biological control BTSD. Spray weekly with pyrethrin, rotenone, ryania, or neem (when registered for use on food plants) to control adults and larvae. Experimental biological controls for larger gardens include spined soldier bugs (release at rate of two to five bugs per square yard [one to four bugs per sq m] of plants) or the tiny parasitic wasp *Edovum puttleri*, which should be released in time to attack second-generation larvae.

Ostrinia nubilalis

CORN BORER, EUROPEAN

European corn borers chew on leaves, tassels, and ears of corn; they may also attack other garden vegetables.

DESCRIPTION: Adult females are pale, yellowish brown moths, with 1-inch (2.5 cm) wingspans and dark, zigzag patterns across the wings; males are darker. Larvae are beige, up to 1 inch (2.5 cm) long, with small brown dots on each segment and brown heads. Eggs are white to tan.

RANGE: Throughout northern and central United States, central and eastern Canada.

PLANTS AFFECTED: Corn; also bean, pepper, potato, tomato, and other plants, including flowers.

DAMAGE: Young caterpillars feed on leaves, in corn tassels, and beneath husks on ears. Older larvae burrow into corn stalks and feed in tassels and ears. Damaged stalks are weakened and often break.

LIFE CYCLE: Larvae overwinter in plant stems left in fields; they complete pupation in early spring. Adults emerge in June and lay masses of 15–20 overlapping eggs on undersides of leaves from late June to mid-July. Eggs hatch in a week; larvae feed for 3–4 weeks. One to three generations per year.

PREVENTION: Plant resistant corn cultivars. Rotate crops. Attract parasitic flies and wasps with nectar and pollen plants. Shred and compost corn stalks in fall or till them in immediately after harvest.

CONTROL: Remove tassels from two-thirds of your corn plants before pollen sheds; this eliminates many larvae in the tassels. Spray BTK on leaf undersides. Apply granular BTK or mineral oil in tips of ears. Spray pyrethrin, ryania, or sabadilla.

Diatraea grandiosella

CORN BORER, SOUTHWESTERN

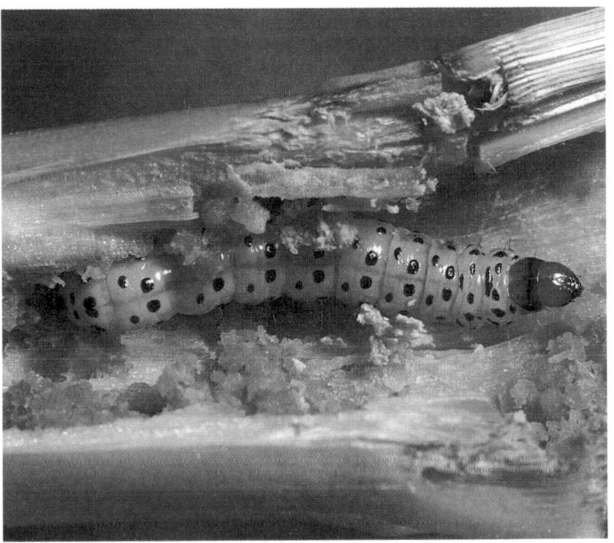

Southwestern corn borers feed within the stems and roots of corn and other grasses, causing stalks to weaken and break.

DESCRIPTION: Adult females are pale beige, lightly marked moths with 1¼-inch (3 cm) wingspans; males are darker. Larvae are white caterpillars with brown heads; the summer form of larvae is covered with brown spots, whereas the overwintering form is all white. Eggs are cream to reddish brown.

RANGE: Throughout southern United States and corn-belt states.

PLANTS AFFECTED: Corn, sorghum, and some grasses.

DAMAGE: Larvae bore into leaf whorls, stalks, and roots of corn plants, weakening stems and causing them to break easily.

LIFE CYCLE: Larvae overwinter in the roots of corn stubble and complete pupation in early June. Moths emerge in about a week and lay eggs in overlapping rows on leaves. First-generation larvae bore into the leaf whorls and later into the stalks, where they pupate. Adults emerge in early August and lay eggs. The second-generation larvae bore into stalks, then down to the roots, where they overwinter. Two or more generations per year.

PREVENTION: Plant corn early in the season. Plant resistant corn cultivars. Attract birds and native parasitic wasps with nectar and pollen plants.

CONTROL: After harvest, cut off corn stalks at soil level, and remove and shred them. Cultivate stubble deeply in fall.

Heliocoverpa (=Heliothis) zea

CORN EARWORM

Corn earworms—also known as tomato fruitworms—feed on silks and kernels of corn or buds, leaves, and fruit of tomatoes.

Adult female corn earworms lay eggs on leaves or on the corn silks. Check the tips of ears regularly for any signs of damage.

DESCRIPTION: Adults are light tan moths with 1½–2-inch (4–5 cm) wingspans. Larvae are light yellow, green, pink, or brown, 1–2 inches (2.5–5 cm) long, with white and dark stripes on the sides, yellow heads, and black legs. Eggs are yellow or white, round, and ribbed.

RANGE: Throughout North America; not hardy in Canada and northern United States, but migrates from Southern regions in spring.

PLANTS AFFECTED: Corn and tomato; also bean, cabbage, peanut, pepper, squash, and sunflower.

DAMAGE: In corn, larvae feed on fresh silks, then move down the ears eating kernels and leaving trails of excrement. Early corn in the North is least affected. In tomatoes, larvae eat buds, chew large holes in leaves, and burrow into the ripe fruit. On other plants, larvae chew holes in leaves.

LIFE CYCLE: Pupae overwinter in the soil, usually only surviving the winter in the southern United States. Adults emerge in early spring and can migrate long distances. Females lay eggs singly on undersides of leaves or on tips of corn ears. Eggs hatch in 2–10 days; larvae feed for 2–4 weeks, then pupate in soil. Adults emerge in 10–25 days. One to four generations per year.

PREVENTION: Plant corn cultivars with tight husks such as 'Calumet' or 'Country Gentleman', to prevent larvae from entering. Attract native parasitic wasps and predatory bugs by interplanting crops with pollen and nectar plants. Avoid leaving lights on at night near a corn patch, as this attracts adult moths to the area.

CONTROL: After silks start to dry, apply one of the following to the tip of each ear: BTK sprays, granular BTK, insect parasitic nematodes, or 20 drops of mineral oil. Open corn husks and dig out larvae in the tip before they damage the main ear. Release purchased lacewings or minute pirate bugs early in the season to attack eggs and small larvae. Paint a mixture of pyrethrin and molasses as bait (use 3 parts water to 1 part molasses) around base of cornstalks to attract and kill emerging adults. Spray neem (when registered for food crops); spray ryania as a last resort. For large corn patches, use pheromone traps to monitor the arrival of moths in the area; time sprays to coincide with the period when most eggs should be hatching.

Diabrotica longicornis

CORN ROOTWORM, NORTHERN

Northern corn rootworms burrow into corn roots. If infestations are severe, plants fall over, especially in windy areas.

DESCRIPTION: Adults are yellowish green, elongated beetles, ¼ inch (6 mm) long, with brown antennae and feet; sometimes head and thorax are brown. They are very active. Larvae are slender, up to ½ inch (1 cm) long, wrinkled, and white with a light brown head.

RANGE: North central United States, from New York to Colorado; related species in Western states (see Cucumber beetle, spotted entry).

PLANTS AFFECTED: Corn.

DAMAGE: Larvae feed on corn roots, causing severe damage. Adults feed on pollen and corn silk, damaging ears and interfering with pollination. Larvae also spread bacterial wilt disease.

LIFE CYCLE: Females lay eggs on soil around corn roots in late summer and fall. Eggs hatch the following spring, and larvae migrate through the soil to corn roots. They feed until early summer, then pupate in the soil. Adults emerge in July and August. One generation per year in most areas.

PREVENTION: Larvae only survive on corn and cannot migrate far in search of food, so crop rotation is very effective. Plant early so plants have a good root system before rootworms emerge. Conserve predatory ground and rove beetle populations with permanent borders and groundcovers.

CONTROL: Cultivate soil well after harvest and again before seeding to kill eggs and larvae. Apply insect parasitic nematodes to soil.

Diabrotica undecimpunctata howardi

CUCUMBER BEETLE, SPOTTED

Spotted cucumber beetles munch on a wide range of plants. The larvae, known as Southern corn rootworms, feed mostly on corn.

DESCRIPTION: Adults are greenish yellow, elongated beetles, ¼ inch (6 mm) long, with 11 black spots. Larvae are slender, white, and up to ¾ inch (2 cm) long, with brown heads and brown patches on first and last segments.

RANGE: Throughout southern United States and Canada, east of Rocky Mountains.

PLANTS AFFECTED: Corn, cucumber, peanut, potato, and many other plants, including ornamentals.

DAMAGE: Larvae feed on roots, often killing young plants; older plants are weakened and fall down easily. Adult beetles eat holes in leaves and chew on fruit skin. Larvae and adults transmit cucumber mosaic virus and bacterial wilt diseases.

LIFE CYCLE: Adults spend the winter under crop debris, emerging in spring to lay eggs in soil close to plants. When eggs hatch, larvae feed in roots and crowns of plants for 2–4 weeks, then pupate. One or two generations per year in Northern areas, three in the South. Northern populations migrate north and south with changing seasons.

PREVENTION: Plant resistant cucumber, squash, and melon cultivars. Rotate garden crops with cover crops. Remove and destroy crop debris to eliminate overwintering sites. Cover plants with floating row covers (hand-pollinate flowers to get fruit).

CONTROL: Spray or dust plants with pyrethrin or rotenone to control adults. Apply insect parasitic nematodes to soil weekly to control larvae.

Acalymma vittatum

CUCUMBER BEETLE, STRIPED

Striped cucumber beetles spread diseases like wilt and viruses as they feed, causing double damage to plants.

DESCRIPTION: Adults are yellow, elongated beetles, ¼ inch (6 mm) long, with black heads and three wide black stripes on wing covers. Larvae are slender white grubs, up to ¾ inch (2 cm) long, brownish on the ends.

RANGE: West to Colorado and New Mexico in the United States; west to Saskatchewan in Canada.

PLANTS AFFECTED: Cucumber, melon, and squash; also corn, pea, and blossoms of many plants.

DAMAGE: Adults feed on leaves, young shoots, stems, and flowers; they also eat holes in fruit. Larvae feed on roots of cucumber and its relatives, stunting or killing plants.

LIFE CYCLE: Adults overwinter in grass and other vegetation, emerging in April to early June. They feed on weed pollen for 2 weeks, then move to crop plants to lay eggs in soil at base of plants. Eggs hatch in 10 days, and larvae burrow down to feed on roots. They feed for 2–6 weeks and pupate in early August. Adults emerge in 2 weeks and feed on blossoms and fruit. One to two generations per year in the North, up to four generations in the South.

PREVENTION: Plant resistant cucumber, squash, and melon cultivars. Cover plants with row covers (hand-pollinate flowers to get fruit). Mulch with deep straw to stop beetles moving between plants.

CONTROL: Spray or dust with pyrethrin or rotenone when adults are seen feeding on pollen in flowers. Apply parasitic nematodes to soil to control larvae.

Noctuidae

CUTWORMS

Cutworms are gray or brown caterpillars that live in the soil. At night, these pests sever the stems of unprotected seedlings.

DESCRIPTION: Adults are brownish or gray moths with 1½-inch (4 cm) wingspans. Larvae are fat, greasy gray or dull brown caterpillars with shiny heads; found in the soil.

RANGE: Throughout North America.

PLANTS AFFECTED: Most early vegetable and flower seedlings and transplants.

DAMAGE: Caterpillars feed at night on young plant stems at the soil line. You'll find the severed plants lying on the ground in the morning; seedlings may be completely eaten. During the day, caterpillars rest below the soil surface, curled beside the damaged plant stems.

LIFE CYCLE: Adults emerge and lay eggs on grass or soil from early May to early June. Eggs hatch in 5–7 days. Larvae feed on grass and other plants for 3–5 weeks, then pupate in soil. Adults emerge in late August to early September. Some species overwinter as eggs that hatch during the first warm days and feed on the earliest seedlings. One generation per year; a late second generation may damage crops in warm fall weather.

PREVENTION: Use cutworm collars on transplants to shield stems. Set out main crops later in the season.

CONTROL: Scatter moist bran mixed with BTK and molasses a week before setting out plants to attract and kill larvae. Apply insect parasitic nematodes to the soil. Dig around the base of damaged transplants in the morning and destroy hiding larvae.

Scolytus multistriatus and *Hylurgopinus rufipes*

ELM BARK BEETLES

Elm bark beetles and their larvae live in galleries that they carve in a radiating pattern under the bark of elm trees.

DESCRIPTION: Adults are shiny, cylindrical, dark brown beetles, 1/10 inch (2.5 mm) long, with rows of fine punctures along wing covers; the head is curved down under a broad thorax. Larvae are fat, C-shaped grubs with brown heads, living under bark.

RANGE: Most of the United States except north central states; southern Ontario and New Brunswick, Canada.

PLANTS AFFECTED: Elm.

DAMAGE: Larvae and adults do not cause serious damage directly, but adults spread Dutch elm disease, which is devastating. Adults carry the disease fungi on their bodies and infect healthy trees when they bore into bark.

LIFE CYCLE: In spring, overwintering adults emerge from holes in bark. They feed in crotches of elm twigs, then move to recently cut, dead, or dying elms. They carve galleries between the wood and inner bark and lay eggs. Each larva feeds in a separate branch of the gallery and pupates in a cell at the end. Adults emerge in 10–14 days. Some species overwinter under the bark as larvae, others as adults. One to three generations per year.

PREVENTION: Plant new elm cultivars resistant to Dutch elm disease, such as 'Prospector' and 'Frontier'. Maintain healthy trees.

CONTROL: Bury or burn all diseased or dying elms to eliminate sources of disease. Trap adult beetles with pheromone traps.

Chrysobothris femorata

FLATHEADED APPLETREE BORER

Flatheaded appletree borers tunnel under the bark of young or stressed trees; vigorous plants are less susceptible to damage.

DESCRIPTION: Adults are flat, dark bronze beetles, 1/2 inch (1 cm) long. Larvae are white, legless grubs, up to 1 1/4 inches (3 cm) long, with a brown retracted head and one wide segment behind head.

RANGE: Throughout the United States and eastern Canada; similar species on the Pacific Coast.

PLANTS AFFECTED: Most fruit, shade, and forest trees.

DAMAGE: Adults feed on leaves. Larvae tunnel into sapwood of young trees and under bark of older trees, forming galleries packed with sawdust castings. Gummy sap runs from attacked bark, which turns dark and dies; the tree dies if bark is killed entirely around trunk. Borers occur in greatest numbers on sunny side of tree.

LIFE CYCLE: Grubs overwinter in chambers 1 inch (2.5 cm) deep in the wood and pupate in spring. Adults emerge May to July and lay eggs in cracks in bark. When eggs hatch, the grubs tunnel under bark for the rest of summer, but usually cannot complete development on vigorous trees. One generation per year; sometimes 2 years are required.

PREVENTION: Avoid injuring bark; remove injured limbs promptly. Protect trunks of young trees with white latex paint diluted with an equal amount of water to prevent sunscald and reduce borer attacks. Wrap trunks of young trees with paper or burlap for the first year to prevent attack.

CONTROL: In late summer or early fall, cut out larvae from under dark patches of dying bark.

Chrysomelidae

Flea beetles

Flea beetles have enlarged hind legs that enable them to jump like fleas. They scatter quickly when disturbed.

DESCRIPTION: Adults are small, black, brown, or bronze beetles, 1/10 inch (2.5 mm) long. Larvae are thin, white, legless grubs with brown heads; they live in soil.

RANGE: Throughout North America.

PLANTS AFFECTED: Most vegetables, especially cabbage family plants, potato, and spinach; also flowers and weeds.

DAMAGE: Adults chew small, round holes through leaves, which look like they have been peppered with fine shot. Adults are most damaging in early spring, and seedlings may be killed by beetles feeding, although larger plants usually survive. Larvae feed on plant roots. Adults may spread viral diseases.

LIFE CYCLE: Overwintering adults emerge from the soil in spring. They feed and lay eggs on plant roots, then die by early July. Eggs hatch in a week, and larvae feed for 2–3 weeks. They pupate in the soil, and adults emerge in 2–3 weeks. One to four generations per year.

PREVENTION: Plant susceptible crops as late as possible. Cover seedlings with floating row covers or fine mesh until adults die off. Flea beetles prefer full sun, so interplant to shade susceptible plants.

CONTROL: Spray pyrethrin or rotenone to control adults; use neem (when registered for food crops). Drench roots with insect parasitic nematodes to control larvae.

Synanthedon spp.

Fruit borers

Fruit borers produce small holes and spots of "sawdust" along trunks and branches. Look for symptoms before buying plants.

DESCRIPTION: Adults are moths but look wasp-like. They have clear wings marked with dark patterns and smooth black or black-and-yellow striped bodies 1 inch (2.5 cm) long. Larvae are pale yellow or white with dark heads, found in canes or crowns.

RANGE: Throughout North America.

PLANTS AFFECTED: Related species attack blackberry, currant, gooseberry, raspberry, and rhododendron.

DAMAGE: Larvae boring into the pith of stems kill or weaken canes, causing them to break easily. Larvae in crowns girdle canes and destroy new shoots.

LIFE CYCLE: Larvae overwinter in canes and pupate in early May; adults emerge in 2 weeks. Eggs are laid on canes and hatch in 10 days. Larvae tunnel in canes all summer and remain there for winter. They pupate in the cane, after making an exit hole for the moth that will emerge later. Rhododendron crownborer larvae spend the winter in crowns and work their way up into plant stems by July. They pupate under bark, several inches above the soil line; adults emerge in a month.

PREVENTION: Examine plants carefully for signs of borer damage before purchasing; look along trunks and branches for small holes and little spots of "sawdust." Maintain vigorous plants.

CONTROL: Prune out and burn canes with borers, and destroy seriously infested plants; smash remaining stubs of plants with a mallet to kill pupae and larvae. Try summer oil spray to kill eggs.

Cynipidae

GALL WASPS

Gall wasp larvae feed on leaves and stems. The resulting galls serve as food and protection for the larvae within.

DESCRIPTION: Rarely seen, adults are tiny brown or reddish wasps, 1⁄20–1⁄10 inch (1–2.5 mm) long, with short antennae. Larvae are legless white grubs living inside plant galls.

RANGE: Western United States and Canada; some species occur in the East.

PLANTS AFFECTED: Oak, rose, and thistle; some other plants.

DAMAGE: Plants respond to larval feeding by producing enlarged masses of cells that become galls. These do not seem to harm the plant, but may be unsightly. Galls are attached to stems or leaves and have a variety of shapes, including round, star-shaped, or conical; they may be smooth, spiny, or covered with mossy tendrils. Oak galls ("oak apples") are rich sources of tannin and were once used to make writing ink.

LIFE CYCLE: Overwintering adults emerge from the previous season's gall, which may be on roots, attached to fallen leaves, or still on the plant. Females lay eggs on the host plant in early spring. When the eggs hatch, the feeding larvae stimulate the gall formation. Adults emerge in summer and lay eggs that form overwintering galls.

PREVENTION: Maintain vigorous plants.

CONTROL: Usually galls are few and control is not necessary. If galls on roses or shrubs are numerous, prune out and destroy the galls early in the season, before adults emerge.

Acrididae

GRASSHOPPERS

Grasshoppers seldom cause damage to gardens, but they can be a problem when nearby agricultural areas are infested.

DESCRIPTION: Adults are brown, yellow, or green, 1–2 inches (2.5–5 cm) long, with leathery forewings and enlarged hind legs for jumping; many have brightly colored underwings. Nymphs are similar to adults but are smaller, and have short or rudimentary wings.

RANGE: Throughout North America.

PLANTS AFFECTED: Primarily cereals and grasses, though adults will eat any plant.

DAMAGE: Economic damage is usually to field crops, on rare occasions when large grasshopper populations build up and devastate large areas; garden plants in outbreak areas will also be damaged by grasshoppers chewing foliage.

LIFE CYCLE: In late summer, females deposit elongated masses of eggs in burrows in the soil. Eggs hatch in spring, and nymphs develop for 40–60 days, then molt to the adult stage. Adults feed until killed by cold weather.

PREVENTION: Conserve natural enemies—blister beetles, ground beetles, predatory flies, birds, and parasitic nematodes; these usually suppress populations. Build birdhouses to attract birds. In areas with high grasshopper populations, cover garden plants with floating row covers.

CONTROL: Cultivate gardens in fall to kill overwintering eggs. Aerial sprays of naturally occurring grasshopper diseases (*Nosema locustae* or *Beauvaria bassiana*) are good for use over large areas.

Lymantria dispar

GYPSY MOTH

Gypsy moth larvae feed voraciously on leaves and can quickly defoliate deciduous and evergreen trees.

Female gypsy moths lay yellowish egg masses on trees and other objects in fall. The overwintering eggs hatch in spring.

DESCRIPTION: Adult females are almost-white moths that are 1 inch (2.5 cm) long, with thin, brown markings on their wings and heavy, furry bodies. Although they have wings, they are unable to fly. Males are smaller, darker, and strong fliers. Larvae are up to 2½ inches (6 cm) long; they have five pairs of blue dots and six pairs of red dots on their backs and are covered with tufts of long hairs.

RANGE: Eastern and central United States; eastern Canada; isolated outbreaks have occurred in California, Oregon, Washington, and British Columbia.

PLANTS AFFECTED: Many trees and shrubs, including conifers.

DAMAGE: Larvae feed on leaves, chewing large holes; in heavy infestations, trees are completely defoliated. Deciduous trees can leaf out again, but repeated defoliations may eventually kill them; a single defoliation kills conifers. Some people are allergic to the hairs on larvae and may experience allergic reactions when gypsy moth populations are high.

LIFE CYCLE: Eggs overwinter on tree trunks and hatch in May. Larvae crawl up trees and feed until mid-July, then pupate for several weeks. Adults emerge in late July to early August. Males locate females by detecting the female sex pheromones. After mating, the females crawl up nearby trees or other objects to deposit egg masses under a yellowish furry covering. One generation per year. Dispersal of this introduced species is usually by humans moving egg masses or other life stages on camping and outdoor equipment, trucks, and ships.

PREVENTION: It is crucial to prevent further spread of this pest by checking trailers, boats, camping gear, and other outdoor equipment for egg masses or larvae before leaving an infested region. Attract predators and parasites, which are important controls, especially tachinid flies, ground beetles, and parasitic wasps.

CONTROL: Use pheromone traps, which catch males, to determine whether populations are present; where moth populations are low, placing enough traps over a large area may prevent males from mating. In outbreaks, spray BTK two to three times at 1–2-week intervals in spring to kill caterpillars, or spray neem. Wrap burlap tree bands on orchard and yard trees, check daily, and destroy larvae hiding under bands; or use sticky tree bands to trap larvae, renewing glue frequently. In fall, search for and destroy egg masses on tree trunks, sides of buildings, fence posts, and outdoor equipment.

Artogeia (=Pieris) rapae

IMPORTED CABBAGEWORM

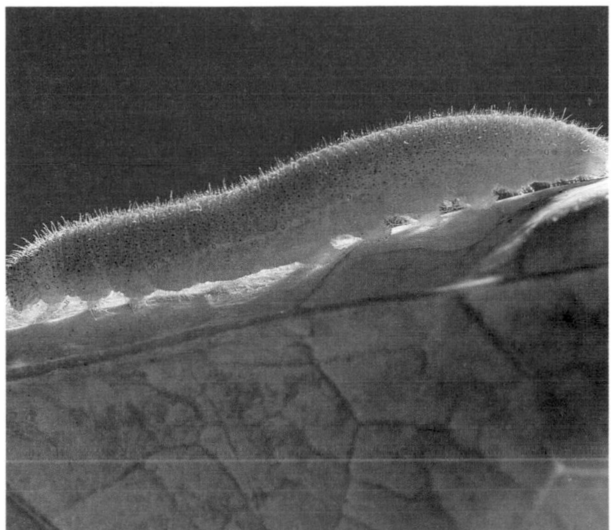

Imported cabbageworms often hide in broccoli heads. Soak harvested heads in salty water before cooking to drive out the pests.

DESCRIPTION: Adults are common white "cabbage butterflies," with 1½-inch (4 cm) wingspans; the forewings have black tips and two to three black spots. Larvae are velvety green caterpillars with a fine yellow stripe down the back. Eggs are tiny yellow cones.

RANGE: Throughout North America.

PLANTS AFFECTED: Broccoli, cabbage, cauliflower, and related plants.

DAMAGE: Larvae eat large, ragged holes in leaves and heads of cabbage and chew florets of cauliflower and broccoli. As they feed, they produce quantities of dark green droppings.

LIFE CYCLE: Pupae spend the winter in garden debris. Adults emerge in early spring and lay eggs on the undersides of leaves. Larvae feed for 2–3 weeks, then pupate in garden trash on soil surface. The adults emerge in 1–2 weeks. Three to five overlapping generations per year. All ages of larvae may be present all season.

PREVENTION: Attract or conserve parasitic wasps and other natural enemies, including yellow jacket wasps (which consume large numbers of caterpillars). Cover plants with floating row covers.

CONTROL: In light infestations, handpick larvae and eggs. Place yellow sticky traps among host plants to catch female butterflies. To control larvae, spray with BTK at 1–2-week intervals. As a last resort, spray ryania or sabadilla.

Macronoctua onusta

IRIS BORER

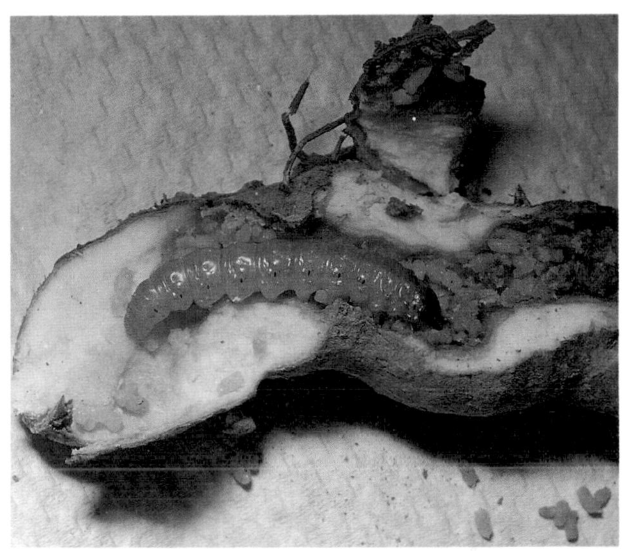

Iris borers tunnel into leaves and rhizomes, injuring foliage and buds. Damaged rhizomes are prone to diseases.

DESCRIPTION: Adults are "miller moths" with a 2-inch (5 cm) wingspan; they have dark brown forewings and yellowish hind wings. Young larvae are greenish, later becoming pinkish with brown heads. They are up to 1½–2 inches (4–5 cm) long, with a light stripe down the back and rows of black dots along the sides.

RANGE: Eastern United States west to Iowa; Quebec and eastern Ontario, Canada.

PLANTS AFFECTED: Iris.

DAMAGE: Where it occurs, it is the most serious pest of iris. Young larvae tunnel in the leaves, leaf sheaths, and buds, then bore down into the iris crowns and rhizomes as they develop. Soft rots usually follow larval damage.

LIFE CYCLE: Eggs overwinter on old leaves and hatch in late April to early May. Larvae enter leaves and feed for several weeks, then pupate in soil near the rhizomes. Adults emerge in late August to early September and lay eggs for winter. One generation per year.

PREVENTION: Remove and destroy dead iris leaves and stems in late fall to eliminate overwintering eggs.

CONTROL: Dig infested rhizomes. If plants are valuable, dig out the larvae and pupae, then dust the rhizomes with sulfur before replanting to prevent soft rot.

Popillia japonica

JAPANESE BEETLE

Japanese beetles feed ravenously on the leaves and flowers of many different plants. Birches and roses are favorite targets.

The larvae of Japanese beetles are white grubs with brown heads. Larvae feed on grass roots and can damage your lawn.

DESCRIPTION: Adults are blocky, metallic blue-green beetles, ½ inch (1 cm) long, with tufts of white hairs along the sides of the abdomen. They have bronze-colored wing covers and long legs with large claws. Larvae are fat, dirty white, C-shaped grubs up to ¾ inch (2 cm) long, with brown heads; they are found in sod.

RANGE: The United States west to Mississippi River and Iowa; occasionally in California.

PLANTS AFFECTED: Wide range of vegetables, especially asparagus, bean, corn, okra, onion, rhubarb, and tomato; also many flowers and ornamentals.

DAMAGE: Adult beetles feed during the day, especially in warm weather and on plants in full sun. They chew on flowers and skeletonize leaves, which wilt and drop; if populations are large, beetles may completely defoliate plants. Larvae feed on roots of turf and other grasses, causing irregular patches of dead or wilted grass in spring and again in fall. Turf may be torn up by crows, racoons, and other animals searching for larvae.

LIFE CYCLE: Larvae overwinter deep in the soil and move toward the surface in spring to feed on roots. They pupate in May and June, and the adults emerge in late June to July, with peak numbers of beetles present on plants in July. The beetles feed on plants until late summer, then burrow under grasses and lay eggs. The eggs hatch into larvae that feed until cold weather arrives, then burrow farther into the soil to avoid freezing. One generation every 1–2 years.

PREVENTION: Plant ornamentals not attractive to the beetles, such as larch, white birch, chrysanthemums, and most evergreens. Cover garden plants with floating row covers. Conserve and attract native species of parasitic wasps and flies with nectar and pollen plants. Allow lawn to dry out well between waterings in midsummer, or stop watering and allow lawn to go dormant in summer, so beetle eggs dry out.

CONTROL: In early morning, handpick beetles, vacuum them from plants with a hand-held vacuum cleaner, or shake them from plants onto ground sheets and drown them in soapy water. Apply milky disease (*Bacillus popilliae*) or insect parasitic nematodes to sod to kill larvae. Aerate lawn with spiked sandals in late spring and late fall to kill larvae while they are close to the surface. Organize a community-wide trapping program to reduce adult beetle populations over the entire area (placing traps in a single yard has been shown to be ineffective). Spray plants attacked by beetles with ryania or rotenone.

June/May beetles

June beetles—also known as May beetles—are large nocturnal insects. The white larvae cause serious damage to plant roots.

DESCRIPTION: Adults are blocky-looking beetles, ¾ inch (2 cm) long, with the tip of their abdomen showing behind the wing covers. Most are shiny brown or black; some have stripes on the back or fine hairs over the body. Larvae are fat, C-shaped, white grubs with dark heads.

RANGE: Throughout North America.

PLANTS AFFECTED: Larvae feed on roots of corn, potato, strawberry, and garden transplants; also grasses. Adults feed on leaves of oak, elm, beech, maple, poplar, willow, and other trees and shrubs.

DAMAGE: Adults chew on leaves; high numbers may defoliate trees. Larvae chew on roots, which may cause severe damage in years of large broods.

LIFE CYCLE: Females lay eggs in soil; eggs hatch in 2–3 weeks. For the first summer, grubs feed on decaying vegetation; they hibernate in soil over winter and feed on plant roots the second summer. After hibernating again, they feed until June of the third summer, then pupate for 2–3 weeks. Adults remain in earthen cells in the soil until the spring of the fourth year, when they emerge to feed and lay eggs. The largest broods appear in 3-year cycles; some species have 1- or 4-year life cycles.

PREVENTION: Grow nectar and pollen plants to attract native predators and parasites.

CONTROL: Apply milky disease (*Bacillus popilliae*) or parasitic nematodes to soil to control grubs where infestations are severe.

Lace bugs

Lace bugs are tiny white insects that usually feed on the undersides of leaves. Rhododendrons and azaleas are common targets.

DESCRIPTION: Adults are oval- or rectangular-shaped bugs, ⅒ inch (2.5 mm) long, with a lacy pattern on the wings and unusually wide, flattened extensions on the thorax. Nymphs are smaller and darker and may be covered with spines. Eggs are inserted in leaf tissue along a midrib on the underside, with a cone-like cap projecting from the leaf.

RANGE: Throughout North America.

PLANTS AFFECTED: Flowers, ornamental trees, vegetables, and many garden plants.

DAMAGE: Both adults and nymphs suck juices from the undersides of leaves and from flowers. They produce small dark spots of excrement and cause yellowish patches or a speckled white or gray blotchy appearance on the leaf surface. Lace bugs usually appear in groups.

LIFE CYCLE: Most species overwinter in the egg stage, although some overwinter as adults under the bark of trees. Eggs hatch into nymphs that feed on plant juices on underside of leaves for several weeks until molting to adults. Three or more generations per year.

PREVENTION: Maintain healthy plants.

CONTROL: To control both adults and nymphs, spray insecticidal soap, neem, superior oil (not on chrysanthemum flowers), pyrethrin, or, as a last resort, rotenone.

Cicadellidae

LEAFHOPPERS

Leafhoppers are small, brightly colored pests. They often feed on stems and the undersides of leaves, causing a mottled look.

Leafhoppers can move quickly when disturbed, making control difficult. Soap, oil, or pyrethrin sprays may work.

DESCRIPTION: Adults are wedge-shaped, slender, 1/10–1/2 inch (2.5–12 mm) long. Many species have a broadly triangular head or a pronounced forward point to the head. Most are either brown or green, and some have bright bands of color on wings. All species have well-developed hind legs and can jump rapidly into flight when disturbed. Nymphs are similar to adults, but paler in color and wingless; they hop rapidly when disturbed.

RANGE: Throughout North America; more than 2,700 native species.

PLANTS AFFECTED: Most fruits and vegetables, especially apple, bean, cucumber and related plants, eggplant, grape, and potato; also some flowers and weeds.

DAMAGE: Both adults and nymphs suck juices from stems and undersides of leaves, leaving a mottled appearance. Their toxic saliva causes some plants to react with severe leaf distortions—including warty, crinkled, or rolled edges—or stunted growth. Plants may have tipburn (called "hopper burn" on potatoes) and yellowed, curled leaves with white spots on the undersides. As they feed, leafhoppers excrete sticky honeydew on leaves below. Fruit may be spotted with drops of excrement and honeydew (you can wash this off). Many species spread viruses and other disease-causing organisms.

LIFE CYCLE: Adults overwinter, usually on or about wild host plants, and start laying eggs when leaves begin to appear on trees. Some species do not survive winter in the northern United States and Canada; they migrate over long distances from the South every summer. Females lay eggs in rows or clusters, usually in the tissue of leaves and stems. The eggs hatch in 10–14 days, and nymphs develop for 1–4 weeks. Most species have two to five generations per year. The first frosts in fall usually kill off nymphs; some leafhoppers overwinter as eggs.

PREVENTION: Maintain vigorous plants, which will recover quickly from leafhopper attacks. Attract and conserve natural enemies—parasitic flies, damsel bugs, minute pirate bugs, lady beetles, lacewings, parasitic wasps, and spiders—that are important controls.

CONTROL: Some damage is tolerable, and control measures are usually not necessary in gardens. Apply dormant oil sprays to kill adults overwintering on fruit trees. Wash nymphs from plants with a strong spray of water. To control nymphs, spray with insecticidal soap or pyrethrin while nymphs are still small; as a last resort, spray rotenone or sabadilla.

Agromyzidae

Leafminers

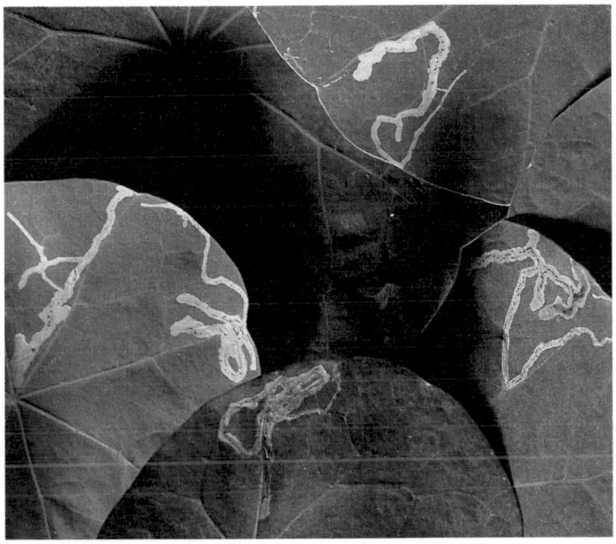

Leafminers tunnel within leaves, causing foliage to look unsightly. They often damage beets, chard, and columbines.

DESCRIPTION: Adults are black or black-and-yellow flies, 1/10 inch (2.5 mm) long; you'll rarely see them. Larvae are pale green, stubby, translucent maggots found in tunnels in leaves. Eggs are white and cylindrical.

RANGE: Throughout North America.

PLANTS AFFECTED: Bean, beet, cabbage, chard, lettuce, pepper, tomato, and other vegetables; also many ornamentals, especially chrysanthemum and nasturtium.

DAMAGE: Larvae tunnel through the leaf tissue, making hollowed-out, curved, or winding mines. Larval damage may destroy seedlings; on older plants, larvae are often a nuisance rather than a serious problem. Mines are unsightly on ornamentals.

LIFE CYCLE: Adults emerge from overwintering cocoons in early spring and lay eggs side by side in clusters on undersides of leaves. Larvae mine leaves for 1–3 weeks, then pupate for 2–4 weeks in the leaf or drop to the soil to pupate. Two to three generations per year; more in greenhouse crops.

PREVENTION: Cover seedlings with floating row covers; maintain covers all season if pests are numerous. Remove nearby dock or lamb's-quarters, which are wild hosts for beet leafminers. Attract native parasitic wasps, which usually suppress leafminers.

CONTROL: Handpick and destroy mined leaves and remove egg clusters as soon as they are visible in spring. Spray neem or avermectin, when available.

Pseudococcidae

Mealybugs

Mealybugs are most commonly seen as the soft, oval, waxy white females that attack fruits, ornamentals, and foliage plants.

DESCRIPTION: Adult females are soft, oval, segmented, 1/10 inch (2.5 mm) long, with a pinkish body covered by white waxy fluff. Males are tiny two-winged insects that are rarely seen. Nymphs are similar to females but much smaller.

RANGE: Most species occur in southern United States; long-tailed mealybug is widespread. All species found in greenhouses throughout North America.

PLANTS AFFECTED: Apple, citrus, and other tree fruit; avocado, grape, and potato; also ornamentals and tropical foliage plants.

DAMAGE: Adults and nymphs suck plant juices on all parts of plant, particularly new growth. Leaves wither and turn yellow, and fruit drops prematurely. Mealybugs excrete honeydew on leaves that supports growth of sooty mold.

LIFE CYCLE: Females lay eggs in a cottony white mass. The eggs hatch in 10 days and "crawlers" wander away to find feeding sites on the plant, where they develop for 1–2 months or longer. Several generations per year; more in greenhouses.

PREVENTION: Attract native parasitic wasps, which often keep populations in check outdoors.

CONTROL: Knock mealybugs from plants with a strong stream of water or spray with insecticidal soap. Release mealybug destroyer (*Cryptolaemus montrouzieri*) for citrus, grapes, or indoor plants. Release the parasitic wasp *Leptomastix dactylopii* to control mealybugs on citrus.

Epilachna varivestis

MEXICAN BEAN BEETLE

Mexican bean beetles are often mistaken for beneficial lady beetles, but the distinctive larvae make identification easy.

Adult beetles lay oval yellow eggs on the undersides of plant leaves. Check for egg masses regularly and squash them.

DESCRIPTION: Adults are oval, yellowish brown to copper-colored beetles, ¼ inch (6 mm) long, with 16 black spots arranged in three rows across wing covers. They look much like beneficial lady beetles. Larvae are fat, yellowish orange grubs up to ⅓ inch (8 mm) in length, with no legs, and with six rows of long, branching spines protruding from their segments. Eggs are yellow ovals.

RANGE: Most areas east of Rocky Mountains.

PLANTS AFFECTED: Cowpea, lima bean, snap bean, and soybean.

DAMAGE: Both larvae and adults feed from the underside on leaf tissue between the veins; they skeletonize the leaves, leaving behind a characteristic lacy appearance. In severe attacks, production of pods may be reduced and completely defoliated; plants may be killed. The greatest damage occurs in July and August. Bean beetles are most abundant in weedless fields.

LIFE CYCLE: Adults overwinter in garden debris or in leaf litter in nearby fields. Some emerge to feed by the time the first bean leaves are up, while others straggle out of hiding over a period of several months. In spring, the beetles feed for a couple of weeks, then females lay eggs on end in clusters of 40–60, on undersides of bean leaves. Eggs hatch in 5–14 days, and larvae feed for 2–5 weeks. They pupate in a case attached to the underside of a leaf, and adults emerge in about a week. Upon emergence, new adults are solid yellow; they soon darken and the spots become visible. One to four generations per year. In late summer, large numbers of beetles disperse from fields.

PREVENTION: Plant resistant cultivars, such as 'Wade' and 'Logan' snap beans and 'Black Valentine' lima bean. In Southern areas, plant early-season bush beans to avoid main beetle generations; Northern gardeners will find early plantings grow slowly and suffer more damage from early generation of beetles. Cover plants with floating row covers until plants are well grown. Leave a few flowering weeds between rows to attract native predators and parasites, or interplant with flowers and herbs. Remove debris and dig under crop residues as soon as plants are harvested to remove overwintering sites.

CONTROL: Plant soybeans as a trap crop; destroy the plants when they are infested with beetle larvae. In small bean patches, handpick larvae and adults and crush egg masses daily; if done diligently, this will considerably reduce damage from the second generation. Release spined soldier bugs (*Podisus maculiventris*) to control the early generation. Release the parasitic wasp *Pediobius foveolatus* when weather warms, to control second generation. Spray weekly with pyrethrin, sabadilla, rotenone, or neem (when registered for food plants), ensuring that undersides of leaves are thoroughly covered.

MITES, SPIDER

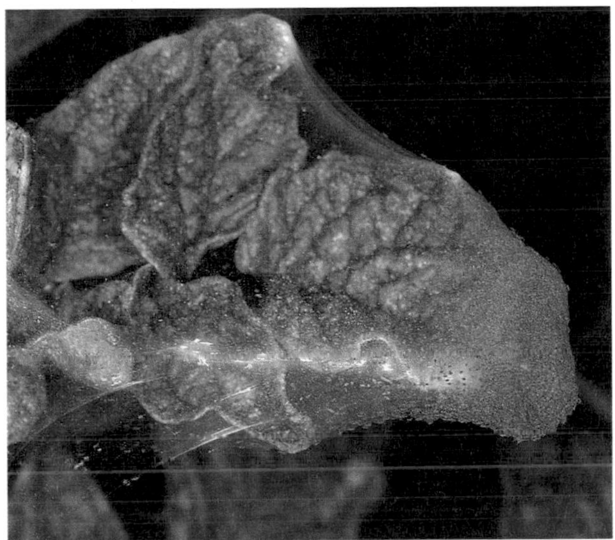

Spider mites often spin fine webbing on leaves; severe infestations may enclose whole leaves and shoots.

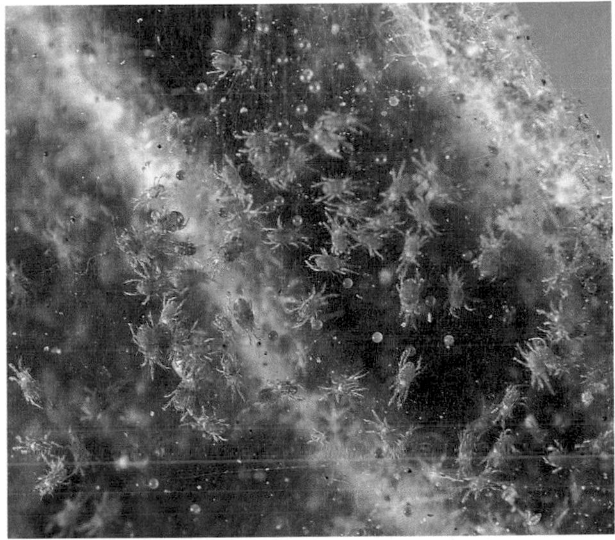

If your plants have yellow-speckled foliage, grab a magnifying glass and look for these tiny pests on the undersides of leaves.

DESCRIPTION: Adults are minute, eight-legged mites 1/75–1/50 inch (less than 0.5 mm) long. They have fine hairs on the body, which is reddish, pale green, or yellow. Overwintering two-spotted mites are dark crimson with brown side patches; summer form is pale green. Most, but not all, species spin fine webs on leaves and shoots. Nymphs are similar but smaller than adults; earliest stages have six legs. Eggs are minuscule pear-shaped spheres found on webbing or leaf hairs.

RANGE: Throughout North America; two-spotted spider mite most common.

PLANTS AFFECTED: Many vegetables, including bean, cucumber, eggplant, melon, and tomato; also fruit trees and ornamentals, including houseplants.

DAMAGE: Both adults and nymphs pierce plant cells and suck the juice from the undersides of leaves. Their feeding weakens plants, causes leaves to drop, and reduces harvest by stunting fruit. Damage first appears as yellow speckled areas on leaves; extremely fine webbing may or may not be visible on undersides of leaves. When the infestation is advanced, leaves become bronzed or turn yellow or white with brown edges. Webs may cover both sides of leaves and eventually encase growing tips; long strings of webbing bearing hundreds of mites may hang down from branch tips and disperse on the wind. Spider mite outbreaks can be severe and rapid in hot, dry conditions; in low humidity, spider mites feed more to avoid drying up, which leads them to lay more eggs and speeds their development.

LIFE CYCLE: Eggs or adults overwinter in crevices in bark or in garden debris. Adults or early nymphs emerge in early spring. Eggs hatch in 1–8 days, and nymphs develop to adults in 5–10 days. Many overlapping generations occur every season; reproduction continues year-round on houseplants and in greenhouses.

PREVENTION: Maintain high humidity in greenhouse crops and around houseplants. Preserve native predatory mites in orchards by avoiding use of pesticides, including sulfur, as much as possible.

CONTROL: Spray dormant oil on fruit trees to kill overwintering eggs. In gardens or greenhouses, rinse plants with water and mist them daily to suppress reproduction of mites. Release predatory mites *Metaseiulus occidentalis* or *Typhlodromus pyri* on fruit trees, *Phytoseiulus persimilis* or similar species on vegetables, strawberries, flowers, and houseplants; consult your local suppliers for the best species for your conditions. Spray insecticidal soap, pyrethrin, or, as a last resort, rotenone. On ornamentals, other spray options include neem or avermectin, when available. On woody shrubs and trees, spray superior oil.

NEMATODES

Nematodes can be harmful or beneficial. Some parasitize soil-dwelling pests; other species cause lesions on roots and leaves.

DESCRIPTION: Nematodes are slender, translucent, unsegmented worms. Most plant-damaging species are under 1/50 inch (0.5 mm) long.

RANGE: Throughout North America.

PLANTS AFFECTED: Corn, lettuce, pepper, potato, tomato, and other plants are susceptible to root nematodes. Alfalfa, chrysanthemum, onions, rye, and other plants are attacked by leaf nematodes.

DAMAGE: Feeding by root nematodes causes lesions and galls on roots and stimulates excessive root branching. Above ground, plants wilt, growth is stunted, and plants may die. Leaf nematodes cause leaf galls or lesions and distorted leaves. (There are also many beneficial species of nematodes.)

LIFE CYCLE: Females lay eggs in masses, or eggs may remain inside the female to hatch when she dies. Most species have a mobile larval stage that moves through the soil on a film of water to infect the plant. The adult stage is reached after several molts. Life cycle takes 3–4 weeks.

PREVENTION: Rotate crops attacked by root nematodes with nonsusceptible crops.

CONTROL: To suppress root-feeding nematodes, grow cover crops of *Tagetes minutum* marigolds in infested soils. Or turn under green manure crops while growth is green to stimulate soil fungi that parasitize nematodes. Solarizing (covering moist soil with clear plastic for the summer) will heat soil and kill nematodes. Drench soil with neem.

Choristoneura rosaceana

OBLIQUEBANDED LEAFROLLER

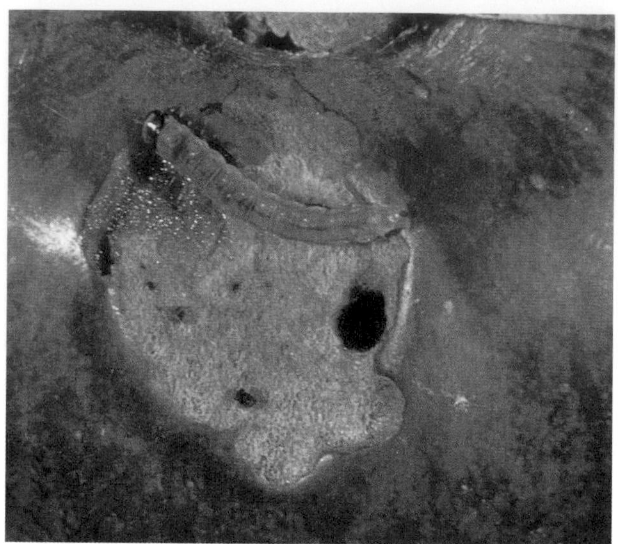

Obliquebanded leafrollers feed on leaves and buds early in the season; later generations are destructive to fruit crops.

DESCRIPTION: Adults are reddish brown moths, with 3/4-inch (2 cm) wingspans; a light and dark V pattern shows on the wings when folded. Larvae are pale green with black heads, 5/8–1 inch (15–25 mm) long. Eggs are greenish.

RANGE: Throughout North America.

PLANTS AFFECTED: Apple, rose, other related fruit; ornamental trees and shrubs.

DAMAGE: Young larvae mine into leaves early in spring; later they move to the tips of branches to spin webs and roll leaves around themselves. They feed on enclosed buds, leaves, and developing fruit. Later in the season, second-generation larvae are most damaging to fruit.

LIFE CYCLE: Larvae overwinter in tough silken cocoons on tree bark and resume feeding in spring. They pupate on tree bark, and adults emerge in June. Females lay eggs in overlapping masses on undersides of leaves; eggs hatch in 2–3 weeks. Larvae mine in leaves, then move to branch tips to spin webs. One generation per year; two generations in warmer regions.

PREVENTION: Attract and conserve native parasitic wasps; also attract woodpeckers, which feed on cocoons during winter.

CONTROL: Spray BTK, pyrethrin, or rotenone when larvae are still young, before they spin webs. Handpick webbed leaves and buds; on small trees, destroy egg masses on undersides of leaves.

Delia antiqua

Onion Maggot

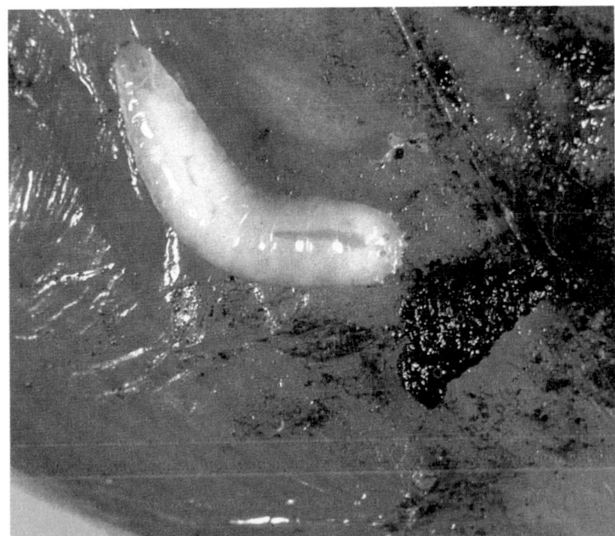

Onion maggots are a problem in Northern gardens. Infestations are worst in cool, wet weather. Damaged bulbs often rot.

DESCRIPTION: Adults are gray flies, ¼ inch (6 mm) long. Larvae are white maggots, ⅓ inch (8.5 mm) long, found burrowing in onion bulbs.

RANGE: Throughout northern United States; southern Canada.

PLANTS AFFECTED: Onion and shallot; garlic and leek somewhat susceptible.

DAMAGE: Maggots burrow into developing onions, killing young plants and hollowing out or stunting older plants. A single maggot can kill over a dozen seedlings during its development. A late generation may infest bulbs in storage.

LIFE CYCLE: Pupae overwinter in soil. Adults emerge from mid-May to late June and lay eggs at the base of plants. Eggs hatch in a week; maggots burrow into roots for 2–3 weeks, then pupate in soil nearby. Adults emerge in 1–2 weeks. Two generations per year; a third occurs in some areas.

PREVENTION: Rotate crops. Cover seedlings with floating row covers. Plant onion sets late to avoid first generation. Plant red onions and Japanese bunching onions, which may be somewhat resistant. Conserve native ground and rove beetles. Sprinkle rows liberally with ground cayenne peppers, ginger, dill, or chili powder to repel females.

CONTROL: Drench soil with insect parasitic nematodes to control maggots. Plant cull onions among seedling rows as a trap crop; pull and destroy 2 weeks after they sprout.

Grapholitha molesta

Oriental Fruit Moth

Oriental fruit moth larvae burrow into the tips of twigs early in the season; later generations attack both shoots and fruit.

DESCRIPTION: Adults are gray moths with mottled forewings and wingspans of ½ inch (1 cm). Larvae are white to pinkish gray with brown heads, up to ½ inch (1 cm) long. Eggs are flat and white.

RANGE: Eastern United States; Pacific Northwest; Ontario, Canada.

PLANTS AFFECTED: Most fruit trees.

DAMAGE: Larvae bore into twigs early in season, causing them to wilt and die. Midsummer larvae bore into developing fruit, leaving gummy castings on fruit. Late-summer larvae enter at the stem end of maturing fruit and bore into the pit or center.

LIFE CYCLE: Larvae overwinter in cocoons on bark or weeds or in soil. They pupate in early spring, and adults emerge in early May to mid-June. Eggs hatch in 10–14 days, larvae feed for 2–3 weeks, then pupate. A second generation appears in mid-July; a third by late August in Northern states. Three to four generations per year in the North, six to seven generations in the South.

PREVENTION: Plant early peach and apricot cultivars, such as 'Floragold' (apricots) and 'Earligrande' (peaches); harvest fruit before midsummer larvae attack. Attract native parasitic wasps and flies with flowering cover crops around trees.

CONTROL: Destroy overwintering larvae by cultivating soil 4 inches (10 cm) deep around trees before trees bloom. Spray superior oil to kill eggs and larvae. Spray ryania as a last resort.

Synanthedon exitiosa and *S. pictipes*

PEACHTREE BORERS

Peachtree borers chew on inner bark near ground level. Their entrance holes exude masses of gummy sawdust.

DESCRIPTION: Adults are narrow moths with 1¼-inch (3 cm) wingspans and blue-black bodies. Males have narrow yellow bands across the body; female *S. exitiosa* have one broad orange band, which is lacking in *S. pictipes*. Larvae are white grubs, up to 1 inch (2.5 cm) long, with dark brown heads.

RANGE: Throughout North America.

PLANTS AFFECTED: Peach; occasionally plum, prune, cherry, apricot, and nectarine.

DAMAGE: Larvae bore beneath bark at the base of a tree, as well as into main roots near the surface. Young trees may be killed; older trees are less affected.

LIFE CYCLE: Females lay eggs on trees or in soil close to trunks. Eggs hatch in 12 days; larvae bore under bark, then overwinter in bark or soil. They resume feeding in spring, and pupate in soil by late June or July; their silken cocoons are usually within a few inches of the trunk. Moths emerge in 2–3 weeks. One generation per year; some with 2-year life cycles.

PREVENTION: Maintain vigorous trees. Prevent mechanical injuries. Attract native parasitic wasps and predators with nectar and pollen plants.

CONTROL: In late summer and fall, inspect tree trunks from about 1 foot (30 cm) above ground level to 2–3 inches (5–7.5 cm) below ground level. Remove borers by digging them out with a knife or by inserting a flexible wire into entrance holes. Cultivate around the trunk to expose and destroy pupae.

Cacopsylla (=Psylla) pyricola

PEAR PSYLLA

Pear psylla are tiny insects that attack the leaves of pears and quinces. They may also spread diseases as they feed.

DESCRIPTION: Adults are dark reddish brown, ⅒ inch (2.5 mm) long, with green or red markings and transparent wings folded roof-like over the back. Nymphs are small, oval, yellow with red eyes, and wingless. Eggs are pear-shaped and yellow.

RANGE: Eastern United States and Canada; Pacific Northwest and California.

PLANTS AFFECTED: Pear and quince.

DAMAGE: A major pest of pears, psylla spread diseases—such as "pear decline" virus and fireblight—and suck plant juices, causing leaves to turn yellow from the toxic saliva. On heavily infested trees, leaves turn brown and drop, and fruit is stunted or drops prematurely. Psylla secrete honeydew, which supports sooty mold growth.

LIFE CYCLE: Adults overwinter under bark and leaf litter; they emerge in spring to lay eggs on fruit spurs and buds. Eggs hatch in 2–4 weeks; by full bloom, numerous minute nymphs are present on stems and undersides of leaves. Early-stage nymphs are covered with a droplet of honeydew. Nymphal development takes 1 month. Three to five generations per year.

PREVENTION: Conserve and attract native beneficial insects, such as earwigs, damsel bugs, minute pirate bugs, and other predators.

CONTROL: Spray dormant oil as soon as leaves drop in fall or just before buds swell in spring. Spray insecticidal soap to control nymphs.

Conotrachelus nenuphar

PLUM CURCULIO

Plum curculios are serious pests on many kinds of fruit trees; they are the worst pest on apples in many Eastern areas.

DESCRIPTION: Adults are brownish gray "snout beetles," ⅕ inch (5 mm) long, with hard, warty wing covers and white hairs on body. Larvae are plump, white grubs ⅓ inch (8 mm) long, with brown heads. Eggs are round and white.

RANGE: Eastern North America.

PLANTS AFFECTED: Most tree fruits and blueberry.

DAMAGE: Feeding and egg-laying by adults damages fruit skin. Larvae tunnel in fruit, usually causing it to rot or drop prematurely.

LIFE CYCLE: In spring, adults move to trees to feed and lay eggs under crescent-shaped cuts in fruit skin as leaves and blossoms appear. Eggs hatch in 5–10 days, and larvae feed for 2–3 weeks. When fruit drops, larvae exit and pupate in soil. Adults emerge from late July to late October, feed on ripe or fallen fruit until fall, then migrate to nearby wooded areas or leaf litter to hibernate. One to two generations per year.

PREVENTION: Every other day, collect and destroy all fallen fruit, especially early drops. Or let chickens into the garden or orchard to eat dropped fruit.

CONTROL: Knock beetles onto a ground cloth by sharply tapping branches with a padded stick; destroy beetles. Where severe infestations occur, apply a mixture of pyrethrin, ryania, and rotenone when you first see feeding or egg scars on developing fruit; repeat in 7–10 days. (Do not apply this mixture before petals drop, as it kills pollinators.)

Macrodactylus subspinosus

ROSE CHAFER

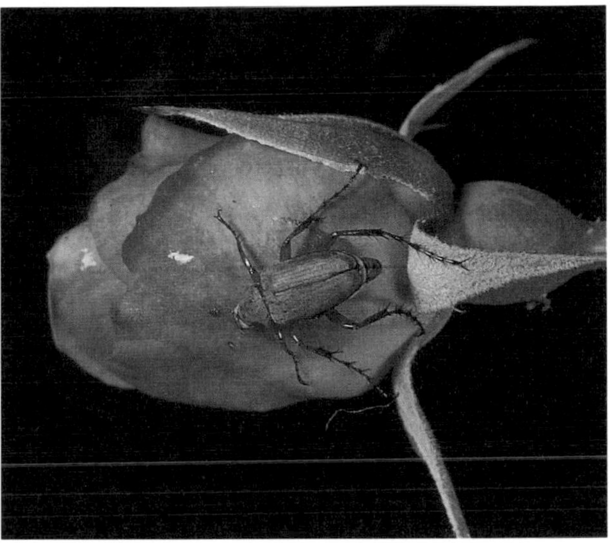

Rose chafers feed on many kinds of plants. They are especially damaging to developing grapes and cherries and to rosebuds.

DESCRIPTION: Adults are reddish brown beetles, ⅓ inch (8 mm) long, with wing covers bearing small, yellowish hairs; the body is black on the underside. Larvae are small white grubs, found in the soil.

RANGE: Throughout North America; most common west of Rocky Mountains.

PLANTS AFFECTED: Blackberry, grape, raspberry, strawberry, and tree fruit; also garden vegetables and ornamentals such as dahlia, hollyhock, iris, peony, poppy, and rose.

DAMAGE: Adult chafers chew on flowers, leaves, and fruits, but are usually damaging only when exceptionally numerous. Damage is more severe in areas with sandy soils. Larvae feed on roots of grass and weeds, doing little noticeable damage.

LIFE CYCLE: Larvae overwinter in the soil and pupate in spring. Adults emerge in late May to early June. Females lay eggs in groups of 6–25 in the soil among weeds and grasses until early July. Eggs hatch in about 2 weeks, and larvae feed on roots until fall, then burrow deeper in the soil. One generation per year.

PREVENTION: Cover smaller plants with floating row covers until July.

CONTROL: Cultivation destroys eggs and pupae in soil; it is especially effective against pupae if continued into early June. If large numbers of chafers are present, spray pyrethrin or rotenone. Drench soil with insect parasitic nematodes to kill larvae.

Saperda candida

ROUNDHEADED APPLETREE BORER

Roundheaded appletree borers tunnel under bark near ground level (girdling the tree) or into heartwood (weakening it).

DESCRIPTION: Adult borers are striped beetles, ¾ inch (2 cm) long, with white undersides and long antennae. Larvae are creamy white grubs with a puffy appearance and a dark head; they have one slightly larger segment behind the head.

RANGE: Eastern United States and Canada; west to Texas and Nevada.

PLANTS AFFECTED: Apple, crab apple, cherry, hawthorn, mountain ash, pear, plum, and quince.

DAMAGE: Larvae are very destructive to apples, boring under bark near ground level or into heartwood. Young trees near infested mountain ash or hawthorn are most likely to be attacked. Adults feed on bark of twigs but cause little damage.

LIFE CYCLE: Adults emerge in June and start laying eggs a week later in the bark, just above soil line. Eggs hatch in about 2–3 weeks. In large trees, larvae burrow into sapwood the first year, overwinter in burrows in soil, and feed in heartwood the second year. Larvae burrow directly into heartwood of young trees. In the third spring, larvae pupate in a feeding gallery inside the tree, and adults emerge several weeks later. A complete life cycle takes 2–4 years.

PREVENTION: Remove wild host plants near garden or orchard.

CONTROL: Impale larvae in holes by probing with a length of fine, flexible wire. Try injecting insect parasitic nematodes in borer holes.

Neodiprion spp.

SAWFLIES, CONIFER

Conifer sawfly larvae feed together in colonies; they rear up when disturbed. These larvae are serious pests of evergreens.

DESCRIPTION: Adults are stubby, thick-waisted wasps, ¼–½ inch (6–10 mm) long, with dark abdomens and transparent, membranous wings. Larvae are gray-green with light stripes or yellow with black dots, ¾–1 inch (2–2.5 cm) long, with a black, brown, or red head.

RANGE: Eastern United States and Canada; related species in West.

PLANTS AFFECTED: Hemlock, pine, and spruce.

DAMAGE: Larvae chew on conifer needles, especially on upper branches, stripping them bare. They may completely devour the needles or only strip the edges, causing the remaining needles to turn reddish brown and dry up in straw-like clumps. Repeated yearly infestations kill trees.

LIFE CYCLE: Eggs overwinter in needles; they hatch in early spring. Larvae feed on old needles until May or early June, then pupate in cocoons in ground litter beneath trees. Adults emerge in fall, mate, and lay eggs in slits made in needles. Some species overwinter in cocoons, and adults emerge to lay eggs in spring. One generation per year.

PREVENTION: Conserve native parasites and predators, including shrews. These, along with a naturally occurring virus, can suppress populations.

CONTROL: Spread ground sheets under trees to catch larvae as they drop to ground to pupate; collect larvae daily and destroy in soapy water. Spray superior oil (not on blue spruce).

Fenusa spp.

SAWFLIES, LEAFMINER

Leafminer sawfly larvae feed between the upper and lower surfaces of leaves, causing tunnels, blotches, or blisters.

DESCRIPTION: Adults are black, stout-bodied wasps, 1/10–1/6 inch (2.5–4 mm) long, with transparent wings. Larvae are flattened white grubs, with rudimentary legs and a brown head, found in leaf mines.

RANGE: Related species in northern and eastern United States; west to Great Lakes states and Canada.

PLANTS AFFECTED: Elm, birch, and alder.

DAMAGE: Larvae mine between upper and lower surface of leaves, leaving brownish, wrinkled blisters. Early generations are most damaging. The worst damage is caused by larval feeding, which, if severe, removes enough leaf area to weaken trees and make them susceptible to attack by borers and other pests.

LIFE CYCLE: Larvae overwinter in cocoons in the soil and pupate in the spring. Adults emerge by mid-May and lay eggs among unfolding young leaves. Larvae feed in leaves until ready to drop to the soil to pupate. Two to four generations per year.

PREVENTION: Maintain healthy, vigorous trees.

CONTROL: Prune out and destroy mined leaves to reduce the number of larvae that survive to the next generation.

Coccidae

SCALES, ARMORED

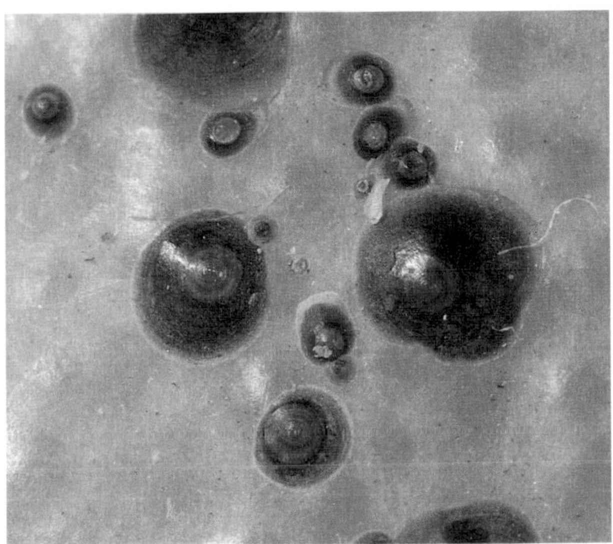

Armored scales may be ash gray, yellow, white, or reddish or purplish brown; some have a distinct dimple in the center.

DESCRIPTION: Adults are circular or oval hard bumps, under 1/10 inch (2.5 mm) long. All secrete an armor of wax in an oyster-shell or circular shape. Early-stage nymphs are mobile crawlers; later stages are legless and sedentary.

RANGE: Southern United States; a few species in Northern regions.

PLANTS AFFECTED: Southern species attack citrus, palm, rose, and tropical ornamentals; Northern species attack fruit and shade trees, currant, grape, raspberry, and ornamental shrubs.

DAMAGE: Scales suck plant juices, weakening plants and causing distortion and injury from the toxic saliva. Severe infestations may kill trees. Scale is the most serious citrus pest.

LIFE CYCLE: Females lay eggs or bear live nymphs; nymphs wander for several hours or days before settling and becoming immobile. Development to adult takes 1 month or more. Most armored scales overwinter as nymphs or eggs on bark of trees. One to two generations per year in the North; up to six generations in warm regions.

PREVENTION: Attract native predators and parasites.

CONTROL: Most pesticides are little use because scales are protected by waxy covering. Dormant and superior oil sprays provide good control. Release the predatory beetles *Chilocorus nigritus* or *Lindorus lophanthae;* for California red scale or oleander scale, release the parasitic wasp *Aphytis melinus*.

Coccidae

Scales, soft

Soft scales are common on fruits, trees and shrubs, and houseplants. Some species produce fluffy white egg sacs.

DESCRIPTION: Adult females are oval or round, soft, legless, wingless bumps, 1/10–1/5 inch (2.5–5 mm) long. Adult males are minute yellow-winged insects. Early-stage larvae are crawlers resembling minute mealybugs; later stages are immobile.

RANGE: Throughout North America.

PLANTS AFFECTED: Citrus, many fruits, ornamental shrubs and trees, and houseplants.

DAMAGE: All stages suck plant sap, weakening plants and causing leaves to yellow and drop. In severe infestations, plants will die. Soft scales secrete honeydew, which supports growth of sooty mold.

LIFE CYCLE: Females of some species lay as many as 2,000 eggs; others give birth to several nymphs per day. Nymphs move around for a short time, then settle down; the females molt to an immobile form. One or two generations per year outdoors; up to six generations on indoor plants.

PREVENTION: Attract native predatory beetles and parasitic wasps with nectar and pollen plants.

CONTROL: Prune and destroy infested branches and twigs. Remove scales from twigs with soft brush or from leaves with soft cloth and soapy water; rinse well. Release the predatory beetles *Chilocorus nigritus* or *Lindorus lophanthae*; for soft brown scale, release the parasitic wasp *Metaphycus helvolus*. Spray dormant oil on fruit and ornamental trees. Spray superior oil (not on citrus after July). Spray pyrethrin or rotenone as a last resort.

Slugs and snails

Slugs lurk in damp places and come out to feed at night. They usually hide under rocks or garden debris during the day.

DESCRIPTION: Adults are soft-bodied, land-dwelling mollusks. Snails have coiled shells on their backs and are 1–1½ inches (2.5–4 cm) long, slugs are without shells. Garden slugs are 1/8–1 inch (3–25 mm) long (longer when they stretch out); banana slugs may be up to 4–6 inches (10–15 cm) long. Most slugs and snails are dark or light gray, tan, green, or black; some have darker spots or patterns. They leave a characteristic slimy trail of mucus behind. Eggs are clear, oval or round, and laid in jelly-like masses.

RANGE: Throughout North America; banana slugs in coastal areas.

PLANTS AFFECTED: Any tender plant or shrub.

DAMAGE: Both slugs and snails feed primarily on decaying plant material. They also eat soft, succulent plant tissue and rasp large holes in foliage, stems, and even bulbs. They may completely demolish seedlings and severely damage young shoots and plants. Snails and sometimes slugs may climb into trees and shrubs to feed. Both are most numerous and damaging in wet years and in regions with high rainfall.

LIFE CYCLE: Adults lay egg masses in moist soil or under rocks or garden debris. Eggs hatch in 2–4 weeks. Slugs grow for 5–24 months before reaching maturity; snails take 2 years to reach maturity.

PREVENTION: Maintain permanent walkways of clover, sod, or stone mulches to harbor ground beetles

SOWBUGS/PILLBUGS

Moisture is less critical to snails, since they are protected by their shells. Snails may climb into trees and shrubs to feed.

and rove beetles, which prey on slugs. Attract birds and protect garter snakes, toads, and lizards—which also eat slugs—and centipedes and fireflies, which eat slug eggs. Repel slugs and snails with copper barrier strips fastened around trunks of trees or shrubs. Use copper, zinc, or metal screen edging for garden beds, first making sure all slugs are removed from the enclosed area. Staple 3-inch (7.5 cm) wide copper bands around edges of greenhouse benches. Wrap commercial snail and slug tapes, which are coated with salt and hot pepper, around tree trunks. Where slugs are not a serious problem, seedlings may be sufficiently protected by wide bands of cinders, wood ashes, or diatomaceous earth, renewed frequently.

CONTROL: Trap slugs and snails under flowerpots, boards, grapefruit rinds, or cabbage leaves; check traps and destroy pests every morning until numbers drop, then check weekly. Set out commercial slug traps with yeast bait; or make traps by burying shallow pans—filled with beer or other fermenting liquids to attract slugs—with the lip flush to the soil surface. Decollate snails (predatory snails that eat other mollusks) are sold for brown-snail control in citrus orchards in some counties in California; these should not be used elsewhere.

Sowbugs—also known as pillbugs—feed mostly on decaying plant material, but they may attack tender seedlings, too.

DESCRIPTION: Adults are gray or brown crustaceans ¼–⅝ inch (6–15 mm) long, with numerous segments of jointed armor. They have seven pairs of barely visible, short legs. Pillbugs curl up into a ball if disturbed. Nymphs look like small adults.

RANGE: Throughout North America.

PLANTS AFFECTED: Seedlings of many plants.

DAMAGE: Sowbugs and pillbugs feed on decaying organic matter. They cause little or no damage to established plants, but if their numbers are high, they can severely damage seedlings by chewing on leaves and fine roots.

LIFE CYCLE: Females carry eggs and young nymphs in a pouch for several weeks. Nymphs and adults prefer moist conditions and cannot survive long on dry surfaces. Often in early spring, with warm rains, they may emerge from their overwintering sites at the same time, so populations seem to explode suddenly. Individuals may live for 3 years.

PREVENTION: Drain wet areas and remove trash, leaf litter, boards, and other debris from foundations and garden beds.

CONTROL: Sprinkle diatomaceous earth around seedlings. Trap sowbugs under stones, boards, or cabbage leaves; destroy every morning. Set out traps made from paper painted with a sticky trap glue, then folded tent-like, with the glue-side down.

Philaenus spumarius

SPITTLEBUG/FROGHOPPER

Spittlebugs produce masses of frothy "spittle" on stems and feed inside. The fast-moving adult form is known as a froghopper.

DESCRIPTION: Adults are oval, frog-faced, and ¼–½ inch (6–10 mm) long. The tan, mottled brown, or black bugs are similar to leafhoppers but stouter, with sharp spines on hind legs. Adults are very active and jump when disturbed. Nymphs are yellow to yellowish green, similar to adults, but wingless; you'll find them inside a foamy mass of "spittle." Eggs are white to beige.

RANGE: Throughout North America.

PLANTS AFFECTED: Strawberry, legume forage crops (such as alfalfa and clover), and nursery plants.

DAMAGE: Froghoppers are rarely a serious problem in gardens. Adults and nymphs suck plant juices, causing stunted, dwarfed, weakened plants with reduced yields. Adults migrate in large numbers from hay fields to nearby crops when hay is cut; at this time a home garden may suddenly be infested with froghoppers.

LIFE CYCLE: Overwintering eggs hatch in mid-April, and nymphs develop for 6–7 weeks in masses of spittle on plant stems. Adults feed for the rest of summer and start to lay overwintering eggs in rows on stems or stubble by early September.

PREVENTION: Conserve native predatory bugs. Cover garden plants with floating row covers when nearby hay fields are cut.

CONTROL: If you saw a high number of nymphs in summer, then till under stubble of forage legumes in fall to kill overwintering eggs.

Choristoneura fumiferana

SPRUCE BUDWORM

Spruce budworm is one of the most damaging forest pests in North America. It will also attack ornamental evergreen trees.

DESCRIPTION: Adults are grayish brown moths, with ⅞–1¼ inch (2.2–3 cm) wingspans and dark brown hind wings fringed with white. Up to ¾ inch (2 cm) long, larvae are dark brown with lighter sides, dark spines, and two rows of white dots along their back. Eggs are green.

RANGE: Throughout north central and eastern United States; in Canada to the Yukon; related species in the West.

PLANTS AFFECTED: Balsam fir and spruce; occasionally Douglas fir, hemlock, larch, and pine.

DAMAGE: Larvae mine in needles, buds, cones, and twigs. Trees often die after 3–5 years of heavy infestations; surviving trees are weakened and susceptible to bark beetle attack.

LIFE CYCLE: Moths lay eggs in overlapping masses on undersides of needles in late June to early August. Eggs hatch in 8–12 days; young larvae disperse throughout the tree, then spin cocoons and hibernate. Larvae emerge the following spring and mine in old needles, then in young buds. As new growth expands, larvae spin webs around tips of twigs and feed inside, pupating by late June. Adults emerge in 10 days. One generation per year.

PREVENTION: Avoid using susceptible plants in areas where spruce and fir are very common.

CONTROL: Spray BTK as soon as you see the tiny larvae in late summer; spray again in early spring when the surviving larvae resume feeding.

Anasa tristis

SQUASH BUG

Squash bugs and their nymphs suck plant sap and may cause vines to wilt. Adults emit an unpleasant smell when crushed.

DESCRIPTION: Adults are oval, dark brown to black, ⅝ inch (15 mm) long, covered with fine, dark hairs, and have a flattened abdomen. Nymphs are pale green; they develop a darker, reddish thorax and abdomen as they mature; older nymphs are covered with a grainy gray powder. Eggs are shiny yellow to brick red ellipses.

RANGE: Throughout North America.

PLANTS AFFECTED: Cucumber, gourd, melon, pumpkin, and squash.

DAMAGE: Both adults and nymphs suck plant juices, causing leaves and shoots to blacken and die back; symptoms may be mistaken for a wilt disease.

LIFE CYCLE: Adults overwinter under garden litter, vines, or boards. Females lay eggs in groups on underside of leaves in spring. Eggs hatch in 1–2 weeks, and nymphs take 4–6 weeks to develop, molting five times before becoming adults. One generation per year.

PREVENTION: Plant resistant squash cultivars, such as 'Early Prolific Straightneck', 'Early Summer Crookneck', 'Royal Acorn', and 'Table Queen'. Support vines off the ground on trellises. Attract native parasitic flies with pollen and nectar plants. Cover young plants with floating row covers (hand-pollinate flowers to get fruit).

CONTROL: Handpick all stages from undersides of leaves. Spray rotenone to control nymphs, or sabadilla to control adults.

Melittia cucurbitae

SQUASH VINE BORER

Squash vine borers tunnel into the bases of vine stems, causing entire vines to wilt suddenly.

DESCRIPTION: Adults are narrow-winged moths, with 1–1½-inch (2.5–4 cm) wingspans. They have olive-brown forewings, clear hind wings, hind legs with long fringes, and a red abdomen with black rings. Larvae are white grubs, up to 1 inch (2.5 cm) long, with a brown head.

RANGE: East of Rocky Mountains; south to Mexico.

PLANTS AFFECTED: Cucumber, gourd, melon, pumpkin, and squash (especially Hubbard squash).

DAMAGE: Larvae bore into vines, chewing inner tissue near the base of the plant and causing vines to wilt suddenly. Girdled vines rot and die. Later in the season, larvae may also feed on fruit.

LIFE CYCLE: Larvae or pupae overwinter in soil. Adults emerge as squash vines begin to lengthen; they lay eggs on stems and leaf stalks near the base of plants. Larvae burrow into stems to feed for 4–6 weeks, then pupate in soil for winter. One generation per year, two in Southern areas.

PREVENTION: Plant early and promote vigorous growth so vines are able to tolerate attack. Cover plants with floating row covers; hand-pollinate flowers to get fruit or uncover when plants start to bloom for pollinators. Plant resistant cultivars such as 'Sweet Mama' squash.

CONTROL: Spray base of plants with rotenone or pyrethrin repeatedly to kill larvae before they enter vines. Slit infested stems, remove borers, and heap soil over the damaged vine to induce rooting.

Pentatomidae

Stink bugs

Stink bugs are shield-shaped insects that may be dull or brightly colored. Adults emit a foul smell when disturbed.

DESCRIPTION: Adults are shield-shaped, ½–⅝ inch (10–15 mm) long, and colored green, tan, brown, or gray; one species has bright red-and-black harlequin markings. Nymphs are oval, similar to adults, but wingless. Eggs are barrel-shaped.

RANGE: Throughout North America.

PLANTS AFFECTED: Bean, cabbage, corn, okra, pea, squash, and tomato; also peach, forage crops, and many weeds.

DAMAGE: Both adults and nymphs suck sap from leaves, flowers, fruit, and seeds. Leaves may wilt and turn brown or have brown spots. Feeding punctures in fruit cause scarring and dimpling known as "catfacing"; pods drop and seed is deformed.

LIFE CYCLE: Adults overwinter in standing stalks of garden residues or in weeds along waste areas. They emerge in spring. Females lay 300–500 eggs in clusters on undersides of leaves. Eggs hatch in a week, and nymphs develop to adults in about 5 weeks. Two or more generations per year.

PREVENTION: Control weeds in the garden to reduce overwintering sites; remove crop residues and till the garden in fall. Attract native parasitic wasps and tachinid flies with pollen and nectar plants.

CONTROL: Handpick all stages; crush egg masses on undersides of leaves. Spray insecticidal soap to control both adults and nymphs. As a last resort, dust or spray with pyrethrin, rotenone, or sabadilla.

Otiorhynchus ovatus

Strawberry root weevil

Strawberry root weevil larvae feed within roots and crowns, causing serious damage. The adults chew on leaves and fruit.

DESCRIPTION: Adults are shiny, nearly black, hard-shelled "snout beetles," ¼ inch (6 mm) long. Their wing covers are fused so they cannot fly. Found in roots, larvae are white, C-shaped, legless grubs with brown heads.

RANGE: Throughout most of North America.

PLANTS AFFECTED: Apple, grape, peach, strawberry, raspberry, and peach; also pine and spruce seedlings in nurseries.

DAMAGE: Adult weevils (also called "strawberry clippers") feed on leaves and fruits, clipping small half circles from the edges of leaves and severing flower stems. The worst damage is caused by larvae boring into crowns and roots of plants. Plants are stunted and may die, often from diseases that enter roots through the wounds.

LIFE CYCLE: Larvae and some adults overwinter in roots; most adults overwinter in nearby weedy or brushy areas. Larvae feed for a while in spring, then pupate; new adults emerge in June. After feeding for 2–3 weeks, they lay numerous eggs near plant crowns. Eggs hatch in 10 days and larvae burrow into the root zone. One generation per year.

PREVENTION: Cover plants with floating row covers.

CONTROL: Spray rotenone to control adults. To control larvae, drench soil with insect parasitic nematodes when larvae are present (in early May, as soon as soil warms, and again in August).

Lygus lineolaris

TARNISHED PLANT BUG

Tarnished plant bugs suck sap from leaves, buds, and fruit, causing silvery brown spots, stunted growth, and stem dieback.

DESCRIPTION: Adults are oval, mottled light green to coppery brown, ¼ inch (6 mm) long; forewings have black-tipped yellow triangles. From the side, there is a downward slant to the rear portion of the wings. Adults move very quickly. Nymphs are yellow-green with five black dots on the body. They look similar to adults but are wingless.

RANGE: Throughout North America.

PLANTS AFFECTED: Most flowers, fruit, vegetables, and weeds.

DAMAGE: Adults and nymphs pierce leaves, buds, and fruits and suck plant juices; nymphs are most damaging. Their toxic saliva causes buds and pods to drop and distorts leaves and shoots. Plants wilt or are stunted, branch tips blacken and die back. Feeding on fruit causes pitted, "catfaced" fruit.

LIFE CYCLE: Overwintering adults emerge from under debris or bark in early spring. They feed on fruit-tree buds, then move to garden plants and weeds to lay eggs in stems or leaves. Eggs hatch in 10 days. Nymphs feed for 3–4 weeks, then molt to adults. Two to five overlapping generations per year.

PREVENTION: Cover plants with floating row covers. Attract predatory bigeyed bugs, damsel bugs, and minute pirate bugs with nectar and pollen plants. Remove crop debris near gardens and orchards.

CONTROL: Release minute pirate bugs or damsel bugs, when available. As a last resort, spray rotenone or sabadilla.

Malacosoma spp.

TENT CATERPILLAR

Tent caterpillars feed in masses and often spin large "tents" of silken webbing in the forks of branches for protection.

DESCRIPTION: Adults are yellowish to brown moths with 1–1½-inch (2.5–4 cm) wingspans and two narrow stripes across the wings. The hairy larvae have a black head and body with a white stripe or rows of dots along the back, and brownish and blue or red marks along the sides. Egg masses are covered with a hardened foamy layer.

RANGE: Throughout North America.

PLANTS AFFECTED: Most deciduous trees and shrubs, especially apple, aspen, and wild cherry.

DAMAGE: Larvae chew on leaves; they may completely defoliate trees in years of high populations. Trees usually leaf out again, but growth may be stunted for several years.

LIFE CYCLE: Females lay eggs on twigs in midsummer; they overwinter and hatch in early spring. Larvae move to nearest branch crotch, where most species spin a silk tent for protection. They pupate in leaf litter after feeding for 5–8 weeks; moths emerge in 10 days. One generation per year.

PREVENTION: Attract native parasitic flies and wasps with nectar and pollen plants; these usually keep populations in check. Do not destroy larvae with white eggs or cocoons attached to their backs; they are hosts for parasites.

CONTROL: Prune branches with tents and destroy them. In winter, remove egg masses from bare branches. While larvae are small, spray BTK weekly. Catch larvae in sticky tree bands.

Thripidae

THRIPS

Thrips are tiny insects that feed on leaves, fruits, and flowers, producing a characteristic silvery appearance.

DESCRIPTION: Adults are minute, elongated insects 1/50–1/25 inch (0.5–1 mm) long with narrow fringed wings; the yellowish, brown, or black adults move very quickly. Nymphs are light green or yellow; they are similar to adults but smaller.

RANGE: Throughout North America.

PLANTS AFFECTED: Many garden plants, flowers, fruit, and shade trees.

DAMAGE: Adults and nymphs suck contents of plant cells, leaving silvery speckling or streaks on leaves. Severe infestations stunt and distort plants, damage flowers, and scar developing fruit. Some species spread tomato spotted wilt virus.

LIFE CYCLE: Adults overwinter in sod, debris, or cracks in bark, becoming active in early spring. Females lay eggs in plant tissue; eggs hatch in 3–5 days. Nymphs feed for 1–3 weeks, then rest in soil or on leaves for 1–2 weeks before molting to the adult stage. Five to 15 generations per year outdoors; generations year-round in greenhouses.

PREVENTION: Attract native predators such as minute pirate bugs, lacewings, and lady beetles.

CONTROL: Spray dormant oil on fruit trees. For onion or western flower thrips, release the predatory mite *Amblyseius cucumeris* or minute pirate bugs. Use bright blue or yellow sticky traps to catch adults. Spray insecticidal soap, pyrethrin, or neem. As a last resort, spray ryania or dust undersides of leaves with sabadilla or diatomaceous earth.

Manduca quinquemaculata

TOMATO HORNWORM

Tomato hornworms are large caterpillars that blend in very well with foliage. They can do serious damage to leaves.

DESCRIPTION: Adults are mottled gray, narrow-winged moths with 4–5-inch (10–12.5 cm) wingspans and rows of orange dots along their plump, furry abdomen. At dusk, they sip nectar from flowers. The green larvae are up to 4 ½ inches (11 cm) long, with a single large horn on their tail and eight diagonal white marks along sides. Eggs are round and yellowish green.

RANGE: Throughout North America.

PLANTS AFFECTED: Eggplant, pepper, potato, tobacco, and tomato.

DAMAGE: Larvae chew large holes in leaves and may completely strip young plants. In severe infestations, larvae also feed on stems and chew large holes in fruit.

LIFE CYCLE: The large, dark brown pupae overwinter in soil, and moths emerge in June and July. Females lay eggs singly on undersides of leaves; eggs hatch in a week. Larvae feed for 3–4 weeks, then pupate in soil. One generation per year in most areas; two or more generations in the South.

PREVENTION: Grow nectar or pollen plants to attract native parasitic wasps, which usually provide sufficient control in most areas.

CONTROL: Handpick caterpillars from foliage; drop them in a pail of soapy water. Spray BTK while caterpillars are still small. Till garden in fall or early spring to destroy pupae. Release lady beetles or lacewings to attack eggs.

Hyphantria cunea

WEBWORM, FALL

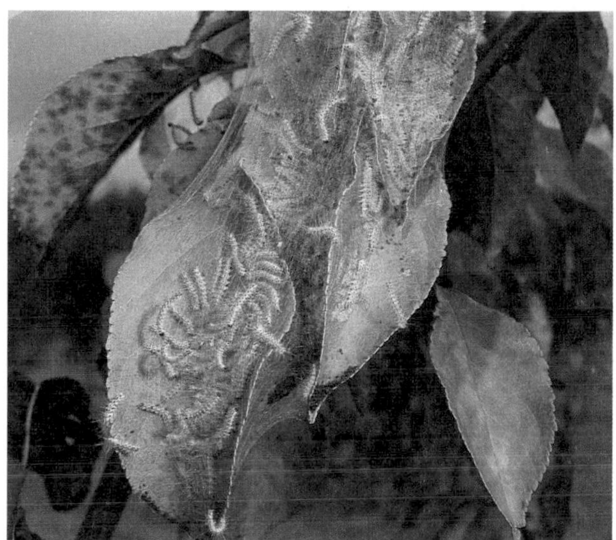

Fall webworms build their unsightly silken nests near branch tips and feed ravenously on the foliage within.

DESCRIPTION: Adults are pure white moths, with 2–2½-inch (5–6 cm) wingspans and black dots on the forewings; the abdomen is yellow with black spots. Larvae are beige, covered with dense yellow to brown hairs, and have tufts of long white hairs on their sides.

RANGE: Throughout United States; southern Canada.

PLANTS AFFECTED: Many deciduous trees and shrubs.

DAMAGE: Larvae chew on leaves and spin large, conspicuous, dirty white webs over the ends of branches; sometimes several branch tips are enclosed by one web.

LIFE CYCLE: Pupae overwinter in tightly woven cocoons under soil debris or tree bark. Adults emerge in May to June and lay eggs in masses covered with hairs on undersides of leaves; eggs hatch in a few days. Groups of larvae feed together through June and July (4–6 weeks) inside the web, which extends as the foliage inside is consumed. Last-stage larvae wander all over the tree, then pupate in soil debris. One to two generations per year.

PREVENTION: Attract native parasitic wasps with nectar or pollen plants.

CONTROL: Prune and destroy branches with webs. Spray BTK on leaves around web while larvae are small or when older larvae start wandering outside web to feed. Catch larvae in sticky tree bands as they leave to pupate.

Achyra rantalis

WEBWORM, GARDEN

Garden webworms spin webbing around leaves and feed on the undersides of enclosed foliage until the leaves are skeletonized.

DESCRIPTION: Adults are brown moths, with ¾-inch (2 cm) wingspans and pale gold and gray marks on wings. Larvae are pale green to nearly black, up to ¾ inch (2 cm) long, with a dark or light stripe down the back and three dark spots on the side of each segment. When disturbed, larvae drop from plants on silk threads.

RANGE: Throughout North America.

PLANTS AFFECTED: Most vegetables, especially bean and pea; also strawberry and some weeds.

DAMAGE: Caterpillars spin silk webbing around leaves and skeletonize foliage. When large numbers of webworms are present, they cover plants with webs and cause severe defoliation.

LIFE CYCLE: Larvae or pupae overwinter in cocoons in soil near host plants. Moths emerge from spring to midsummer and lay masses of 5–50 eggs, which hatch in 3–7 days. Caterpillars feed for 3–4 weeks, then pupate for 7–10 days. Two to five generations per year.

PREVENTION: Grow nectar and pollen plants to attract native parasitic wasps, which usually suppress webworm numbers.

CONTROL: Knock caterpillars from plants into a pail of soapy water (they drop readily); destroy webbing. Spray BTK on leaves when larvae are very small, before webbing protects them from sprays. As a last resort, spray pyrethrin or rotenone. Till garden in fall to kill pupae.

Aleyrodidae

Whiteflies

Whiteflies are tiny insects that congregate and feed on the undersides of leaves. They fly up in a cloud when disturbed.

DESCRIPTION: Adults are powdery white and 1/25 inch (1 mm) long. Larvae are flattened, legless, translucent scales 1/30 inch (0.8 mm) long on undersides of leaves. Eggs are tiny gray or yellow cones.

RANGE: Throughout North America in greenhouses; most species outdoors in California, Florida, Gulf states, and the West Coast.

PLANTS AFFECTED: Citrus, ornamentals, and vegetables, especially cucumber and tomato relatives.

DAMAGE: Nymphs and adults suck plant juices, weakening plants. They secrete honeydew, which supports growth of sooty mold on leaves and fruit. Feeding can spread plant virus diseases.

LIFE CYCLE: Females lay eggs on underside of leaves; eggs hatch in 2 days into tiny, mobile scales. After a few days, these become immobile; they continue to feed on plant juices until they pupate. The complete life cycle takes 20–30 days at room temperature. Numerous generations per year; all winter in greenhouses and warm climates.

PREVENTION: Attract native parasitic wasps, lacewings, lady beetles, and pirate bugs.

CONTROL: Capture adults on yellow sticky traps. Vacuum adults from leaves. Release the parasitic wasp *Encarsia formosa* (indoors) to control greenhouse whitefly. Spray with insecticidal soap, kinoprene (Enstar), summer oil, or garlic oil to control nymphs. As a last resort, spray pyrethrin, ryania, or rotenone.

Limonius spp.

Wireworms

Wireworms burrow into and feed on newly planted seeds and underground plant parts, like roots, bulbs, and tubers.

DESCRIPTION: Adults are elongated, brown or black beetles 1/3–3/4 inch (8–20 mm) long, with fine, lengthwise grooves on wing covers. The adults are often called "click beetles" because they produce a sharp click as they flip onto their feet. Larvae are yellow to brown, leathery, jointed, and worm-like, up to 1½ inches (4 cm) long.

RANGE: Throughout North America.

PLANTS AFFECTED: Gladiolus and other corms, potato, and most vegetables.

DAMAGE: Adults feed on leaves and flowers but cause little damage. Larvae bore into seeds or roots, stunting or killing plants. Wireworms are worst in newly turned sod and for a few years thereafter.

LIFE CYCLE: Adults lay eggs in plant roots in early spring; eggs hatch in 3–10 days. Larvae spend 2–6 years feeding near the soil surface while soil is cool in spring and fall. They burrow deeper in hot weather and again in late fall. Mature larvae pupate in late summer. One generation every 2–6 years.

PREVENTION: Delay planting tubers and corms until soil is very warm; keep soil bare until planting.

CONTROL: To destroy larvae, cultivate soil weekly for 4–6 weeks in fall, or allow chickens to run on infested ground. Raw potato or carrot pieces buried 2–6 inches (5–15 cm) in soil attract some species; check traps every few days and destroy wireworms. Insect parasitic nematodes may give some control of larvae.

B E N E F I C I A L S

Aphidoletes aphidimyza

APHID MIDGE

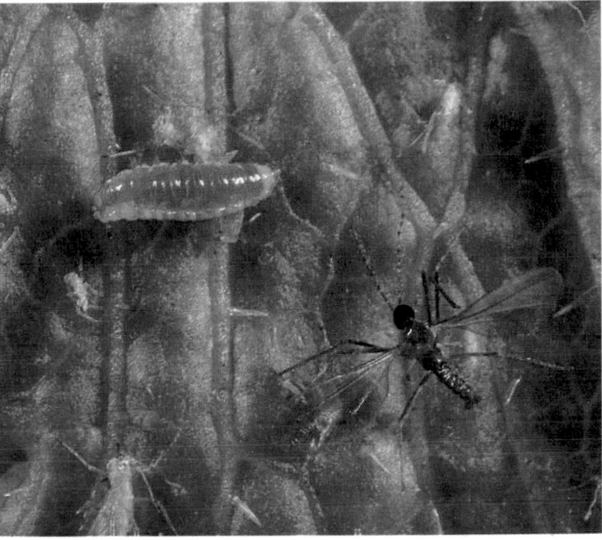

Aphid midges are tiny, long-legged flies. Their orange larvae are excellent predators of aphids in gardens and greenhouses.

DESCRIPTION: Adults are tiny, delicate, long-legged flies, 1/16 inch (2 mm) long; they are active at night. Larvae are light to dark orange maggots, up to 1/8 inch (3 mm) long. Eggs are minute orange ovals.

RANGE: Throughout North America; also sold commercially.

BENEFICIAL EFFECTS: Aphid midge larvae are common, hardy, extremely effective aphid predators, known to feed on more than 60 species of aphids. They paralyze the aphids with toxic saliva and suck their body fluids.

LIFE CYCLE: Females lay their eggs at night on undersides of leaves among aphids. Eggs hatch in 2–3 days, and the larvae feed on aphids for 3–5 days. Larvae drop to the ground and burrow into the soil to pupate; adults wiggle to the surface and emerge in 2–3 weeks. The last generation in fall overwinters as larvae in soil. Three or more generations per year.

HOW TO ATTRACT: Plant pollen and nectar plants to attract adult midges. Shelter the garden from strong winds with a windbreak. Provide a source of water in dry weather. If you want to supplement native populations, buy 200–300 cocoons for a small garden, orchard, or greenhouse and release once in early spring; for larger areas, release three to five cocoons per plant or five to ten per orchard tree.

Reduviidae

ASSASSIN BUGS

Assassin bugs are effective predators of many different garden pests, including aphids, caterpillars, and beetles.

DESCRIPTION: Adults are somewhat flattened, oval, ½–1 inch (1–2.5 cm) long, with narrow, somewhat conical heads and stout, curving beaks; wings are crossed and folded flat over the back. Some have an elaborately flared or sculptured thorax. Most can inflict a painful bite if caught, and some species squeak when handled. Nymphs are similar to adults but are smaller and wingless. Some nymphs are brightly marked; others camouflage themselves by sticking debris or trash to their bodies.

RANGE: Throughout North America; more than 110 native species.

BENEFICIAL EFFECTS: Assassin bugs are voracious general predators that help suppress pest populations by feeding on flies, mosquitoes, beetles, large caterpillars, and other insects (even bed bugs).

LIFE CYCLE: The females lay their eggs singly or in clusters in crevices, under stones, or in other shelters. The nymphs feed on insects, growing in size and molting several times until fall; they overwinter in a pre-adult stage and continue development to become adults the following June. One generation per year.

HOW TO ATTRACT: Avoid pesticide use in the garden.

Geocoris spp.

BIGEYED BUGS

Bigeyed bugs attack a variety of garden pests, including caterpillars. They feed on nectar when pests are scarce.

DESCRIPTION: Adults are stubby little bugs, ⅛–¼ inch (3–6 mm) long, with large eyes; they are black or pale yellowish green, with minute black spots on head and thorax. Nymphs are similar to adults but are smaller and wingless. Adults and nymphs move very rapidly. They may be mistaken for tarnished plant bugs.

RANGE: Western North America.

BENEFICIAL EFFECTS: Both adults and nymphs are predators on aphids, leafhoppers, plant bugs, spider mites, and small caterpillars. They are very valuable native predators in orchards and field crops, such as alfalfa and cotton.

LIFE CYCLE: Females insert eggs into the tissue of plant stems and undersides of leaves. Eggs hatch in 2 weeks and nymphs develop for 4–6 weeks before molting to adults. Adults overwinter in garden trash or other protected areas. Two to three generations per year in most areas.

HOW TO ATTRACT: Bigeyed bugs prefer to lay eggs on soybeans, pigweed, and goldenrod, so attract them by interplanting crops with soybeans and growing the wild plants in borders. Avoid using pesticides.

Braconidae

BRACONID WASPS

Braconid wasps are so tiny that you rarely see them. But you will see their white-to-brown cocoons on parasitized hosts.

DESCRIPTION: Adults are slender, black or brown 1/10–1/2-inch (2.5–10 mm) long mini-wasps, with a characteristic narrow waist. They do not sting. Larvae are soft, pearly white grubs found feeding inside or on other insects.

RANGE: Throughout North America; more than 2,000 native species; some sold commercially.

BENEFICIAL EFFECTS: Most braconids parasitize aphids or moth and beetle larvae; some attack flies and other insects. Braconid wasps are important native parasites of such pests as codling moths, elm bark beetles, cabbageworms, hornworms, corn borers, armyworms, green peach aphids, and others. Many species develop as parasites inside the host insect; others paralyze the host and the wasp larvae develop as external parasites.

LIFE CYCLE: Females inject eggs into host insects, singly or in large numbers. The larvae feed inside the host, but the host does not die until the wasp larvae have completed development. They spin cocoons, usually nearby or on the dead host, then pupate. Most species overwinter as newly hatched larvae inside a living host. Life cycles are usually short; several generations occur per year.

HOW TO ATTRACT: Females need nectar to sustain them while laying eggs, so grow nectar plants with small flowers, such as dill, parsley, wild carrot, corn spurry, mustard, white clover, lemon balm, stinging nettle, and yarrow.

Bombus spp.

BUMBLEBEES

Bumblebees are important native pollinators of fruit and vegetable crops. Protect these insects to keep garden yields high.

DESCRIPTION: Adults are large, plump, black-and-yellow, fuzzy bees, 1/2–1 inch (1–2.5 cm) long. They are able to fly in very cool weather. Larvae are fat, white grubs, found in cells in the nest.

RANGE: Throughout North America; also sold commercially.

BENEFICIAL EFFECTS: Bumblebees are extremely important wild pollinators for a variety of fruit and seed crops. Bumblebee colonies are sold commercially for use in greenhouses to pollinate tomatoes and peppers.

LIFE CYCLE: Queen bumblebees emerge from their overwintering sites in soil or leaf litter in May. They make a nest on or below the ground, in a deserted mouse nest, in a hole in a rock wall, or in a similar refuge. The queen lays 8–12 eggs, each in an individual cell made of pollen. She feeds the developing larvae pollen and honey until they mature in 3–4 weeks to become workers. The workers collect pollen and nectar to rear the next two or three broods of eggs laid by the queen. In fall, young queens develop in the colony, fly away to mate, and the colony breaks up.

HOW TO ATTRACT: Protect bees by minimizing spraying or by spraying only in evenings after bees return to their nest. Plant pollen and nectar flowers, and allow dandelions to bloom to provide early pollen.

CENTIPEDES AND MILLIPEDES

Centipedes prey on many kinds of soil-dwelling pests. Unlike millipedes, centipedes have one pair of legs for each body segment.

Millipedes are slow moving and feed mostly on decaying plant material, although they sometimes damage seedlings.

DESCRIPTION: Long, slender, segmented soil-dwellers, ½–3 inches (1–7.5 cm) long, with many legs. Centipedes have one leg per segment; millipedes have two legs per segment. Centipedes have long legs and move more quickly than millipedes; they may be light brown to black and tend to have a flattened appearance. Millipedes have short legs and some curl up when disturbed; they are generally dark brown or gray and cylindrical. Centipedes have poisonous "claws" behind their head that they use to grab prey; smaller species are usually harmless to people; larger species can inflict a painful bite.

RANGE: Throughout North America.

BENEFICIAL EFFECTS: Centipedes are generally good predators of soil-dwelling pests and insects, including slugs, worms, and fly pupae. They may also feed on earthworms, but overall centipedes are considered to be beneficial. Millipedes primarily feed on decaying plant material, such as dead leaves, manure, or compost. They are beneficial in breaking down organic matter, but may occasionally feed on plant roots, germinating seeds, and seedlings. They may also chew on fruits that rest on the ground, like strawberries and tomatoes.

LIFE CYCLE: Both centipedes and millipedes lay their eggs in soil. The resulting nymphs are similar to adults but are shorter and have fewer segments.

HOW TO ATTRACT: Preserve centipede populations by avoiding the use of pesticides. They prefer moist habitats, such as under boards or in compost piles. Millipedes are commonly found in soil or under rocks and garden debris. Control of millipedes is not necessary unless populations are unusually high. To reduce millipede numbers, allow the soil surface to dry out around seedlings. Further dry the surface by sprinkling wood ashes, diatomaceous earth, or cinders along rows of germinating seeds. Keep fruit off the ground with straw mulches.

Nabidae

DAMSEL BUGS

Damsel bugs attack many of our worst garden pests, including aphids, thrips, leafhoppers, and small caterpillars.

DESCRIPTION: Adults are elongated, gray or brown bugs, ⅓–½ inch (8–10 mm) long, with long piercing beaks tucked under the head. They move rapidly, and some can fly long distances. Nymphs are slender, wingless, and smaller than adults.

RANGE: Throughout North America; at least 48 native species.

BENEFICIAL EFFECTS: These are robust, voracious predators of aphids, thrips, plant bugs, leafhoppers, treehoppers, small caterpillars, and other insects. They are important native predators, very common in unsprayed fields and orchards.

LIFE CYCLE: Adults overwinter in protected areas and emerge in April and May. Females lay eggs in plant tissue; eggs hatch in a week, and nymphs immediately begin feeding, often on prey larger than themselves. Nymphs develop for 3–4 weeks until molting to adults. Two or more overlapping generations per year.

HOW TO ATTRACT: Collect damsel bugs from alfalfa fields, using a sweep net, and release them around your garden or orchard. Avoid the use of pesticides in the garden.

Carabidae

GROUND BEETLES

Ground beetles are fast-moving predators of slugs, snails, and other soil-dwelling pests. They are active mostly at night.

DESCRIPTION: Adults are large, iridescent, blue-black or purplish brown beetles, ¾–1 inch (19–25 mm) long, with long legs; the thorax is usually narrower than the abdomen. They are active at night, hiding under stones and boards by day; they run very quickly when disturbed. Larvae are dark brown or black, with ten segments, tapering markedly toward the rear; they have large mandibles for grasping prey.

RANGE: Throughout North America; more than 2,270 native species.

BENEFICIAL EFFECTS: Ground beetles are common voracious predators of slugs, snails, cutworms, cabbage maggots, codling moth pupae, and other pests that spend part of their life cycle in the soil. Some pursue prey on plants, such as potato beetle larvae, and up trees, such as gypsy moth and tent caterpillars. One beetle larva can eat more than 50 caterpillars. Adults may live for 2–4 years.

LIFE CYCLE: Overwintering adults emerge in spring from a pupal cell in soil and lay their eggs in soil. When eggs hatch, larvae feed on insects and slugs for 2–4 weeks, then pupate in soil. Adults remain in soil for the winter. One generation per year.

HOW TO ATTRACT: Plant permanent beds and perennials among garden plants for stable habitats. Plant white clover as a groundcover in orchards. Make permanent stone, sod, or clover pathways throughout your garden to provide refuges.

Apis mellifera

HONEYBEE

Honeybees are appreciated by all for their honey, but they're prized by gardeners for pollinating fruit and vegetable crops.

DESCRIPTION: Adults are fuzzy, gold-and-black striped bees, ¾ inch (2 cm) long, with transparent wings; they are often seen visiting flowers. Larvae are white grubs found in wax combs in beehives.

RANGE: Throughout North America; domesticated, escaped, and wild colonies common.

BENEFICIAL EFFECTS: Honeybees are extremely important pollinators of fruit, vegetables, and agricultural crops; it is estimated that over 80 percent of pollination is done by domestic honeybees.

LIFE CYCLE: Bees live in social colonies numbering up to 20,000 bees. Queen bees lay eggs in wax cells in the hive, and workers feed and care for larvae. Larvae destined to become new queens are fed a special diet of royal jelly. Males mate with new queens, who leave with a swarm of workers to start new colonies. Bees overwinter clustered in hives to keep warm, living on stored honey.

HOW TO ATTRACT: Plant pollen and nectar plants that bloom before or after the main fruit bloom (so they do not attract bees away from fruit flowers). Provide a water source in dry weather, such as a pail of water with a piece of plywood floating on the surface. Avoid spraying fruit trees when flowers are blooming. If you must apply a botanical insecticide, spray in evenings, after bees return to their hive.

Syrphidae

HOVER FLIES

Hover flies—also known as flower flies—may resemble honeybees, but hover flies only have one pair of wings and don't sting.

DESCRIPTION: Adults are robust, shiny, yellow-and-black or white-and-black striped flies, ⅜–⅝ inch (9.5–15 mm) long, with large eyes. They hover over flowers like miniature hummingbirds. Larvae are gray or greenish, somewhat translucent, slug-like maggots up to ½ inch (1 cm) long. Eggs are tiny white cylinders.

RANGE: Throughout North America; more than 870 native species.

BENEFICIAL EFFECTS: Hover-fly larvae are hardy, native predators of most aphid species; one larva will eat 400 aphids during its development. They are common in orchards and are particularly strong fliers, good at finding aphid colonies, even in windy areas.

LIFE CYCLE: Pupae overwinter in the soil and adults emerge very early in spring; they are often seen collecting pollen from pussy willows. Females lay their eggs singly or in small groups among aphid colonies. Eggs hatch in 2–3 days and larvae feed on aphids for up to 2 weeks, depending on the temperature. They drop to the soil to pupate; adults emerge in 2 weeks. Three to seven overlapping generations per year.

HOW TO ATTRACT: Plant pollen and nectar flowers throughout the garden. Allow flowering weeds such as wild carrot and yarrow to grow in waste areas or between crop plants.

Ichneumonidae

ICHNEUMON WASPS

Ichneumon wasps are thin-waisted flying insects. Their large ovipositors look like stingers, but they're harmless to people.

DESCRIPTION: Adults are slender, thin-waisted, usually dark-colored wasps, 1/10–1½ inches (2.5–40 mm) long, with long antennae. Some species have long thread-like ovipositors (for laying eggs) that are often mistaken for stingers. Larvae are white, tapering grubs that are parasitic in other insects.

RANGE: Throughout North America; more than 3,350 native species.

BENEFICIAL EFFECTS: Ichneumons are an extremely important family of native biological controls. They lay their eggs inside other host insects, such as caterpillars, sawfly and beetle larvae, and other pests. The larvae develop as parasites and kill the host. Adult females also kill hosts by stinging them and feeding on body fluids.

LIFE CYCLE: Females inject one or more eggs inside host eggs or larvae. The wasp larvae develop inside, eventually killing the host, then pupate in the killed insect or beside it. Many species overwinter as mature larvae in cocoons; some species of adult females overwinter. Most species have one to three generations per year; some have up to ten generations in warmer regions.

HOW TO ATTRACT: Plant pollen and nectar flowers in gardens; allow flowering weeds such as wild carrot and yarrow to remain in waste areas and hedgerows. Grow flowering cover crops in orchards.

Chrysoperla (=Chrysopa) spp.

LACEWINGS

Lacewing adults feed mostly on pollen and nectar, but their larvae are voracious predators of aphids and other pests.

DESCRIPTION: Adults are delicate, green or brown insects, ½–¾ inch (1–2 cm) long, with small heads and large eyes. Their wings are transparent and covered with a network of fine veins. Larvae are spindle-shaped, mottled yellow or brown, with tubercles (small knobbly protuberances) on their sides and large, curved mandibles (mouthparts); they resemble tiny alligators.

RANGE: Throughout North America; more than 145 native species; two species sold commercially.

BENEFICIAL EFFECTS: Lacewings are common native predators in gardens and orchards. Larvae feed on aphids, thrips, mealybugs, scales, moth eggs, small caterpillars, other soft-bodied insects, and also mites. The adults are usually not predators.

LIFE CYCLE: Adults or pupae overwinter; adults emerge in spring and lay eggs singly on tips of long stalks; eggs hatch in 4–7 days. Larvae feed for about 3 weeks, then spin cocoons and pupate for 5–7 days. Adults emerge from a hole cut in the top of cocoon. Three to six overlapping generations per year.

HOW TO ATTRACT: Plant pollen and nectar flowers to attract adults; allow some flowering weeds to grow between garden plants. Provide a water source during dry weather. When using purchased lacewings, distribute the eggs widely throughout the garden; larvae are cannibalistic when crowded. A minimum order of 500–1,000 eggs is sufficient for the average garden.

Coccinellidae

LADY BEETLES

Lady beetles—also known as ladybugs or ladybirds—are among the most well-known beneficial insects.

Along with the adults, the alligator-like larvae of lady beetles prey on aphids, spider mites, mealybugs, or soft scales.

DESCRIPTION: Adults are shiny, round beetles, 1/16–3/8 inch (2–9.5 mm) long, with short legs and antennae; the head is hidden beneath the front of the thorax. Common species are ash gray with dark spots or pale yellow to dark reddish orange with or without black spots; some species are solid black or black with two red spots. Larvae are generally spindle-shaped, up to 3/8 inch (9.5 mm) long, usually with short spines, warts, or tubercles (small, knobbly protuberances) on each segment; most are a dark color with yellow, red, or white spots. Eggs are white or yellow ovals.

RANGE: Throughout North America; more than 400 native species. Convergent lady beetle (*Hippodamia convergens*) is sold widely; other species also available commercially.

BENEFICIAL EFFECTS: Lady beetles belong to one of the most beneficial families of insects. They are common and often numerous in gardens and orchard trees. Both adults and larvae feed on aphids and other small, soft-bodied pests, as well as on insect eggs. Larvae of many species consume 200–300 aphids during their development; adults eat 300–400 aphids over a month. Some species prefer mealybugs (see Mealybug destroyer entry). *Stethorus* spp. and *Scymnus* spp. are important predators of spider mites in crops; *Chilocorus* spp. and *Lindorus* spp. prey upon soft scales. *Rodolia cardinalis* is a highly successful species imported to control cottony cushion scale in the California citrus industry. (A few lady beetle species, such as Mexican bean beetle and squash beetle, are plant pests.)

LIFE CYCLE: In spring, overwintering adults migrate to find food; after feeding for a few days, they lay eggs on end in clusters of 12–25 among aphids or other prey. Eggs hatch in 3–5 days, and larvae feed for 2–3 weeks, then pupate on a plant stem or leaf. Adults emerge in 7–10 days. In fall, adults overwinter in leaf litter, wooded areas, or other protected sites; in the West, convergent lady beetles migrate to the Sierra Nevada Mountains to collect in large groups for winter. At that time they are easily caught for sale. Two to four overlapping generations per year.

HOW TO ATTRACT: Provide food for adults by planting pollen and nectar flowers, especially angelica and dill; allow a few weeds, such as dandelion, wild carrot, and yarrow, to grow among garden plants. Purchased convergent lady beetles are effective in controlling aphids in greenhouses if all vents are screened to prevent their escape, but they may fly away from gardens. To encourage them to stay, water the garden thoroughly, and wait until nighttime to release the beetles; ample moisture and an ample supply of aphids may entice them to make a home in your garden.

Cryptolaemus montrouzieri

MEALYBUG DESTROYER

Mealybug destroyers are actually a type of lady beetle. The hairy white larvae closely resemble their prey.

DESCRIPTION: Adults are oval lady beetles, ⅓ inch (8.5 mm) long, with black wing covers; the head and tip of the abdomen are coral colored. Larvae are cream colored, segmented, and covered with long, waxy hair; they resemble mealybugs. Eggs are yellow ovals.

RANGE: Native to California and West Coast; sold commercially.

BENEFICIAL EFFECTS: Both adults and larvae are effective predators on all stages and species of aboveground mealybugs found on citrus, grapes, greenhouse ornamentals, and houseplants.

LIFE CYCLE: Females lay eggs in masses among mealybug fluff. Eggs hatch in 8–10 days, and larvae eat eggs and young mealybugs for 3 weeks. They pupate on plants, and adults emerge in 2–3 weeks. Adults overwinter in mild coastal climates; generations continue year-round indoors, although they reproduce very slowly in winter. Four to six overlapping generations per year; more indoors.

HOW TO ATTRACT: Conserve native populations by avoiding use of pesticides. To use purchased beetles in citrus orchards or vineyards, release 250–500 adults on up to ¼ acre (0.1 ha); release two to five beetles per infested plant in indoor plantings, twice yearly. On houseplants, confine 10–20 adults on an infested plant for 4–5 weeks by draping sheer curtain material over the plant and tying it around the pot.

Orius spp.

MINUTE PIRATE BUGS

Minute pirate bugs will attack almost any insect, but they commonly feed on thrips, spider mites, and small caterpillars.

DESCRIPTION: Adults are quick-moving, black-and-white patterned bugs, ¼ inch (6 mm) long, with wings folded flat over the abdomen. Nymphs are shiny, oval, and up to ⅕ inch (5 mm) long. They are wingless until the final molt to adults; their color changes from yellow to orange to mahogany brown as they grow.

RANGE: Throughout North America. *O. tristicolor* and *O. insidiosus* sold commercially.

BENEFICIAL EFFECTS: All stages of pirate bugs are voracious predators of thrips, spider mites, small caterpillars, leafhopper nymphs, other small insects, and insect eggs. They are adept at finding prey deep inside flowers and are particularly good thrips predators. Adults also feed on pollen.

LIFE CYCLE: Females insert eggs into plant stems or leaf tissue. Eggs hatch in 3–5 days; nymphs feed on insects in flowers and on undersides of leaves for 2–3 weeks until molting to adult stage. Mated females overwinter in crevices of bark, weeds, and plant residues; males die before winter. Two to four generations per year.

HOW TO ATTRACT: Grow pollen and nectar plants, especially goldenrod, daisies, yarrow, and alfalfa. Collect pirate bugs on goldenrod in fall and move them to the garden. In greenhouses, release purchased or wild-collected pirate bugs at rate of one adult per one to five plants.

Phytoseiidae

Mites, predatory

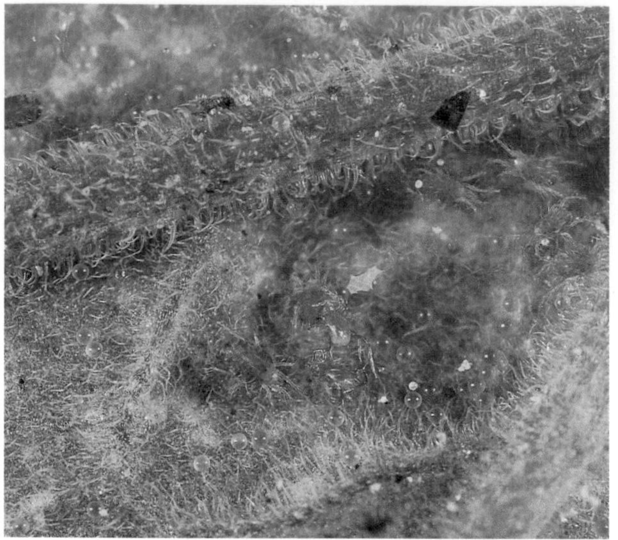

Predatory mites may look like pest mites, but up close you'll see that the predators move faster and have fewer hairs.

DESCRIPTION: Adults are minute, beige to reddish tan, fast-moving mites, 1/50 inch (0.5 mm) long. Nymphs are similar but smaller and lighter colored than adults.

RANGE: Throughout North America; several species sold commercially.

BENEFICIAL EFFECTS: Phytoseiid mites are valuable native predators of spider mites, especially two-spotted spider mite, European red mite, and citrus red mite. Some also feed on pollen, thrips, cyclamen mites, and rust mites.

LIFE CYCLE: Overwintering females emerge from crevices in bark or soil litter and lay eggs on leaves among prey. Eggs hatch in 3–4 days, and nymphs molt several times until they reach the adult stage in 5–10 days. There are numerous overlapping generations.

HOW TO ATTRACT: Avoid the use of pesticides. Sustain native populations by sprinkling pollen (especially from ice plant, cattail, or dandelion) on plants. In apple orchards and on strawberries, release *Metaseiulus occidentalis, Amblyseius fallacis,* or *Typhlodromus pyri* to control various species of spider mites. In greenhouses, use *Phytoseiulus persimilis* or other recommended species to control spider mite (except on tomato, where they are trapped by sticky hairs on plant stems). Release *Amblyseius cucumeris* to control onion thrips and western flower thrips in peppers and cucumbers.

Mantis religiosa

Praying mantid

Praying mantids are large, dramatic-looking insects with large forelimbs that are usually poised for attack.

DESCRIPTION: Adults are very large, narrowly streamlined insects, 2–3 inches (5–7.5 cm) long, with long legs and prominent eyes in a triangular head. The large forelegs bear rows of sharp spines and are held up in readiness to capture prey. Wings are folded flat on top of the abdomen. Nymphs are similar to adults but smaller and wingless. The eggs are housed in a frothy-looking grayish case.

RANGE: Eastern and southern United States; north into Ontario, Canada.

BENEFICIAL EFFECTS: Mantids eat any insect they can catch. As general predators in the garden, they feed on both pests and harmless or beneficial species, including butterflies and honeybees; if they find no other prey, they will eat each other.

LIFE CYCLE: Females glue a case of 50–400 eggs in a sticky gray mass to stems or twigs where eggs harden and remain for winter. Nymphs, which are very small at first, emerge in early spring; they feed on larger and larger insects as they mature. One generation per year in Northern areas.

HOW TO ATTRACT: To protect the more than 20 native species, avoid using pesticides, and do not release purchased mantid eggs (these are not native species in most areas). Provide permanent plantings for overwintering sites.

Staphylinidae

ROVE BEETLES

Rove beetles are fast-moving beneficials that often hold the tip of their abdomen bent upward, as if preparing to sting.

DESCRIPTION: Adults are slender, elongated, quick-moving insects, 1/10–1 inch (2.5–25 mm) long, with stubby wing covers extending only over the first three segments on the abdomen. They are usually brown or black; some are shiny, others have dense hairs, and a few species have bright markings. Most are active at night. Larvae look like adults without wings.

RANGE: Throughout North America; more than 3,100 native species.

BENEFICIAL EFFECTS: Most species scavenge on decaying organic materials and are beneficial decomposers in the ecosystem. Many species are predators of aphids, springtails, mites, nematodes, slugs, snails, fly eggs, and maggots, making them valuable allies in gardens. A few species parasitize cabbage maggots and other fly larvae. Parasitic species, such as *Aleochara bilineata* and *A. bimaculata* may control up to 80 percent of cabbage maggots in a field.

LIFE CYCLE: Most species overwinter as adults, becoming active in the spring and laying eggs in the soil. Larvae pass through three molts as they feed, then pupate in a cell in the soil.

HOW TO ATTRACT: Maintain permanent beds and plantings in the garden to protect populations. Interplant with cover crops, mulch planting beds, or make stone or plank walkways in your garden to provide daytime shelters.

Cantharidae

SOLDIER BEETLES

Soldier beetles frequently linger around flowers, feeding on nectar, pollen, and small insects like aphids.

DESCRIPTION: Adults are elongated, soft-bodied, parallel-sided beetles, 1/3–1/2 inch (8–10 mm) long, with characteristic leathery wing covers bearing fine hairs. Adults are mostly dark gray, brown, or yellow; some body parts—such as the thorax or legs—may be red, orange, or bright yellow. Larvae are flattened, elongated, covered with velvety hairs, and are usually dark colored.

RANGE: Throughout North America; more than 450 native species.

BENEFICIAL EFFECTS: Both larvae and adults are native predators of aphids, caterpillars, corn rootworms, grasshopper eggs, beetle larvae (especially cucumber beetles), and other insects, including harmless and beneficial species. Adults fly very well and are active during the day; larvae search for prey in the soil and on low-growing plants.

LIFE CYCLE: Overwintering larvae pupate in spring in cells in the soil. Adult females lay eggs in the soil; after the eggs hatch, they remain inactive for a short period before larvae start to develop. One or two generations per year.

HOW TO ATTRACT: Plant goldenrod, hydrangea, and catnip to attract adults; they also feed on pollen and nectar from milkweed and wild parsley. Plant perennials or permanent beds in the garden to provide refuges and protect pupating beetles.

SPINED SOLDIER BUG

Spined soldier bugs resemble pesky stink bugs. Look for the long, pointed "shoulders" to identify this beneficial.

DESCRIPTION: Adults are shield-shaped bugs, ½ inch (1 cm) long, grayish brown, and covered with black flecks; they have sharp points on their thorax. They are very similar to pests known as stink bugs. Nymphs are oval and similar to adults but are wingless. Eggs are metallic bronze and barrel-shaped.

RANGE: Throughout North America; also sold commercially.

BENEFICIAL EFFECTS: Both adults and nymphs feed on many species of hairless caterpillars, including tent caterpillars, fall armyworms, cabbage looper, imported cabbageworm, and sawfly larvae. They also feed on beetle larvae, particularly those of the Mexican bean beetle and Colorado potato beetle.

LIFE CYCLE: Overwintering adults emerge in spring. Females lay up to 500 eggs in their lifetime, in clusters of a dozen on leaves. Nymphs hatch out in a few days and drink water or plant juices for a short period, then become predators for the rest of their lives. Nymphs develop into adults in 6–8 weeks; adults live for 5–8 weeks. One to two generations per year.

HOW TO ATTRACT: Maintain permanent beds of perennials in your garden to provide shelter. Try releases of two to five bugs per square yard (one to four bugs per sq. m) of beans to control bean beetles. In the potato patch, release spined soldier bugs as the plants are sprouting to control potato beetle larvae.

TACHINID FLIES

Tachinid flies feed mainly on nectar and honeydew, but their larvae are effective parasites that feed inside host insects.

DESCRIPTION: Adults are robust, ⅓–½-inch (8–10 mm) long flies that are gray, brown, or black with lighter, sometimes colorful, markings. Some may be mistaken for large houseflies. Larvae are white maggots found feeding inside host insects.

RANGE: Throughout North America; more than 1,280 native species.

BENEFICIAL EFFECTS: Among this valuable group of beneficial flies are the most important natural enemies of many caterpillars, including cutworms, codling moths, hornworms, earworms, armyworms, tent caterpillars, cabbage loopers, and gypsy moth larvae; some also attack sawflies, squash bugs, stink bugs, and grasshoppers.

LIFE CYCLE: Females lay their eggs or deposit a newly hatched larvae on the skin of a caterpillar where the maggots can burrow into the host. Some species lay eggs on the leaf where caterpillars will eat them along with the leaf material. As the fly maggots develop inside, they eventually kill the host, then pupate inside the corpse or in the soil nearby. One to three generations per year.

HOW TO ATTRACT: Plant dill, parsley, sweet clover, and other herbs to attract adults; allow a few weeds, such as wild carrot and yarrow, to flower in the garden. Do not destroy caterpillars with white eggs stuck to their backs: They will not cause further damage and will produce more tachinid flies.

Cicindelidae

Tiger beetles

Tiger beetles are colorful, metallic-looking, long-legged predators. The adults and larvae eat many kinds of insects.

DESCRIPTION: Adults are brightly colored and patterned beetles, ½–¾ inch (1–2 cm) long, with large eyes and very long, spiny legs. They are among the swiftest runners of all insects. The adults are often attracted to lights at night. Larvae are segmented, S-shaped, and have a pronounced hump in their back, which has strong hooks to anchor them into burrows in the soil.

RANGE: Throughout North America; 108 native species.

BENEFICIAL EFFECTS: Both adults and larvae prey on a wide variety of insects. Beetles capture their prey by running them down; larvae dig into burrows in the soil and wait there to seize passing insects, which they drag into the burrow to eat. Although they feed on some desirable species, tiger beetles are generally considered beneficial.

LIFE CYCLE: Females lay eggs singly in burrows in the soil; when larvae hatch, they lie in wait for passing prey. Larvae develop for several years, digging deep into the soil every fall to overwinter. Adults also overwinter in burrows. One generation every 2–3 years.

HOW TO ATTRACT: Maintain permanent beds in the garden as refuges. To avoid killing adult beetles, do not leave outdoor lights on all night in summer and do not use insect light traps in the yard.

Vespula spp.

Yellow jackets

Yellow jackets may be the bane of picknickers everywhere, but these creatures also help to control garden pests.

DESCRIPTION: Adult wasps are ½–¾ inch (1–2 cm) long, with shiny, yellow-and-black striped abdomens and two pairs of transparent wings. Larvae are white grubs, found inside cells in paper nests.

RANGE: Throughout North America.

BENEFICIAL EFFECTS: Adult wasps seize large numbers of caterpillars, flies, beetle grubs, and other insects to feed their young. They also feed on nectar, fruit juices, and picnic foods, which cause them to be a nuisance. They may be a threat to people who are allergic to stings.

LIFE CYCLE: Queens overwinter under bark or in a protected burrow, emerging in spring to build a small nucleus of paper cells in a mouse burrow, in an old log, or suspended from a tree limb. She lays eggs and captures prey to feed the first brood, which become worker wasps. They take over foraging and feeding from the queen to rear succeeding broods. The colony expands until late summer; then workers die off before winter and the nest falls apart. The queen mates and finds an overwintering site; the old nest is not reused.

HOW TO ATTRACT: Plant nectar flowers and provide water in a shallow container filled with pebbles. People often prefer to remove nests, but this is unnecessary if they are located out of main travel paths. To avoid conflict with yellow jackets, keep picnic food and drinks covered, maintain clean garbage cans, and pick fruit early in the morning.

D I S E A S E S

Anthracnose

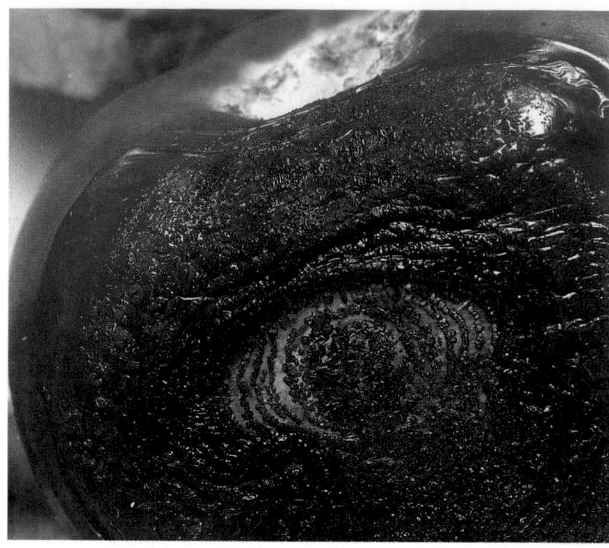

Anthracnose on tomato fruit starts as small, sunken, water-soaked spots that expand and darken as the fruit ripens.

TYPE OF PROBLEM: Fungal.

RANGE: Worldwide.

PLANTS AFFECTED: Many kinds of woody and herbaceous plants; vegetables, particularly bean, cucumber, pepper, squash, and tomato; susceptible trees include dogwood, elm, hawthorn, linden, maple, sycamore, and walnut.

SYMPTOMS: Infection starts as small or large yellow, brown, or purplish spots, often with slightly raised margins, which darken as they age. Spots may eventually merge to cover the entire leaf, giving a scorched appearance; leaves may drop prematurely, and an entire tree can be defoliated. Tips of young tree twigs may be killed before the leaves begin to open; brown spots and patches may appear on young leaves. On fruit, small, sunken spots appear on the surface. Fruit infections lead to fruit rot.

PREVENTION: Plant resistant cultivars. Ensure good air circulation around leaves and stems. Plant in well-drained soil. Prevent drought stress to trees by mulching and watering in dry conditions. Avoid handling beans and other plants when leaves are wet. Prune out succulent growth, such as water sprouts, which is susceptible to attack.

CONTROL: Rake up and burn or destroy infected leaves; prune out dead wood and burn or destroy it. Apply copper sprays in severe infections. A dormant spray of bordeaux mix or lime-sulfur may provide some control.

Venturia inaequalis

Apple scab

Apple scab produces corky areas on apple and crab apple fruit and either green to brown or black spots on the leaves.

TYPE OF PROBLEM: Fungal.

RANGE: Widespread, wherever apples are grown; most severe in the North.

PLANTS AFFECTED: Apple, crab apple, hawthorn, and pear.

SYMPTOMS: Initial infections appear on sepals and undersides of early leaves as light grayish spots, turning to velvety olive green. These progress to chocolate brown and metallic black on leaves and fruit. Later, spots on fruit appear scabby and corky; fruit may by cracked, deformed, or russeted. Infected young fruit and leaves drop early, causing poor fruit-bud development for next year. Disease spreads rapidly in cool, moist summer weather.

PREVENTION: Plant resistant cultivars such as 'Jonafree', 'Liberty', and 'Red Free' apples. Prune and space trees to promote good air circulation. Scab fungi overwinter on dead leaves, so rake up and destroy dropped leaves in fall.

CONTROL: To control scab with sulfur fungicides, spray or dust trees weekly and immediately after rain. Start from the time buds break and continue until 3–4 weeks after petals fall. If early-season treatments are diligently applied, there will be little need for sprays later. Ensure leaves and flowers are thoroughly covered and that rapidly expanding new leaves are protected with sprays. If the disease does strike, copper, sulfur, or lime-sulfur sprays may prevent its spread.

Bacterial spot

Bacterial spot mainly attacks leaves, making circular or elongated patches that are often surrounded by a yellowish halo.

TYPE OF PROBLEM: Bacterial.

RANGE: Widespread, especially in humid regions.

PLANTS AFFECTED: Many woody and herbaceous plants, particularly bean, cucumber, pepper, and tomato; also delphinium, carnation, and gardenia.

SYMPTOMS: Initial symptoms appear as small, yellowish green, water-soaked spots on young leaves. Spots are generally circular, but may be angular or elongated between leaf veins. As disease develops, the straw-colored dead tissue often falls out, leaving shot holes or irregular, ragged holes in leaves. Spots may be so numerous that they produce large areas of dead tissue and destroy most of the plant surface; lower leaves of the plant turn yellow and drop. On green fruit, infection appears as small, scabby, whitish or brownish spots or as black specks and spots; fruit may become cracked and distorted. The disease is favored by wet weather. It is spread by raindrops hitting infected plant material and by handling plants while they are still wet.

PREVENTION: Plant resistant cultivars and clean seed. Practice good garden sanitation; avoid spreading bacteria on equipment. Bacteria survive in the soil, so practice a 3–4-year crop rotation.

CONTROL: Copper sprays, applied at 10–14-day intervals, may suppress the spread of the disease. Remove and destroy infected plants at first sign of disease. On pepper and tomato, try streptomycin spray (Agri-Strep).

Pseudomonas and *Erwinia* spp.

BACTERIAL WILT

Bacterial wilt interferes with water movement in the plant, causing leaves to look limp and vines to wilt.

TYPE OF PROBLEM: Bacterial.

RANGE: Widespread.

PLANTS AFFECTED: Wide range of plants, especially bean, cabbage, cucumber, melon, potato, squash, and tomato.

SYMPTOMS: Initially, individual leaves or all leaves on a side branch may droop or wilt, without yellowing; they may recover overnight. This is soon followed by the leaves wilting then the plant collapsing. Leaves and stems shrivel and dry out without turning brown. When infected stems are cut and pulled apart, a sticky, whitish bacterial ooze is often visible on the cut surface. On cucumbers and related plants, diagnose the disease by pressing two cut ends of the stem together; then slowly draw them apart and look for a fine, sticky thread of ooze. The centers of cut tomato stems appear water-soaked; later they turn brown and the stem may become hollow. Insects—including cucumber beetles, flea beetles, and grasshoppers—can spread the disease as they feed.

PREVENTION: Plant resistant cultivars. Cover cucumbers and related plants with floating row covers to prevent cucumber beetles and grasshoppers from feeding on plants (hand-pollinate flowers to get fruit). Rotate plantings of tomatoes, peppers, and potatoes with less-susceptible crops.

CONTROL: Remove and destroy any infected plants as soon as you see them.

Dibotryon morbosum

BLACK KNOT

Black knot is a common problem on wild plums and cherries, but it can cause dark stem swellings on cultivated trees, too.

TYPE OF PROBLEM: Fungal.

RANGE: Widespread, but primarily eastern United States and Canada.

PLANTS AFFECTED: Cherry and plum ('Stanley' and 'Damson' are very susceptible).

SYMPTOMS: Large, highly visible, elongated, rough, knotty swellings appear on twigs and branches. In spring, the knots are a velvety, olive green color; later in the season, knots become hard and tar black. The swellings arise along the sides of larger branches or may wholly girdle twigs and branches. Knots continue to expand each year, giving a grotesque appearance to branches. If the tree has not died after several years of infection, it is likely to be severely stunted and unproductive.

PREVENTION: Destroy wild plums and cherries near orchards to reduce the source of infectious spores brought by the wind and on birds' feet.

CONTROL: The fungus produces spores in winter and summer; control programs are aimed at winter spores, which infect trees just before they are in full bloom. In late winter, prune infected branches and twigs 4–6 inches (10–15 cm) below the knots; disinfect pruners between cuts in a bleach solution and burn prunings. Apply dormant and delayed dormant sprays of bordeaux mixture or lime-sulfur at weekly intervals before buds begin to grow.

Guignardia bidwellii

BLACK ROT

Black rot can affect all parts of the grape plant, causing dark spots on leaves and shoots and shriveled fruits.

TYPE OF PROBLEM: Fungal.

RANGE: United States and Canada east of Rocky Mountains; most severe in warm, humid regions.

PLANTS AFFECTED: Grape.

SYMPTOMS: In late spring, numerous circular red spots appear on young, rapidly growing leaves, mostly on upper side. Later, as the spots enlarge, they become brown or grayish tan with a brown margin and black specks in a ring around the margin. On shoots, tendrils, stalks, and leaf veins, spots are purple to black, slightly sunken, and elongated. When grape berries are about half grown, whitish or tan round spots appear and enlarge rapidly. They are surrounded with an outer ring of brown with a black margin, giving a "bird's-eye" effect. The whole berry soon rots, shrivels, and hardens, becoming a coal black mummy. In hot, humid weather, the entire crop may be destroyed.

PREVENTION: Plant resistant cultivars. Keep weeds down around vines; prune and space plants to promote good air circulation and rapid drying of leaves. Burn annual prunings and any overwintering grape berries left on vines.

CONTROL: Prune out and burn infested fruit and other plant material. Spray bordeaux mixture or copper fungicides before and after bloom and again 10 days later; where black rot is a severe problem, spray again in early June.

Diplocarpon rosae

BLACK SPOT

Black spot is a bane of rose growers everywhere. The characteristic black blotches are surrounded by yellow patches.

TYPE OF PROBLEM: Fungal.

RANGE: Widespread.

PLANTS AFFECTED: Rose.

SYMPTOMS: Small to large circular black spots appear on leaves. The spots have fringed margins and may run together to form large irregular spots. Severely affected leaves may turn yellow and drop. Under humid conditions, particularly susceptible roses can be almost entirely defoliated. The fungus produces infectious spores throughout the season, causing repeated infections in warm, wet weather.

PREVENTION: Plant resistant cultivars. Site plants where there is good air circulation. Prune to maintain open foliage and avoid wetting leaves unnecessarily.

CONTROL: Remove and destroy infected leaves; prune out canes of diseased plants. Beginning as soon as new leaves appear in spring or at the first appearance of black spot on leaves, spray leaves thoroughly with fungicidal soap or sulfur; repeat at 7–10-day intervals or after every rain. Some gardeners have success spraying with baking soda in water (1 teaspoon baking soda to 1 quart/1 l of water).

Blossom end rot

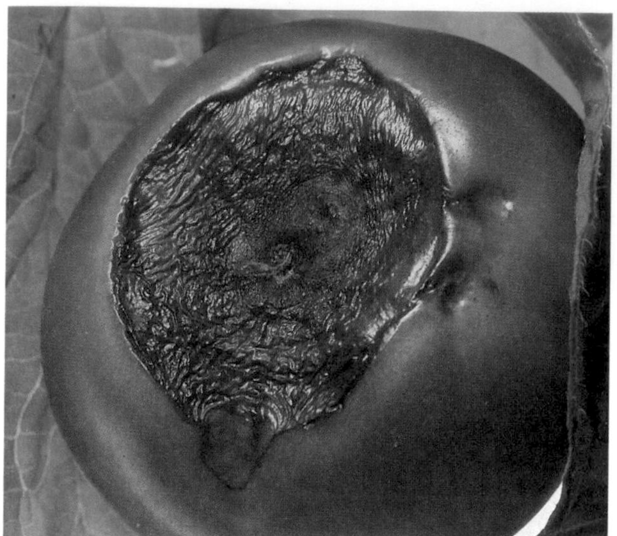

Blossom end rot often affects early-season tomatoes. It starts as a tan patch on the bottom and expands to a dark, sunken area.

TYPE OF PROBLEM: Physiological.

RANGE: Anywhere susceptible crops are grown.

PLANTS AFFECTED: Tomato and pepper.

SYMPTOMS: A water-soaked, and sometimes sunken, brown spot appears on the blossom end of fruit; it enlarges and turns into a leathery brown or black patch. If the problem is severe, the fruit has a flattened or somewhat concave bottom end. The disorder is caused by a calcium deficiency in the plant; although sufficient calcium may be present in soil, not enough is reaching plant tissues. This may be caused by excessive nitrogen fertilization, overly rapid plant growth, or extreme variations in the water available to plants (which in turn may be due to heavy rains, drought, or physical injury to roots). The problem is worse in hot, dry weather, especially if plants are growing rapidly.

PREVENTION: Maintain an even supply of moisture with regular watering and deep mulches. Avoid overfertilizing with nitrogen. Protect roots by using mulch, rather than cultivation, to control weeds. Test your soil periodically and correct nutrient imbalances.

CONTROL: At first sign of blossom end rot, pay extra-close attention to watering and mulching. Plants usually grow out of the problem later in the season when conditions are corrected. Spraying with seaweed extract may help supply some calcium to affected plants.

Botrytis cinerea

Botrytis blight

Botrytis blight often attacks flowers first. The petals show a fuzzy gray or white growth; then they collapse and turn brown.

TYPE OF PROBLEM: Fungal.

RANGE: Worldwide.

PLANTS AFFECTED: Wide range of plants; especially tomato, lettuce, and cucumber in greenhouses; flowers of begonia, cyclamen, dahlia, geranium, peony, and rose.

SYMPTOMS: The first symptoms you see may be water-soaked spots on leaves, flowers, or stems; these spots quickly develop fuzzy gray or whitish growth. Infections often begin as blossom blights because aging petals are particularly susceptible. Damage soon spreads to entire flowers and stems, which collapse as the flowers dry and turn brown; if fruit is present, it may also rot. Infected foliage and stems become soft and watery; later the plant tissue appears light brown, cracks open, and the fuzzy gray mold appears. In head lettuce, rot begins on stem or on lower leaves in contact with soil, spreading upward as a slimy rot into the head.

PREVENTION: Botrytis spores are always present, but do not germinate until exposed to high humidity; disease develops where injury to tissues provides entry. Promote good air circulation by pruning and spacing plants; in greenhouses, increase heating and ventilation to dry plant leaves early in the day. Avoid injuring plants; control insect pests.

CONTROL: Remove and destroy infected plants or plant parts. Increase ventilation in greenhouses. Prune to aid air circulation around infected plants.

Botrytis cinerea

Botrytis fruit rot

Botrytis fruit rot produces a fluffy, light-colored mold on soft fruits like grapes, strawberries, and raspberries.

TYPE OF PROBLEM: Fungal.

RANGE: Worldwide.

PLANTS AFFECTED: Wide range of fruits and vegetables, including root crops; especially apple, strawberry, grape, and bramble berries; also bean, cucumber, greenhouse tomato, and pepper.

SYMPTOMS: A characteristic gray, tan, or whitish fluffy mold grows on berries and other fruit; when disturbed, a puff of gray spores scatters. Infected fruit has water-soaked spots, which later appear light brown and crack as the fungus grows; on berries, the entire fruit becomes water-soaked and rots. On apples, infections appear first as a blossom end rot; the apple rots and infections may spread to other touching apples. On tomato, infections appear first as "ghost spots," small brown spots of dead tissue surrounded with a pale halo, often slightly raised.

PREVENTION: Botrytis fruit rot develops only under particularly cool and moist conditions and where injury to tissues gives spores an opening. Promote good air circulation by pruning and spacing plants; in greenhouses, increase heating and ventilation to dry leaves early in the day; avoid injuring plants; control insect pests. Before storing onions, make sure they are well cured and dry. Plant berry cultivars that are least susceptible to Botrytis.

CONTROL: Destroy infected fruit or other plant material; increase ventilation in greenhouses or prune to aid air circulation around infected plants.

Monilinia fructicola

Brown rot

Brown rot forms a brownish mold on fruit surfaces, often in concentric rings. Affected fruit may drop or hang on the tree.

TYPE OF PROBLEM: Fungal.

RANGE: Worldwide; in humid areas, wherever stone fruit is grown.

PLANTS AFFECTED: Almond, apricot, cherry, peach, and plum; sometimes apple and pear.

SYMPTOMS: Initial infections appear on blossoms as brown spots, which spread rapidly to the whole flower and stem; the dying tissue is covered with a brownish gray mold. Twigs may be girdled and killed by sunken, brown cankers. Rapidly spreading, small, circular brown spots appear on fruit as it matures; eventually grayish tufts of fungal growth break the fruit skin, often in concentric rings on the surface. The fruit finally completely rots, shrivels, and turns into a corrugated mummy, either remaining on the tree or falling to the ground.

PREVENTION: Plant resistant cultivars. Prune to ensure good air circulation. Avoid overfertilizing with nitrogen. Control insects that puncture fruit (such as tarnished plant bugs and stink bugs). Handle ripe fruit carefully to prevent bruising; store it in clean containers and refrigerate immediately.

CONTROL: Prune and destroy infected blossoms and twigs. Collect fallen fruit mummies and those still on the tree; destroy to remove overwintering sites for fungus. Spray with sulfur just before blossoms open and again after petals fall to protect developing fruit; spray again just before harvest to protect fruit in storage.

Gymnosporangium juniperi-virginianae

CEDAR-APPLE RUST

Cedar-apple rust on apples starts as yellow spots on the upper surfaces of leaves and fruit; the spots later turn orange.

TYPE OF PROBLEM: Fungal.

RANGE: Throughout North America.

PLANTS AFFECTED: Eastern red cedar, other *Juniperus* species, and apple; similar diseases affect hawthorn and quince.

SYMPTOMS: The fungus alternates between cedar and apple host plants. It first appears as a small greenish brown swelling on the cedar needles; the following year, it enlarges and grows to a hard, brown gall, 1½–2 inches across (4–5 cm), on the tip of a cedar branch. Although unsightly, galls are usually not damaging. The following spring, when conditions are warm and wet, the galls absorb water, swell up, and produce startling jelly-like horns up to 1 inch (2.5 cm) long. These produce spores that infect nearby apple trees. Infection first appears as tiny yellow spots on upper surface of leaves and on fruit; these later turn orange. Brown spots may appear on the lower leaf surface. Infected fruit show a large depressed area with raised orange rust spots, often in concentric rings.

PREVENTION: Plant rust-resistant species or cultivars of apples (such as 'Freedom' or 'Liberty') and junipers (*Juniperus* spp.). Although rarely practical, where possible, avoid planting junipers and apples within 4 miles (6.5 km) of each other.

CONTROL: Remove and destroy galls on junipers and infected foliage and fruit on apples. Protective fungicides are of little use.

Coccomyces sp.

CHERRY LEAF SPOT

Cherry leaf spot appears as many tiny dark spots on upper leaf surfaces; symptoms may spread to leaf stems and fruit.

TYPE OF PROBLEM: Fungal.

RANGE: Worldwide; especially severe in humid climates.

PLANTS AFFECTED: Sweet and sour cherries and plum.

SYMPTOMS: Early symptoms are numerous tiny reddish to purplish black spots on the upper surface of leaves. These may appear on leaf stems and fruit in severe infections. There are corresponding raised, waxy bumps on the underside of the spots on the leaves. After humid weather, these produce a white moldy growth. The centers of the spots eventually dry and fall out, leaving a shot-hole effect, which is most obvious on plum. Usually, entire leaves turn yellow and drop early in the season and fruit may drop prematurely. If leaf drop is severe, the trees are weakened and may die back in following seasons. Sour cherry is most susceptible, sweet cherries and plums less so. Nursery stock is most commonly and seriously affected.

PREVENTION: Plant resistant cultivars, such as 'Northstar' sour cherry. In fall, rake up and burn fallen leaves to remove overwintering sites for fungus. Prune to promote good air circulation.

CONTROL: Spraying sulfur, starting at petal fall, may reduce severity of attack. An additional sulfur spray applied after harvest may prevent premature leaf drop.

Plasmodiophora brassicae

CLUB ROOT

Club root is a common soilborne disease of cabbage and its relatives. The fungus causes root swellings and wilted plants.

TYPE OF PROBLEM: Fungal.

RANGE: Widespread, wherever cabbage family plants are grown; especially in soils with low pH.

PLANTS AFFECTED: Cabbage family plants, including turnip and mustard, and ornamentals such as alyssum, candytuft, and stocks.

SYMPTOMS: Aboveground, plants appear to wilt and turn yellow, although they may recover overnight. Plants gradually become stunted and young plants often die; older plants may survive but will be unproductive. Roots are characteristically distorted, gnarled, and enlarged into spindle-shaped galls; the entire root system or just a few roots may be infected. Roots are unable to function normally, and galls often become infected by other fungal diseases as the damage progresses.

PREVENTION: Avoid introducing the disease by planting only transplants grown in sterile potting mix. Plant resistant cultivars. Test soil; add lime if necessary to maintain a neutral soil pH. Practice long (more than 7 years) rotations between cabbage family crops. Plant in well-drained soil.

CONTROL: Remove and destroy infected plants, including wild mustard or related weeds. Apply lime to soil to raise pH above 7.2, which inhibits spores from germinating. Clean tools after using them in infected soil because the organisms remain in soil for many years. Soil solarization for 6–7 weeks may provide control.

CONSTRUCTION DAMAGE

Construction damage—tree injuries due to regrading around roots or damage by trucks—is easier to prevent than to fix.

TYPE OF PROBLEM: Environmental.

RANGE: Anywhere there is construction.

PLANTS AFFECTED: Trees and shrubs.

SYMPTOMS: Trees wilt and grow poorly. The tips of branches may die back. Some trees die completely after 1 or more years of slow decline. Evergreens may produce a large crop of cones before dying. Trees may become diseased from fungi or bacteria that gain entry through bark and root wounds.

PREVENTION: Clearly mark or flag all trees to be preserved during a construction project; fence them off, if possible, at least as far out as the branches reach. Do not pile excavated soil against trunks or raise the soil level over roots. Do not let heavy equipment travel near trunks, even temporarily, because the weight of machinery on the soil causes compaction and can break roots. If possible, keep blasting to a minimum; it tears and disrupts fine roots of neighboring trees.

CONTROL: Cut back top foliage and branches to compensate for reductions in root area, especially if trenches for utilities or landscape grading have severed roots. Cut off damaged bark and smooth edges of wounds to promote healing. Water weekly during dry weather and fertilize carefully (do not overfertilize). Stake trees with injured roots that may blow over in strong winds.

Ustilago maydis

Corn smut

Corn smut galls are edible and prized by some as a delicacy, but they can be a problem if you want a good corn crop.

TYPE OF PROBLEM: Fungal.

RANGE: Wherever corn is grown; most severe in warm and moderately dry areas.

PLANTS AFFECTED: Corn; sweet corn is particularly susceptible.

SYMPTOMS: In the early stages, soft, fleshy, irregular galls covered with a greenish white membrane appear on leaves, stems, ears, and tassels. Later, the galls turn dark brown and are filled with dark powdery spores, which disperse on the wind when the membrane breaks. Ears and tassels may be aborted or converted to a smut gall; plants may be barren and stunted. Disease development is favored by dry conditions and high temperatures. When corn seedlings are infected, minute galls form on the plants; seedlings may remain stunted or die.

PREVENTION: Plant partially resistant cultivars such as 'Aztec', 'Merit', or 'Viking' (complete resistance is unknown). Follow 1 year of corn with 5–7 years of other crops. Smut fungi overwinter in soil and crop litter, so clean up garden debris in fall. Avoid overfertilizing with nitrogen. Cultivate carefully to prevent plant injury. Control insects that attack corn. Ensure plants have an even supply of moisture; apply mulch and irrigate during dry conditions.

CONTROL: Remove and destroy infected plant parts as soon as you see smut galls. Do not use affected plants to make compost.

Agrobacterium tumefaciens

Crown gall

Crown gall forms knobbly tumors on roots near the soil line. It affects more than 60 families of woody and herbaceous plants.

TYPE OF PROBLEM: Bacterial.

RANGE: Worldwide.

PLANTS AFFECTED: Most common on fruit trees, bramble berries, and grape.

SYMPTOMS: Tumors or galls of various shapes and sizes form on roots and crowns of plants. Early symptoms appear as soft, whitish growths on roots, especially near the soil line. These begin in a wound and resemble normal callus tissue, but develop more quickly. Later, the surface darkens and becomes increasingly convoluted. Galls may become quite hard and knotty or remain spongy. Occasionally, tumors are found above ground on stems and shoots. Tumors may rot in fall and grow back the following year. Infected plants grow slowly, yield poorly, and may be prone to winter injury. In severe infections, plants may die.

PREVENTION: Inspect stock carefully for signs of galls before buying. Soak or dip healthy cuttings and nursery stock in a solution containing beneficial bacteria (*Agrobacterium radiobacter*), which may help prevent disease bacteria from infecting the plants.

CONTROL: Destroy infected plants. For mild infections, prune off disease galls and disinfect pruning equipment afterward with a 10 percent bleach solution (1 part bleach to 9 parts water). Avoid planting susceptible plants, particularly nursery stock, in infected soil for several years (rotate with corn or cereal grains).

Cytospora spp.

CYTOSPORA CANKER

Cytospora canker, also known as Valsa canker, is a problem on fruit trees; affected limbs may break when loaded with fruit.

TYPE OF PROBLEM: Fungal.

RANGE: Worldwide.

PLANTS AFFECTED: More than 70 species of woody plants, particularly apple, peach, pear, plum, spruce, maple, poplar, and willow.

SYMPTOMS: Cankers on large branches and trunks appear first as a circular area of dying bark. The area becomes brownish and sunken, often with a raised ring of callus tissue around it. Particularly in fruit trees, the dead tissue exudes gum that flows down the trunk. Later the bark dries and separates from the underlying wood and the healthy bark. The cankers grow larger each year and become large, rough swellings. Infected branches often break from the weight of fruit or in a windstorm. Twigs and branches die back once cankers completely girdle them.

PREVENTION: Plant resistant cultivars. Cytospora is most severe on trees under stress from poor growing conditions or from injury. Maintain vigorous growth, but apply nutrients carefully to prevent winter injury caused by fertilizing trees too late in the season. Avoid wounding trees with heavy pruning. Protect trunks from sunscald.

CONTROL: During dry weather, remove cankerous tissue and prune away and burn infected branches.

DAMPING-OFF

Damping-off is a common challenge for gardeners who start seeds indoors. It can also attack direct-sown seed in cool wet soil.

TYPE OF PROBLEM: Fungal.

RANGE: Worldwide.

PLANTS AFFECTED: Seeds and seedlings of most plants.

SYMPTOMS: Infected seeds do not germinate but turn brown and mushy. Germinating seeds may be attacked before seedlings emerge from the soil. Infection on seedlings first appears as a darker, water-soaked area on the stem at the soil line. Damage spreads quickly, and seedlings fall over as the stems collapse. Infected older plants have stem lesions that cause stunted growth or death.

PREVENTION: Damping-off fungi spread most quickly in cool, wet soils, so start seeds in well-drained conditions at the best temperature for good growth. Do not overwater and avoid crowding plants; maintain good air circulation around seedlings. Incorporate finished compost from a hot compost pile into seedling mixes to inoculate them with beneficial fungi that suppress damping-off. Cover seedlings with a thin layer of sand, perlite, vermiculite, or peat moss to keep the surface dry and to suppress fungal growth. If you've had problems in the past, plant seeds in a sterile soil-less potting mix.

CONTROL: Infected seedlings usually die. Sometimes, you can save remaining plants in a flat by making conditions as warm and as dry as possible. Strengthen plants with seaweed extract solution. Treating flats with a "tea" made from horsetail may aid in suppressing the fungi.

Peronosporaceae

Downy mildew

Downy mildew mostly attacks leaves, causing yellow spots on the upper surfaces and gray or white spots below.

TYPE OF PROBLEM: Fungal.

RANGE: Worldwide.

PLANTS AFFECTED: A wide range of plants, especially cabbage, cucumber, lettuce, grape, onion, and squash.

SYMPTOMS: The infection usually appears first on the oldest leaves. Small, angular, pale yellow spots appear on the upper surface of leaves between the leaf veins; a growth of white or gray mildew appears on the underside of leaves directly under the spots. Later, infected leaf tissue withers and dies, and the mildew spots turn dark gray. As the infected areas enlarge, they may join to form very large, dead areas on leaves and lead to defoliation. Fruit from infected plants is stunted, with an off flavor. Downy mildew also attacks shoots and fruit, which show the characteristic whitish mildew.

PREVENTION: Downy mildew spreads quickly in humid, cool (60°–72°F/16°–22°C) conditions. Prune and space plantings to promote good air circulation. Provide good ventilation in greenhouses. Plant resistant cultivars. Clean up garden waste after harvest to remove overwintering sites for fungus.

CONTROL: When weather conditions favor the disease, spray liquid copper fungicide or bordeaux mixture weekly (test spray on a few leaves first to check for plant damage).

Alternaria spp.

Early blight

Early blight produces irregular brown spots on the leaves of tomatoes and potatoes. It may spread to the fruits or tubers.

TYPE OF PROBLEM: Fungal.

RANGE: Worldwide, but less common in drier climates in western North America.

PLANTS AFFECTED: Primarily potato and tomato; occasionally eggplant and pepper.

SYMPTOMS: Brown spots with a characteristic bull's-eye pattern, up to ½ inch (1 cm) wide, usually appear first on oldest leaves. Later, the spots enlarge and merge; severely infected leaves die and fall off. Elongated lesions may also appear on stems. On tomato fruit, lesions are leathery and sunken. On potato tubers, sunken circular lesions have gray to purplish edges; shallow areas of a brown or black dry rot may show under the lesions.

PREVENTION: Early blight is worst on plants stressed by drought, insect attack, or nutrient deficiencies, so provide the best growing conditions and control pests. Buy and plant hot-water-treated tomato seed and certified disease-free potatoes. Choose cultivars with some resistance. Practice a 3-year rotation with nonsusceptible crops.

CONTROL: At first sign of infection, spray with a copper fungicide; repeat at 7–10-day intervals. Destroy severely infected plants. Mound soil over potato tubers to prevent leaf infections from spreading to roots. Harvest only after the potato plants have died and skins of tubers have toughened. Cure potatoes at 50°–60°F (10°–16°C) for several weeks to allow bruises to heal before storage.

Erwinia amylovora

FIRE BLIGHT

Fire blight is a devastating disease that causes shoots to turn brown or black. Dead leaves cling to blighted branches.

TYPE OF PROBLEM: Bacterial.

RANGE: Worldwide; most severe on pear in eastern United States.

PLANTS AFFECTED: Apple, pear, quince, and related plants in the rose family.

SYMPTOMS: Flowers are usually affected first, becoming water-soaked, then brown and shriveled. Symptoms soon spread to leaves, then shoots, which suddenly turn brown or black and curl up. Leaves remain hanging on twigs and look like they have been scorched by fire. Affected shoots bend downward, and young fruit blackens but remains on the stem. Sunken cankers with a sharp margin or crack around the edge may appear on branches and trunks; they may girdle the tree, causing its death.

PREVENTION: Plant least-susceptible cultivars such as 'Liberty' apples or 'Douglas' pears. Avoid overfeeding and severe pruning; these can lead to rapid, succulent shoot growth, which is most susceptible to fire blight.

CONTROL: During winter, when the disease is dormant, cut down and burn severely infected trees; prune out and burn infected shoots and branches. In summer, remove and burn infected suckers, shoots, and twigs, cutting at least 6–12 inches (15–30 cm) below the lowest visible infection. Spray with copper sulfate or bordeaux mix when tree is dormant. Apply streptomycin (Agri-Strep) sprays to control blossom blight phase of disease; apply one to four sprays at 5–7-day intervals, just before wet periods, if possible.

Fusarium spp.

FUSARIUM WILT

Fusarium wilt can cause serious damage to vegetables, flowers, and some shade trees. A few stems or whole plants may wilt.

TYPE OF PROBLEM: Fungal.

RANGE: Most destructive in warm regions of United States; usually only in greenhouses in Northern regions.

PLANTS AFFECTED: Wide range of plants, especially dahlia, melon, pea, pepper, and tomato.

SYMPTOMS: Infections usually appear first as yellow patches on older leaves. Later, these turn brown and may affect the entire leaf. Leaves yellow and stems wilt over the entire plant or just on one side; leaves drop prematurely and plants usually die. Plants usually have a brownish discoloration on lower stem and upper roots; insides of stems are also discolored. Brown to black lengthwise streaks may show when stems are cut lengthwise. Disease is most prevalent under warm conditions.

PREVENTION: Plant resistant cultivars where available. Fertilize and water evenly to promote vigorous growth. Crop rotation is of limited value, since spores can remain in soil for several years; try leaving at least 4 years between susceptible crops. Mulch to keep soil cool in hot weather.

CONTROL: There is no control once plants are infected. Remove and destroy infected plants, including the roots; disinfect tools afterward with a 10 percent bleach solution (1 part bleach to 9 parts water). Use soil solarization to treat infected soil before replanting; to solarize, cover moist soil with clear plastic during the summer months.

Iron deficiency

Iron deficiency produces a characteristic yellowing between the green leaf veins. It is usually due to a high soil pH.

TYPE OF PROBLEM: Physiological.

RANGE: Anywhere susceptible crops are grown.

PLANTS AFFECTED: Acid-loving plants are most susceptible, including azalea, blueberry, holly, oak, and rhododendron; also tomato, peach, and other plants growing in alkaline soils.

SYMPTOMS: Youngest leaves on upper shoots are first affected, becoming light yellow to nearly white between the veins; veins remain a normal green color. Plants are stunted and yield poorly. If deficiency is severe, leaf tissue may brown and die.

PREVENTION: Iron deficiency appears when the soil is naturally too alkaline (has a high pH) or because it has been overlimed or excess lime is leaching from nearby concrete foundations. Plants in acid soils high in manganese also may become deficient in iron. Have soil tested and follow recommendations for adjusting pH. Where soils are naturally alkaline, plant acid-loving plants in raised beds amended with compost, aged manure, or peat. Manure and compost soil amendments supply iron and help to keep the pH balanced; peat moss lowers pH.

CONTROL: At first sign of yellowing leaves, work compost or aged manure into the soil around the plant (top-dress, but do not dig around the shallow roots of rhododendrons and azaleas). Treat soil with sulfur to reduce pH if necessary. Spray leaves with seaweed extract for a temporary cure; then amend the soil as explained under "Prevention" above.

Phytophthora infestans

Late blight

Late blight is a destructive disease that attacks potatoes, tomatoes, and their relatives, causing fast-spreading leaf spots.

TYPE OF PROBLEM: Fungal.

RANGE: Wherever potatoes are grown.

PLANTS AFFECTED: Potato, tomato, and related plants.

SYMPTOMS: Damage first appears as irregular, water-soaked, grayish areas with a greasy sheen, usually at tips or edges of lower leaves. These expand rapidly during moist weather; a zone of whitish mold appears around the margin of the patches on the underside of leaves. Under moist conditions, all aboveground parts of plants rot away so quickly that they look frosted; dying foliage has an unpleasant smell. On tomato, water-soaked grayish green spots on fruit enlarge and spread; lesions become dark brown, firm, and wrinkled, with a definite margin. Infected potato tubers have irregular, purplish black or reddish brown blotches that extend about ½ inch (1 cm) into the flesh; they soon rot in the field or in storage.

PREVENTION: Plant resistant cultivars and certified disease-free seed potatoes. Thoroughly clean up and destroy all crop residues to remove overwintering sites for fungus.

CONTROL: Apply bordeaux mix every 4–5 days when weather is wet and nights are cool, ensuring thorough coverage of new leaves as they expand. Blight is difficult to control unless weather turns hot and dry. Cut affected potato vines just below soil surface and remove them 2 weeks before harvest to prevent the disease from spreading to tubers.

Lawn mower damage

Lawn mower damage is easy to avoid with common-sense preventive measures, like tree guards and careful trimming.

TYPE OF PROBLEM: Environmental.

RANGE: Anywhere.

PLANTS AFFECTED: Any tree or shrub.

SYMPTOMS: Injury appears as horizontal cuts in the bark of trunks and branches, caused by lawn mowers and weed trimmers colliding with the trunk. Repeated injuries may cause the branch to die back and, in extreme cases, may even kill the tree. Such injuries are open invitations for disease organisms and boring insects to enter, which may cause the eventual death of the tree or shrub.

PREVENTION: Be careful cutting around trees with power tools; use hand tools to clip close to trunks. Protect plants by installing plastic trunk guards; this is especially important in areas where string trimmers are used regularly, as it is difficult to judge where the string is at all times. Or eliminate the need to trim close to trees by installing a no-mow strip around trees in lawns. Apply a 1–2-foot (30–60 cm) wide circle of heavy leaf mulch, gravel, or groundcover plantings around each tree; a wider strip may be necessary where riding mowers are used. Flag small trees or shrubs that might not be noticeable when mowing, especially in tall grass.

CONTROL: Cut away all the damaged bark to clean out the wound; smooth the edges of the cut to speed healing.

Exobasidium spp.

Leaf gall

Leaf gall fungi form unsightly blisters on azalea leaves. Handpicking young galls is a simple and effective control.

TYPE OF PROBLEM: Fungal.

RANGE: Southeastern United States.

PLANTS AFFECTED: Azalea, camellia, and rhododendron.

SYMPTOMS: Leaves of affected plants may show yellow or reddish spots or turn light green to white; they become thickened over a portion or over the entire leaf. The surface of the leaf may appear blistered, deformed, and curled. Whole flowers, or parts of flowers, and seed pods may be deformed into waxy, thickened galls, which later harden and turn brown. In moist weather, the surface of affected parts is covered with a pinkish or whitish fungal growth.

PREVENTION: Always propagate from disease-free plants. Plant least susceptible species and cultivars. Maintain vigorous plants.

CONTROL: Prune out and destroy galls and other infected plant tissue as soon as you see them, ideally before they turn white. In areas with severe leaf-gall problems, apply copper sprays just before leaves start to open and again 2–3 weeks later.

LEAF SCORCH

Leaf scorch is often caused by drought and excessive heat. It is a particular problem on plants close to buildings and pavement.

TYPE OF PROBLEM: Environmental.

RANGE: Widespread, especially in hot or arid regions.

PLANTS AFFECTED: Most plants, especially street trees and plants in hanging baskets.

SYMPTOMS: The margins and tips of leaves begin to yellow and turn brown. Leaves or entire plant may wilt; leaves may roll inward. Plant growth can be stunted and, in the worst cases, plants may die. Scorched appearance may also be due to potassium deficiency or leafhopper damage.

PREVENTION: In dry periods, provide water to plants not tolerant of drought. Water deeply at weekly or longer intervals; avoid frequent light watering, which encourages shallow root development. Use mulches to shade soil and retain moisture. Plants in planters and hanging baskets are particularly susceptible to heat and drought damage because of the smaller volume of soil. Incorporate plenty of peat moss and compost in planter soil mixtures to retain water; water frequently or install automatic drip systems for large numbers of baskets or window boxes. Avoid planting heat-susceptible trees, such as maples and horse chestnut, in a site where excessive heat will be reflected from pavement or buildings in summer.

CONTROL: If possible, remedy drought or heat conditions immediately; provide plants with the best care to speed their recovery.

LIGHTNING DAMAGE

Lightning damage can be hard to diagnose, unless you know that a plant has been hit. Look for branch dieback and split bark.

TYPE OF PROBLEM: Environmental.

RANGE: Most common in thunderstorm areas.

PLANTS AFFECTED: Any plant may be hit, particularly tall or isolated trees, such as elm, maple, oak, pine, and poplar; also plants in open fields.

SYMPTOMS: Trees hit by lightning often have a long scar running the length of the trunk to the ground. In some cases, only the yellowing of leaves and branches dying back indicates that there has been lightning injury to roots; in other cases, a branch or the entire tree may be shattered. In open areas, leaves droop and wilt within a few hours of lightning strike; all plants underneath including weeds are affected in a circular area 10–60 feet (3–18 m) wide. In the center of the area or in the most severe cases, plants rapidly wilt and die. Stems and branches shrink and become flattened and collapse.

PREVENTION: In areas with a lot of thunderstorm activity, it may be worth the expense to install copper lightning protectors on a particularly tall, valuable tree (have a professional install it). In storm belts, plant birch, beech, or horse chestnut, which are rarely struck.

CONTROL: Remove damaged branches and bark from trees not killed by the initial strike; smooth the edges of the wound to prevent colonization by fungal diseases. To aid recovery, water thoroughly and fertilize to promote growth.

Mosaic

Mosaic diseases produce different patterns on different crops, but the control result is the same: Destroy infected plants.

TYPE OF PROBLEM: Viral.

RANGE: Throughout North America.

PLANTS AFFECTED: Wide range of plants; vegetables, especially bean, cucumber, potato, tomato (especially in greenhouses), and tobacco.

SYMPTOMS: Leaves exhibit light yellow or white areas or streaks intermingled with the normal green color; patterns may be described as mottled or streaked, in a ring pattern, a line pattern, or as vein banding (discoloration) or vein clearing. Leaves often have curling edges and may be distorted. Plant growth is slightly or severely stunted, and plants are dwarfed, with shortened stems and excessively curled leaves. Fruit and pods may also be mottled or streaked and stunted.

PREVENTION: Plant resistant cultivars. Control aphids and leafhoppers, which spread viral diseases. Avoid cultivating or handling bean plants while leaves are wet. Buy virus-free stock.

CONTROL: Pull and destroy infected plants. Disease is spread by contact with hands and tools that have touched infected sap, so wash hands and disinfect tools used around infected plants. Milk neutralizes tobacco mosaic virus (which also infects tomato), so dip hands and tools in milk between handling to prevent transmission between plants.

Needlecast

Needlecast attacks many kinds of evergreens, starting at the tips of developing needles and spreading downward.

TYPE OF PROBLEM: Fungal.

RANGE: Widespread.

PLANTS AFFECTED: Many evergreens, especially arborvitae, pine, and western red cedar.

SYMPTOMS: Mottled orange or brown spots, specks, or light and dark bands appear on developing needles. Affected needles turn olive green, yellow, or reddish brown, usually dying from tip first. Severely affected needles may drop by midsummer, and branch tips may die back. Needles on lower two-thirds of young trees are most commonly affected. Plant growth may be slowed; severely infected young trees, especially nursery seedlings, may die.

PREVENTION: Plant hardy trees native to your region; avoid planting exotic pines. Plant trees where there is good air circulation. Provide good growing conditions, including irrigation in drought periods. Protect young trees from frost and cold winter winds.

CONTROL: Rake up and destroy dropped needles. Prune off damaged tips. Where infections are regular and severe, spray with bordeaux mix or copper when new shoots are one-quarter grown and at 2-week intervals thereafter (test spray on several shoots first to make sure it doesn't affect foliage).

Nitrogen deficiency

Nitrogen deficiency starts on the oldest (lowest) foliage, causing leaves to turn yellow; symptoms spread upward.

TYPE OF PROBLEM: Physiological.

RANGE: Widespread, especially in sandy soils.

PLANTS AFFECTED: All plants.

SYMPTOMS: Lower, older leaves first become pale green to yellow; later, the entire plant may be lighter than normal, and lower leaves may turn light brown. Unlike other deficiency symptoms, the light color is relatively even across leaf tissue between veins; veins may show a brownish or purplish cast on underside of leaf. Growth is slow and plants may be stunted, with short, spindly stems. In cases of severe deficiency, leaves may turn light to dark yellow with brown veins and hardened, bronzed stems. Flowers turn yellow and drop; fruits are stunted and woody; yields are reduced and of low quality.

PREVENTION: For vegetables and other heavy-feeding plants, apply yearly applications of nitrogen-rich fertilizer, such as soybean meal or bloodmeal. Grow legume cover crops such as clover or hairy vetch in rotation with vegetables. For plants with lower requirements, annual applications of compost usually provide sufficient nitrogen.

CONTROL: As soon as plants show deficiency symptoms, water with compost "tea" or fish emulsion and dig in supplemental nitrogen fertilizer, such as bloodmeal, around roots. Spraying the leaves with fish emulsion will give plants an immediate boost.

Ceratocystis fagacearum

Oak wilt

Oak wilt spreads quickly. Don't store wood cut from infected trees near healthy oaks; it can harbor disease spores.

TYPE OF PROBLEM: Fungal.

RANGE: North-central United States, from Arkansas and South Carolina to Pennsylvania and Minnesota.

PLANTS AFFECTED: All oaks; red and black oak are most susceptible.

SYMPTOMS: Initially, leaves in the top of the tree wilt and turn yellow or brown, then drop; leaves dry from the tip and edges inward. Symptoms are most pronounced in late spring and early summer. Wilting spreads rapidly in red and black oaks, which may die within weeks. Symptoms spread more slowly in white oaks, which often survive 1–2 years. The bark of trees killed by oak wilt is raised and cracked by mats of fungus growing between the bark and wood.

PREVENTION: Avoid planting oaks as landscape trees in areas where oak wilt is a problem. Prune trees only while they are dormant to reduce the chance of fungi getting into the wound.

CONTROL: There is no control once trees are infected; they should be removed and destroyed immediately, before the fungus produces spores. To save nearby oaks, dig a trench 3–4 feet (1–1.2 m) deep between infected and healthy trees to sever root contacts between trees; this will prevent the fungus from spreading underground from tree to tree. Immediately backfill the trench with soil so healthy roots do not dry out.

Ozone damage

Ozone damage will produce white or tan stippling or flecking on the leaves of susceptible plants, such as this nasturtium.

TYPE OF PROBLEM: Environmental.

RANGE: Any area with smog pollution.

PLANTS AFFECTED: Wide range of plants; particularly alfalfa, bean, blackberry, cereals, citrus, corn, spinach, and tomato; also petunia, pine, sweet gum, and tulip poplar.

SYMPTOMS: Ozone is the most destructive air pollutant. Ozone forms when compounds in car exhaust are exposed to sunlight; naturally high levels of ozone may also occur from lightning. When a layer of warm air, known as an inversion, prevents smog from dispersing, the buildup of ozone may damage plants over a wide surrounding area. Damage appears as stippled, flecked, or mottled areas of pale tissue, mostly on upper leaf surface. Spots may be small or large; they may have a bleached white appearance or may range in color from tan or brown to black. Leaves of citrus, grapes, and vines may drop prematurely, and plant growth is stunted. At low levels, ozone damage may not be noticeable, except as slower plant growth and lower productivity.

PREVENTION: Where damaging ozone levels are a frequent problem, grow plants that are more tolerant, such as beet, lettuce, and strawberry.

CONTROL: There is no control except to support air pollution-reduction programs in your area. Give damaged plants excellent care to aid recovery.

PAN damage

PAN damage starts on the youngest, fastest-growing leaves. It eventually creates a silvery glaze on leaf undersides.

TYPE OF PROBLEM: Environmental.

RANGE: Any area with smog pollution.

PLANTS AFFECTED: Wide range of plants; particularly bean, lettuce, pepper, spinach, and tomato; also dahlia and petunia.

SYMPTOMS: Plants are damaged by exposure to high levels of a pollutant known as PAN (peroxyacyl nitrate) that forms when compounds in car exhaust are exposed to sunlight. When a layer of warm air, known as an inversion, prevents smog from dispersing, the buildup of pollutants may damage plants over a wide surrounding area. The youngest and most rapidly growing leaves are most affected by PAN. A silvery glaze appears on the underside of the leaf, starting as white to bronze spots that spread throughout the leaf. Damage from PAN may be mistaken for injury caused by mites, thrips, frost, or sunscald. Low levels of PAN may not be noticeable, except as slower plant growth and lower productivity.

PREVENTION: Where damaging smog levels are a frequent problem, choose plants that are more tolerant of pollution, such as cabbage, cucumber, and squash, and ornamentals such as arborvitae, English ivy, and sugar maple.

CONTROL: There is no control except to support air pollution-reduction programs in your area. Give damaged plants excellent care to aid recovery.

Taphrina deformans

Peach leaf curl

Peach leaf curl produces distinctive reddish blisters, which spread and cause affected leaves to look distorted.

TYPE OF PROBLEM: Fungal.

RANGE: Widespread.

PLANTS AFFECTED: Peach and nectarine.

SYMPTOMS: Parts of a leaf or entire leaves become thickened, swollen, and distorted, and curl down and inward. Affected leaves have a purple or reddish color, later turning to reddish yellow or gray. Swollen areas turn powdery gray as the fungus produces spores. Later, leaves turn yellow or brown and drop. Blossoms and young fruit may be attacked and usually drop early in the season. The current year's twigs may also be attacked and stunted; in severe infections, twigs may be swollen as well. Disease is worst in years with cool, wet spring conditions while tissue is still young and susceptible; older tissue is more resistant to infection.

PREVENTION: Plant resistant cultivars such as 'Red Haven' peaches. Maintain vigorous trees.

CONTROL: To kill fungus overwintering in bud scales, apply a dormant spray of lime-sulfur, copper, or bordeaux mix after leaves have dropped and again in early spring at the time buds begin to swell. Pick and destroy all affected leaves as soon as symptoms are visible to prevent fungus from reproducing; spray liquid seaweed extracts on remaining leaves at least once a month all season.

Phosphorus deficiency

Phosphorus deficiency is most common on transplants in cool soil, since the roots can't grow quickly in search of nutrients.

TYPE OF PROBLEM: Physiological.

RANGE: Anywhere.

PLANTS AFFECTED: All plants, especially in early spring.

SYMPTOMS: Leaves of affected plants have a blue-green to purplish cast, especially along veins, stems, and twigs. Lower leaves may turn a light bronze color with purplish or brown spots. Shoots may be spindly and shorter and may grow more upright than usual. Plants grow poorly and produce fewer flowers and smaller fruit.

PREVENTION: Make sure your soil has a sufficient supply of phosphorus from compost, well-rotted manure, and other organic materials; amend deficient soils with bonemeal or rock phosphate, which are high in phosphorus. Raise the pH of acid soils by liming to ensure phosphorus is available to plants. Add bonemeal to the soil when setting out bulbs, perennials, shrubs, and trees. Keep transplants warm during the seedling stage; do not set them out until the soil has warmed up.

CONTROL: Symptoms may appear in transplants or seedlings in early spring, especially during a prolonged period of cool weather; plants usually recover as the soil warms and the roots are able to reach and take up sufficient phosphorus. If cool soil is not the cause, dig in compost and bonemeal around deficient plants and water with compost "tea" to aid recovery.

POTASSIUM DEFICIENCY

Potassium deficiency resembles other diseases, making it tricky to diagnose. Check nutrient levels with a soil test.

TYPE OF PROBLEM: Physiological.

RANGE: Anywhere.

PLANTS AFFECTED: All plants.

SYMPTOMS: Older leaves begin to show yellow patches first, with brown tips and many brown spots near the margins. Leaves appear scorched (known as "firing") and have ragged edges as dead tissue from the margins drops away. Symptoms may be confused with bacterial wilt or some fungal leaf diseases; leaf-tissue tests for nutrients can be used to aid in diagnosis. Plant growth is poor, leaves are smaller than usual, and shoots are thinner and shorter between nodes. Root growth is stunted and stalks of plants are weak and blow down readily. In severe cases, young leaves also turn yellow or may be streaked with yellow; shoots may die back from tips. Fruit is stunted or misshapen.

PREVENTION: Test soil periodically to check soil fertility. Ensure soil has a sufficient supply of potassium from compost or well-rotted manure; amend deficient soils with kelp meal, granite dust, greensand, or wood ashes, which are high in potassium. (Use wood ashes sparingly, as they can also raise soil pH dramatically.)

CONTROL: Dig in amendments around roots of plants showing deficiency symptoms, and water with seaweed extract to speed recovery. For deficiencies that appear late in the season, there's not much you can do except correct conditions for next year.

Erysiphaceae

POWDERY MILDEW

Powdery mildew is easy to identify with its characteristic dusty white or gray spots. Lilacs and roses are common targets.

TYPE OF PROBLEM: Fungal.

RANGE: Widespread.

PLANTS AFFECTED: Wide range of plants; particularly damaging to bean, cucumber, and squash; also lilac, phlox, rose, and zinnia.

SYMPTOMS: Powdery white or gray spots appear on leaves, usually on the upper surface first. These spread rapidly to become patches of white and eventually cover the entire surface of leaves, shoots, flowers, and fruit. Although common in humid weather conditions, powdery mildews spread well even in warm, dry climates because the spores do not require a film of water on the leaf to germinate.

PREVENTION: Grow resistant cultivars, when available. Ensure good air circulation around susceptible plants. Compost plant debris at the end of the season to remove overwintering sites for fungi.

CONTROL: Slow the spread of disease by handpicking and destroying infected leaves. Washing leaves of affected plants with water every 1–2 weeks to remove spores has given promising results; be sure to wash undersides of leaves thoroughly as well. Applications of antitranspirants on roses have shown good results. Try a spray of 0.5 percent solution of baking soda (1 teaspoon soda to 1 quart/1 l water). Spray lime-sulfur or spray or dust sulfur weekly; never use these on muskmelon, and test sprays on other squash family plants first to check for leaf damage before spraying your whole crop.

Root rot

Root rot symptoms are most obvious on the aboveground parts of the plant. Look for wilted leaves and branch dieback.

TYPE OF PROBLEM: Fungal.

RANGE: Widespread.

PLANTS AFFECTED: Wide range of plants.

SYMPTOMS: Leaves are smaller than usual, may wilt, and turn yellow or brown; the plant or tree begins to decline gradually or quickly for no obvious reason. Brown or blackened and damaged areas are visible on crowns or roots. Armillaria root rot on trees is indicated by white mats of fungi and dark brown fungal strands found on the roots or growing between the bark and wood.

PREVENTION: Plant resistant cultivars when available. Set out transplants when soil has warmed sufficiently for good growth. Enrich soil with compost. Refrain from cultivating close to roots, which causes injuries and allows disease to enter; use mulches to suppress weeds instead. Plant in well-drained soils; avoid overwatering. Ensure water does not pool around base of trees; plant with soil line slightly higher than surrounding soil level and slope soil away from trunk. Shape irrigation moats to hold water at least 12 inches (30 cm) away from stems or trunks.

CONTROL: Remove and destroy badly infected plants. You may be able to save moderately affected plants by pruning away diseased roots and replanting in well-drained soil. Disinfect tools used on or around infected plants. Soil solarization before planting has shown good results in controlling root rot.

Rust

Rust shows up as light-colored spots on leaf surfaces. Turn the leaves over and you'll see rusty-looking spots underneath.

TYPE OF PROBLEM: Fungal.

RANGE: Widespread.

PLANTS AFFECTED: Wide range of plants; most common on asparagus, bean, blackberry, cereal grains, and raspberry; also carnation, snapdragon, and rose.

SYMPTOMS: Rusty red, orange, yellow, or whitish spots show up on leaves and stems and occasionally on flowers or fruit. Spots may be numerous small, round blisters; on cereals they appear as elongated, rusty brown flecks. The entire underside of rose and bramble leaves may appear bright orange. Spots may become swellings or even galls on leaves or stems. Most infections remain local on the plants and usually do not spread internally. Severely infected plants grow poorly and may die. Spores are spread by the wind, sometimes hundreds of miles, and come down in rainfall to start new infections; infections spread quickly in humid conditions.

PREVENTION: Grow resistant cultivars. Provide good air circulation to permit foliage to dry quickly. Avoid wetting foliage with overhead watering and do not work among plants while leaves are still wet. Compost all garden debris in fall to remove overwintering sites.

CONTROL: Pick and destroy infected leaves to slow the spread of the disease. Spray or dust susceptible plants weekly with sulfur.

*S*ALT INJURY

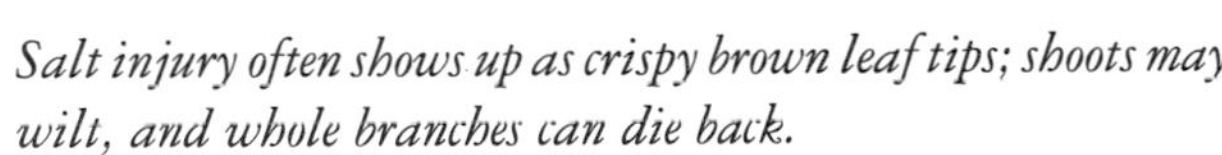

Salt injury often shows up as crispy brown leaf tips; shoots may wilt, and whole branches can die back.

TYPE OF PROBLEM: Environmental.

RANGE: Anywhere; especially in coastal areas or along roads and sidewalks.

PLANTS AFFECTED: Most plants.

SYMPTOMS: Salt buildup in soils from road salt used during winter deicing or from excessive use of fertilizers damages plant roots. This stunts plant growth and causes plants to wilt and leaves to dry up; severely affected plants may die. A white crust on the soil surface indicates salts have accumulated in the soil, often from overfertilizing or poor drainage, especially in container plants. Soils and irrigation water may naturally have high levels of salt in some Western regions. Plants exposed to windblown salt spray or salty road slush have browned leaves, especially around the leaf margins.

PREVENTION: Grow salt-tolerant plants in areas where exposure to salt spray or road salt is unavoidable. Use sand or sawdust instead of rock salt on sidewalks in winter. Avoid overfertilizing, especially in pots and greenhouse beds, and ensure good drainage. Grow dense windbreaks of salt-tolerant vegetation in coastal areas to protect garden plants.

CONTROL: Repot container plants in new soil; trim back damaged roots and leaves. Periodically flush container soil with sufficient water (five to six times the volume of soil) to leach out salts. In areas with poor drainage due to high salt content, apply gypsum to the soil to improve soil structure.

Septoria spp.

*S*EPTORIA LEAF SPOT

Septoria leaf spot starts as tiny yellow specks that gradually enlarge and turn brown; it usually affects lower leaves first.

TYPE OF PROBLEM: Fungal.

RANGE: Worldwide.

PLANTS AFFECTED: Wide range of plants; especially beet, carrot, celery, cucumber family, lettuce, and tomato; also aster, azalea, carnation, chrysanthemum, and marigold.

SYMPTOMS: Leaf spots start as yellowish specks that grow larger and turn light brown or grayish; the spots eventually turn dark brown and are surrounded by a narrow yellow margin. Spots vary in size from barely visible to over ½ inch (1 cm) wide; on some plants, a spot may take up one-third of a leaf. Black specks become visible later inside the spot. On some plants, leaves with a few spots may wilt, turn yellow, and die; on others, leaves may tolerate a large number of spots before wilting.

PREVENTION: Plant only disease-free seed; buy and plant hot-water-treated tomato seed. Clean up and compost all garden debris in fall to remove overwintering sites. Avoid working among plants when leaves are wet. Use 3–4-year crop rotations, keeping related plants together. There are many different species of Septoria, each attacking different host plants, so Septoria on tomato family plants is not likely to attack celery or lettuce.

CONTROL: Remove and destroy infected leaves. Copper sprays may be useful as a last resort. Pull out and destroy severely infected plants.

Slime flux

Slime flux—also known as bacterial wetwood—causes an unsightly ooze that flows down the trunk of damaged trees.

TYPE OF PROBLEM: Bacterial.

RANGE: Widespread.

PLANTS AFFECTED: Many woody plants, especially elm, maple, and poplar.

SYMPTOMS: Fermenting, dark-colored, slimy sap, which may also have a foul smell, oozes from a wound or crack in the bark of a branch, trunk, or crotch of a limb. Wood around the wound becomes dark brown and water-soaked. The flowing sap dries to a light gray or white stain on the bark. Flux appears in trees more than 5 years old, after heartwood has formed; it is often associated with wet soils and mechanical or frost injury to bark or roots. Leaves on one or more branches of young trees may wilt, turn yellow, and drop prematurely; branches on older trees die back slowly. There is a general decline in the health of the tree. You'll usually see symptoms in spring and summer or after wet weather.

PREVENTION: Avoid causing mechanical injury to bark. Use white trunk paint on young trees to prevent sunscald injury on bright winter days. Maintain vigorous growth with good management and soil fertility. Clean out and trim edges of bark wounds with a sharp knife immediately to promote healing.

CONTROL: No control known. Maintain good management and prune away affected limbs and branches. Replace severely affected trees.

Sooty mold

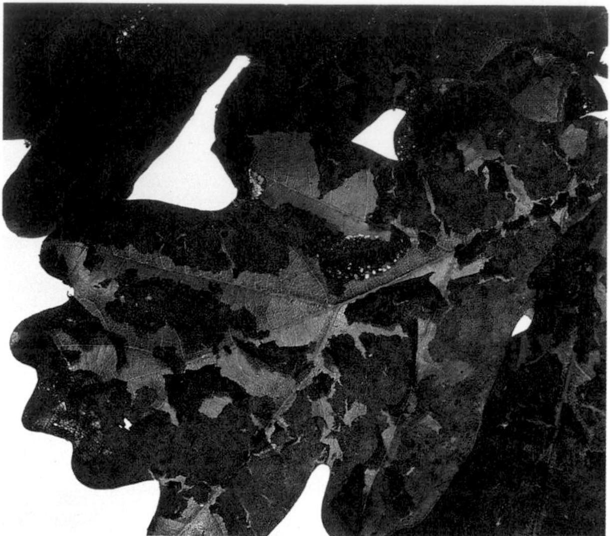

Sooty mold usually doesn't harm plants, but it does indicate a serious infestation of sucking insects like aphids or scales.

TYPE OF PROBLEM: Fungal.

RANGE: Widespread.

PLANTS AFFECTED: Any plant.

SYMPTOMS: Leaves and other plant parts have a dark gray to sooty black layer over the surface; this can be readily wiped off to show the healthy green leaf surface below. Sometimes the fungus forms a papery black layer that can be peeled away from the leaf. The mold grows on the sugars in the sticky honeydew excreted by sucking insects (such as aphids, mealybug, scale, and whitefly) and does not enter the plant tissue. The mold on the leaves does block light to the leaf; if most of the leaf area is covered, it results in poor growth or even the collapse of the plant. Sooty molds spread most quickly in moist, warm conditions.

PREVENTION: Rinse sticky leaves with water to remove honeydew before molds can grow. Control sucking-insect populations.

CONTROL: Control aphids, mealybugs, scale, and whitefly to eliminate source of honeydew. Wash mold from leaves and fruit with a stream of water; to clean harvested fruit, wipe gently with a soft cloth.

Sulfur dioxide injury

Sulfur dioxide injury causes yellowing or browning between the leaf veins; severely affected leaves will shrivel and die.

TYPE OF PROBLEM: Environmental.

RANGE: Widespread, especially in industrial and highly populated areas.

PLANTS AFFECTED: Wide range of plants, especially alfalfa, apple, bean, blackberry, cabbage, pea, and spinach; also conifers, hawthorn, tulip, and violet.

SYMPTOMS: The foliage of plants turns light yellow when low concentrations of sulfur dioxide are present; at higher concentrations, the tissue between leaf veins becomes papery dry and bleached white or straw colored. Grass blades become streaked with light tan or white; needles of conifers turn reddish brown from tips inward.

PREVENTION: Grow sulfur-dioxide-tolerant plants, such as corn, cucumber, onion, and potato; also arborvitae, ginkgo, juniper, maple, pine, privet, and sycamore.

CONTROL: There is no control except to support programs to reduce air pollution and eliminate stack emissions from industrial facilities in your area.

Sunscald

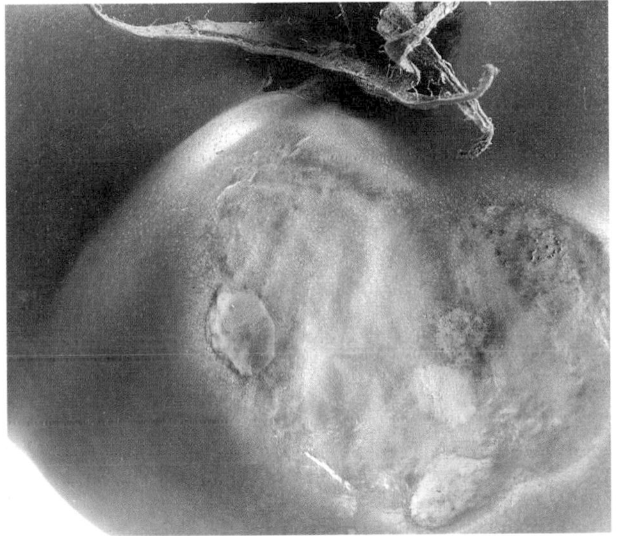

Sunscald can affect any plant part that is suddenly exposed to bright sunshine. Protect plants with shade fabric, if necessary.

TYPE OF PROBLEM: Environmental.

RANGE: Widespread.

PLANTS AFFECTED: Most plants; fruits especially affected are apple, grape, pepper, and tomato.

SYMPTOMS: Leaves develop light green patches, which turn brown and dry out. Seedlings that have not been adequately hardened off to tolerate full sun before transplanting may collapse completely as the stems are injured by sunscald. Fruit may be sunscalded when it is suddenly exposed to bright sun, as happens when disease causes leaves to drop or when foliage is pruned excessively in summer. Water-soaked blisters appear on the fruit skin; these eventually dry up and turn into brown pitted areas surrounded by a grayish white discolored area.

PREVENTION: Harden off tender seedlings gradually to the full strength of the sun. Plant disease-resistant cultivars to avoid leaf drop. Avoid excessive summer pruning; when pruning, always leave leaf cover for developing fruit. Use clothespins to clip squares of light-colored fabric on the sunward side of grape bunches exposed to the sun to protect them from injury. Shade tomatoes and other crops with row cover material or other light fabric.

CONTROL: Shade transplants and seedlings at first sign of injury to allow them to recover. Use damaged fruit as soon as you pick it; the undamaged portion is edible, but it will not store well.

Verticillium spp.

VERTICILLIUM WILT

Verticillium wilt fungi will stay in soil for years, so if the disease does strike, look for resistant cultivars for next year.

TYPE OF PROBLEM: Fungal.

RANGE: Worldwide.

PLANTS AFFECTED: Many woody and herbaceous plants, especially eggplant, melon, pepper, potato, and tomato; also aster, chrysanthemum, and dahlia.

SYMPTOMS: Plants infected with Verticillium wilt look much like those attacked by Fusarium wilt. Plants gradually wilt, turn yellow, and drop leaves, although stems often remain upright. Branches may die one by one, or the whole plant may collapse suddenly. In most cases, Verticillium infections induce wilt at lower temperatures and develop more slowly than Fusarium wilt. Symptoms of Verticillium wilt often appear only on a few branches or on part of a plant, usually on lower or outer branches. If you cut affected stems open, you'll often see a light brown or yellow discoloration extending upward from the base of the stem. In the first year, damage is mild, but it worsens in succeeding years as the disease builds up.

PREVENTION: Plant resistant cultivars; plant certified disease-free potato sets. Avoid cultivating potatoes when tubers are well developed to prevent injury, which increases risk of infection. Clean up and compost garden debris to remove overwintering sites for fungi. Rotation usually isn't effective, since so many plants are susceptible.

CONTROL: Destroy infected plants. Soil solarization before replanting can be effective in warm regions.

WATERLOGGED SOIL

Waterlogged soil can destroy plants that need good drainage. Try raised beds, or look for moisture-loving species.

TYPE OF PROBLEM: Environmental.

RANGE: Anywhere.

PLANTS AFFECTED: Any plant.

SYMPTOMS: When soils are waterlogged, the pores in the soil are filled with water; this excludes the oxygen needed by plant roots, so roots die back and eventually rot as fungi and bacteria attack the dying tissue. Early symptoms show up as poor growth and wilting leaves, even though the soil appears to be quite moist. Potted plants frequently suffer from waterlogged soil as a result of being overwatered or because drainage holes are blocked or lacking in the pots.

PREVENTION: Avoid overwatering potted plants; make sure containers have drainage holes. Naturally heavy, clayey soils are easily waterlogged; mix in compost and other organic matter to improve drainage. Grow plants in raised beds. Ensure even distribution of irrigation water and water according to plant needs.

CONTROL: Severely damaged plants probably will not survive. Improve drainage and soil conditions; reduce watering around less seriously affected plants. Repot houseplants in well-drained soil.

Winter injury

Winter injury can cause shoot tips or whole plants to die back. Water well before cold weather strikes to help prevent damage.

TYPE OF PROBLEM: Environmental.

RANGE: Northern regions.

PLANTS AFFECTED: Most plants, particularly those that are only marginally hardy in your climate.

SYMPTOMS: Cold injury can show up as large brown patches on leaves; branch tips or entire shoots may die back. Evergreens may dry out and turn brown under freezing conditions because the roots cannot get water from frozen ground. Small plants, such as strawberries and perennial herbs and flowers, suffer when frost heaving levers them out of the ground, exposing roots to freezing and drying. Seedlings set out in spring may be chilled by cold weather. Late frosts may damage or kill new growth and early flowers of perennials and woody plants.

PREVENTION: Ensure soil is well watered around perennials and evergreens in fall before cold weather; this is especially important for plants growing near the house under the eaves where soil is usually dry. Shelter evergreens from winter winds with burlap screens or other barriers; spray shrubs with an antitranspirant. Mulch strawberries and other perennials in late fall, when the soil surface begins to freeze. In early spring, protect transplants with hotcaps (plant covers) or floating row covers.

CONTROL: Prune back damaged tissue in spring and provide excellent care to speed recovery. Move tender plants to more sheltered areas or provide more protection in winter.

Yellows

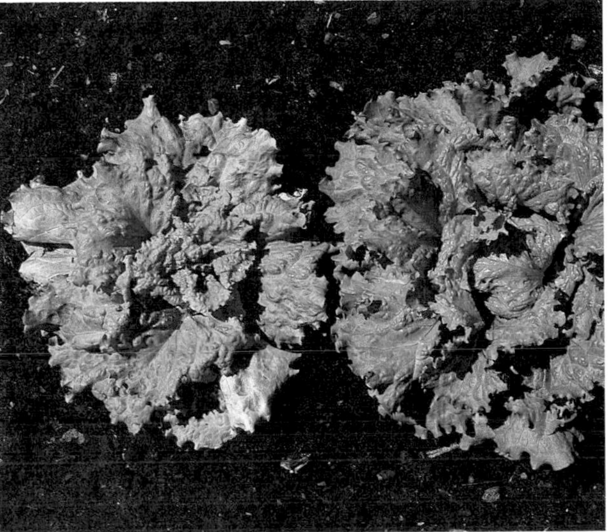

Yellows on lettuce produces light-colored leaves and stunted growth, as shown in the head on the left. Destroy infected plants.

TYPE OF PROBLEM: Mycoplasmalike organisms.

RANGE: Throughout North America; elm yellows occurs in eastern United States.

PLANTS AFFECTED: A wide range of plants, especially aster, carrot, celery, gladiolus, lettuce, potato, tomato, and elm.

SYMPTOMS: Plants generally turn yellow, without the blotching or spots on leaves associated with other diseases. Growth is dwarfed, with abnormal shoot production, usually with smaller than normal spaces between nodes and leaf stems; flowers and stems are distorted or misshapen. Roots of carrots are pale, stunted, and woody with numerous bushy, white, fine roots; carrot leaves are short and bushy and turn from yellow to bronzy purple later in the season. Lettuce is light colored and stunted and does not form proper heads. On elm, leaves wilt, turn bright yellow, and drop; trees usually die within a year. Yellows diseases are transmitted by leafhoppers feeding on plants.

PREVENTION: Cover garden crops with floating row covers to exclude leafhoppers. In areas where aster yellows is a severe problem, remove wild carrot, chicory, dandelion, and wild thistle from the area to reduce wild sources of infection.

CONTROL: Remove and destroy infected plants.

INDEX

The numbers in bold indicate main entries, and the numbers in italic indicate illustrations.

Acalymma vittatum. See Cucumber beetle, striped
Achyra rantalis. See Webworm, garden
Acidity, 20, *20*
Agrobacterium radiobacter, 61
Agrobacterium tumefaciens. See Crown gall
Air circulation, 59, *59*
Air pollution, *49,* 52–53. *See also* PAN damage; Sulfur dioxide injury
Aleochara bilineata, 127
Aleochara bimaculata, 127
Alfalfa, 29
Alkalinity, 20
Amblyseius cucumeris, 114, 126
Amblyseius fallacis, 126
Amelanchier, 67
Anasa tristis. See Squash bug
Animal pests, **65–75**
  damage caused by, 31
  preventing, 36
Animals, beneficial. *See* Beneficial animals
Anthracnose, **130**, *130*
  diagnosing, *50*
  spraying, 63
  symptoms, 51
Antitranspirants, 59
Ant traps, 36
Aphid midge, **117**, *117*
Aphidoletes aphidimyza. See Aphid midge
Aphids, *26,* **78–79**, *78–79*
  damage caused by, 31
  disease carriers, 61
  identifying, *30*
  metamorphosis, 27
  oil sprays, *42*
  predators, 117, 118, 119, 121, 122, 123, 124, 127
  soap spray, *41*
  spraying, 43
  sticky traps, 38
  water spraying, 38
Aphytis melinus, 107
Apis mellifera. See Honeybee
Apple maggot, **79**, *79*
  damage caused by, 31
  sticky traps, 39, *39*
Apples, diseases of, 51
Apple scab, **131**, *131*
  diagnosing, *50*
  spraying, 63
  symptoms, 51
Appletree borer
  flatheaded, 31, **91**, *91*
  roundheaded, 31, **106**, *106*
Armored scales, **107**, *107*
Armyworms, **80**, *80*
  damage caused by, 31
  predators, 119, 128
Artogeia rapae. See Imported cabbageworm
Ash barrier, 37
Asparagus beetle, *26,* 27, **80**, *80*
Assassin bugs, **118**, *118*
Astilbes, *14*

Bacillus lentimorbus, 40
Bacillus popilliae (milky disease), 40, 72, 96, 97
Bacillus thuringiensis, 40
Bacteria
  beneficial, 32, 40, 45, 46
  description, 46
  galls, 50
  rots, 50
  spreading, *47*
  wilt, 50
Bacterial insecticide, 40
Bacterial spot, **131**, *131*
  spraying, 63
  symptoms, 51
Bacterial wetwood. *See* Slime flux
Bacterial wilt, **132**, *132*
  carrier, 61
  diagnosing, *50*
  symptoms, 51
Bagworm, **81**, *81*
Baking soda spray, 62, *62*
Balloons for scaring birds, 71, *71*
Barn swallows, 28
Barriers
  birds, 71
  deer, 68, *68*
  disease carriers, 61
  dogs and cats, 73
  insect pests, 33, **36–37**
  meadow mice, 75
  moles and gophers, 72, *72*
  rabbits, 70, *70*
  woodchucks, 74
Bat houses, 67
Bats, 28, 66–67
Bean beetle, Mexican. *See* Mexican bean beetle
Beauvaria bassiana, 93
Beer traps, *38*
Bees, 27, 28, *28*
  bumblebees, **119**, *119*
  honeybee, **122**, *122*
Beetles. *See also names of species*
  metamorphosis, 27
  spraying, 43
  traps, 36
Beneficial animals, 28, 29, **66–67**
Beneficial insects, **28–29**, *28–29, 32,* 39–40, **117–29**
  attracting, 33, *35*
  spraying, *15*
Beneficial microorganisms, 40, 45
Bigeyed bugs, **118**, *118*
Birdhouses, 67
Birds
  beneficial, 28, 67
  pests, **71**
  preventing, 36
Blackbird, 71
Black knot, 51, **132**, *132*
Black rot, **133**, *133*
Black spot, 55, **133**, *133*
  diagnosing, *49*
  spraying, 62, 63
  symptoms, 51
Black vine weevil, 31, **81**, *81*
Blight, *50. See also* Fire blight
  Botrytis, 51, **134**, *134*
  early, *50,* **140**, *140*
  late, *50,* 51, **142**, *142*
Blissus leucopterus. See Chinch bug
Blister beetles, **82**, *82*
Blood as insects' food, 27
Blossom blights, *47*
Blossom end rot, **134**, *134*
  symptoms, 51
  weather extremes, *48*
Bluebirds, 67
Bluejay, 71
Bombus. See Bumblebees
Borage, 68, *69*
Bordeaux mix, 62, 63
Borer. *See* Appletree borer; Corn borer; Fruit borers; Iris borer; Squash vine borer
Botanical pesticides, 42–43
Botrytis
  blight, 51, **134**, *134*
  fruit rot, **135**, *135*
Braconid wasps, **119**, *119*
Brown canker, 63
Brown rot, *47,* **135**, *135*
  spraying, 63
  symptoms, 51
BT, 40
Buckwheat, 19, 29
Budworm, spruce, **110**, *110*
Bulbs, damage to, 31
Bumblebees, **119**, *119*
Burnet, *16*
Burning diseased plants, 60
Burying diseased plants, 60
Butterflies, metamorphosis, 27
Buying plants, **16–17**, 33
  disease-free, 56
  disease-resistant, 56–57
  pest-resistant, 34
  suitability, 14, 57

Cabbage, 35, *35*
Cabbage looper, **82**, *82,* 128
Cabbage maggot, 27, **83**, *83*
  predators, 121, 127
Cabbageworm, imported. *See* Imported cabbageworm
Cacopsylla pyricola. See Pear psylla
Cages, 36, *68*
California red scale, 107
Camphor cat repellent, 73
Cankerworms, **83**, *83*
Carnivores, 27
Carrot rust fly, **84**, *84*
Carrot weevils, 31
Catbird, 71
Caterpillars, *8. See also names of species*
  handpicking, 38, *76*
  metamorphosis, 27
  spraying, 43
  traps, *36*
Catnip, 29, 73
Cats, **73**, *73, 75*
Cedar-apple rust, 51, **136**, *136*
Cedar waxwing, 71
Celery, *50*
Centipedes, 28, **120**, *120*
Ceratocystis fagacearum. See Oak wilt
Chafer, rose, 31, **105**, *105*
Chemical controls, 62
Cherry, native, 67
Cherry leaf spot, 51, **136**, *136*
Chickadees, 67
Chilocorus nigritus, 107, 108
Chinch bug, **84**, *84*
Choosing plants. *See* Buying plants
Choristoneura fumiferana. See Spruce budworm
Choristoneura rosaceana. See Obliquebanded leafroller
Chrysobothris femorata. See Flatheaded appletree borer
Chrysoperla. See Lacewings
Citrus
  oils, *42,* 43
  repelling cats, 73, *73*
Cleanliness, 34, *34,* 56, 59, *59–60, 74, 75*
Climate, 56
Clover, 19, *19,* 29
Club root, 51, **137**, *137*
Coccomyces. See Cherry leaf spot
Cockroaches, 27
Codling moth, **85**, *85*
  control, *40*
  damage caused by, 31
  predators, 119, 121, 128
  traps, 36
Cold composting, 19
Cold snaps, *53*
Cold stress, 52
Collars, *36,* 37
Colorado potato beetle, **86**, *86*
  control, *40*
  handpicking eggs, 38
  predators, 128
  spraying, 43
Colored sticky traps, 38–39
Color of plants, 17
Companion planting, 35, *35,* 57
Compost, 18–19, *18*
  diseased plants, 60
  mulch, 58
Compost tea, 20, 61
Coneflowers, *29*
Conifer sawflies, **106**, *106*
Conotrachelus nenuphar. See Plum curculio
Construction damage, **137**, *137*
Containers, 16
Convergent lady beetle, 124
Copper fungicide, 61, 63
Copper strips, 33, 37, *37*
Corn borer
  European, 31, **87**, *87*
  predators, 119
  southwestern, **87**, *87*
Corn earworm, **88**, *88,* 128
Corn rootworm, northern, **89**, *89,* 127
Corn smut, **138**, *138*
Cover crops, 19, *19,* 29
Covering plants, 36
Crape myrtle, 56
Crickets, 27
Crioceris asparagi. See Asparagus beetle
Crop rotation, 14, **22–23**, 35, 57
Crown gall, 50, 51, **138**, *138*
Cryptolaemus montrouzieri. See Mealybug destroyer
Cucumber, *35, 50*
Cucumber beetle
  companion planting to prevent, *35*
  disease carriers, 61
  handpicking, 40
  predators, 127
  spotted, **89**, *89*
  spraying, 43
  striped, **90**, *90*
Cultural control of pests, 34
Curculio, plum, **105**, *105*
Cutworms, **90**, *90*
  barriers, 37
  collars, 33, *36*
  damage caused by, 31
  predators, 121, 128
Cydia pomonella. See Codling moth
Cytospora canker, *50,* 51, **139**, *139*

Daisies, *29, 41*
Damping-off, 51, **139**, *139*

Damsel bugs, **121**, *121*
Debris, garden. *See* Garden debris
Deer, **68–69**, *68–69*
Delia antiqua. See Onion maggot
Delia radicum. See Cabbage maggot
Delphinium, 56, *57*
Diabrotica longicornis. See Corn rootworm, northern
Diabrotica undecimpunctata howardi. See Cucumber beetle, spotted
Diatomaceous earth, 37
Diatraea grandiosella. See Corn borer, southwestern
Dibotryon morbosum. See Black knot
Dill, *16,* 29
Diplocarpon rosae. See Black spot
Diseases, **130–55**
  carriers, 61
  control, *54,* **55–63**
  damage caused by, 31
  defining, **46–47**
  desirable, 46
  diagnosing, **48–49**
  identifying, 15, **45–53**
  infectious, 46–47
  look-alikes, **52–53**
  minimizing, **58–59**
  prevention, **56–57**
  spraying, **62–63**
  symptoms, **50–51**
Diversity, 14, *14,* 57
Dogs, 73, *73,* 74
Dormant oil, 42
Downy mildew, 50, 51, **140**, *140*
Drip irrigation, 21, *21,* 58
Drought, *49,* 52
Dusting, 42
Dusts, 37
Dutch elm disease, 51

Early blight, 50, **140**, *140*
Earwigs, 27, *36*
Earworm, corn, **88**, *88,* 128
Edovum puttleri, 86
Elm bark beetles, **91**, *91,* 119
Encarsia formosa, 116
Epilachna varivestis. See Mexican bean beetle
Erwinia. See Bacterial wilt
Erwinia amylovora. See Fire blight
European corn borer, 31, **87**, *87*
Exobasidium. See Leaf gall

Fall armyworms, 128
Fall webworm, **115**, *115*
Fences
  against dogs and cats, 73
  against rabbits, 70, *70*
  against woodchucks, 74, *74*
Fennel, 29, 68
Fenusa. See Sawflies, leafminer
Finch, 71
Fire ants, 43
Fire blight, **141**, *141*
  diagnosing, 50
  spraying, 63
  symptoms,50, 51, *51*
Flatheaded appletree borer, 31, **91**, *91*
Flea beetles, **92**, *92*
  damage caused by, 31
  spraying, 43
  sticky traps, 38
  trap crops, 35
Fleas, 27, 43
Flies, 27, 43
Floating row covers, 33, 36, 61, *70,* 74
Flooding moles and gophers, 72
Flower flies. *See* Hover flies
Flowers
  damage, 31
  diseases, 51
  to attract beneficials, 29
Foxes, *66,* 67
Frightening off. *See* Scaring
Froghopper. *See* Spittlebug
Frost damage, 51, *53*
Fruit
  damage, 31
  diseases, 51
  sunscald, 53
Fruit borers, 31, **92**, *92*
Fruit moth, oriental, **103**, *103*
Fruit rot, Botrytis, **135**, *135*
Fungi
  control with compost, 20, 61
  description, 46
  galls, 50
  leaf curl, 50
  rots, 50
  rusts, 50
  spreading, *47*
  wilt, 50
Fungicidal soap, 63
Fungicides
  biological, 62
  sprays, *63*
Fusarium. See Fusarium wilt
Fusarium wilt, 50, 51, **141**, *141*

Galls
  crown, 50, 51, **138**, *138*
  diagnosing, *50*
  leaf, 50, 51, **143**, *143*
  pruning off, *39*
Gall wasps, **93**, *93*
  damage caused by, 31
  diagnosing, *50*
Garden debris, 34, *34,* 56, 59, *59, 60,* 74, *75*
Garden webworm, **115**, *115*
Garlic
  oil, 42
  repelling cats, 73
  spray, *61, 62*
  woodchuck repellent, 74
Geocoris. See Bigeyed bugs
Gophers, **72**, *72*
Grackle, 71
Grapholitha molesta. See Oriental fruit moth
Grasshoppers, **93**, *93*
  damage caused by, 31
  metamorphosis, 27
  predators, 127, 128
Green peach aphids, 119
Ground beetles, **121**, *121*
Groundhogs. *See* Woodchucks
Growing conditions, 14
Grubs, 27
Guignardia bidwellii. See Black rot
Gymnosporangium juniperi-virginianae. See Cedar-apple rust
Gypsy moth, **94**, *94*
  handpicking, 38
  predators, 128
  prevention, *37*
  traps, 36

Habitat modification
  deer, 68
  dogs and cats, 73
  meadow mice, 75
  moles and gophers, 72
  rabbits, 70
  woodchucks, 74
Handpicking insect pests, 33, 38, *38*
  caterpillars, 76
  with vacuum cleaners, 40
Hawks, 67
Health
  garden, **14–15**
  plants, **16–17**, *16–17*
Heat stress, 52
Helenium autumnale, 59
Heliocoverpa zea. See Corn earworm
Heliothis zea. See Corn earworm
Herbicide drift, 51, 53
Herbivores, 27
Herbs, 16
Hippodamia convergens. See Convergent lady beetle
Homemade pest control, 42
Honeybee, **122**, *122*
Hornworm
  damage caused by, 31
  predators, 119, 128
  tomato, **114**, *114*
  trap crops, *35*
Hot dusts, 42
Hover flies, **122**, *122*
Hylemya brassicae. See Cabbage maggot
Hylurgopinus rufipes. See Elm bark beetles
Hyphantria cunea. See Webworm, fall

Ichneumon wasps, **123**, *123*
Identifying pests, 15, 17
Imported cabbageworm, **95**, *95*
  predators, 119, 128
Inchworms. See Cankerworms
Infectious diseases, 46
Insecticides, 33, 41–43
  bacterial, 40
  botanical, 42–43
  effect on beneficial insects, 29
  soap, 41
Insect pests, **78–116**
  control, **33–43**, **38–43**
  damage identification, **30–31**
  definition, 26
  identifying, 15, 17
  preventing, **34–35**
  symptoms, 31
Insects
  anatomy, *27*
  beneficial (*see* Beneficial insects)
  damage, 30–31, *30–31*
  description, **26–29**
  disease carriers, 61
  feeding habits, 27
  galls, *50*
  life cycles, 26–27, *26*
  metamorphosis, 27
  pests (*see* Insect pests)
Iris borer, **95**, *95*
Iron deficiency, 142, *142*

Japanese beetle, **96**, *96*
  damage caused by, 31
  handpicking, 40
  milky disease, 40
June beetles, **97**, *97*

Kites for scaring birds, 71

Lacebugs, **97**, *97*
Lacewings, *15, 29,* 114, **123**, *123*
Lady beetles, *15,* 28, *28,* 114, **124**, *124*
Ladybirds. *See* Lady beetles
Ladybugs. *See* Lady beetles
Lagerstroemia, 56
Larvae, 27, 29
Late blight, 50, *50,* 51, **142**, *142*
Lavender, 68, *69*
Lawn mower damage, **143**, *143*
Leaf curl, peach. *See* Peach leaf curl
Leaf gall, 50, 51, **143**, *143*
Leafhoppers, **98**, *98*
  damage caused by, 31
  predators, 118, 121, 125
  sticky traps, 38
  water spraying, 38
Leafminers, **99**, *99*
  damage caused by, 31
  identifying, 30
  spraying, 43
Leafminer sawflies, **107**, *107*
Leafroller, obliquebanded, 31, **102**, *102*
Leaf scorch, **144**, *144*
Leaf spot. *See also* Bacterial spot; Black spot; Cherry leaf spot; Septoria leaf spot
  diagnosing, *50*
  spraying, 63
Leaves
  damage, 31
  diseases, 51
  sunscald, 53
Lemon balm, 29
Leptinotarsa decemlineata. See Colorado potato beetle
Leptomastix dactylopii, 99
Lice, 27
Light
  excessive, 53
  insufficient, 52–53
  scorching, *52,* **144**, *144*
Lightning damage, **144**, *144*
Lilac, 56
Lime-sulfur fungicide, 62, 63
Limonius. See Wireworms
Lindorus lophanthae, 107, 108
Lizards, 28
Locating the garden, 14, 57
Looper, cabbage, **82**, *82,* 128
Lovage, 29, *35*
Lygus lineolaris. See Tarnished plant bug
Lymantria dispar. See Gypsy moth

Macrodactylus subspinosus. See Rose chafer
Macronoctua onusta. See Iris borer
Maggots, 27, 127. *See also* Apple maggot; Cabbage maggot; Onion maggot
Malacosoma. See Tent caterpillar
Manduca quinquemaculata. See Tomato hornworm
Manganese deficiency, *53*
Mantis religiosa. See Praying mantid
Marigolds, 73, *73,* 102
May beetles. *See* June beetles
Meadow mice, **75**, *75*
Mealybug destroyer, 99, **125**, *125*
Mealybugs, **99**, *99*
  damage caused by, 31
  predators, 123, 125
  spraying, 43
Melittia cucurbitae. See Squash vine borer
Metamorphosis, 26–27
Metaphycus helvolus, 108

Metaseiulus occidentalis, 101, 126
Mexican bean beetle, **100**, *100*
damage caused by, 31
predators, 128
Mice, meadow, 75, *75*
Microorganisms. *See* Bacteria; Viruses
Midges, 27
aphid, 117, *117*
Mildew. *See also* Downy mildew; Powdery mildew
diagnosing, *50*
spraying, 63
Milky disease, 40, 72, 96, 97
Millipedes, **120**, *120*
Mint, 29, 68
Minute pirate bugs, **125**, *125*
Mites
predators, 123, 127
predatory, 28, 101, 114, **126**, *126*
spider (*see* Spider mites)
Mold, sooty. *See* Sooty mold
Moles, 72, *72*
Monilinia fructicola. See Brown rot
Mosaic, 51, **145**, *145*
Mosquitoes, 27
Moths. *See also names of moths*
metamorphosis, 27
Mulch, 37, 58–59, *58*
living, 19
Mustard, 35
Mylar tape for scaring birds, 71

Nasturtiums, *35*
Native cherry, 67
Needlecast, **145**, *145*
Neem, 43
Nematodes, beneficial. *See* Parasitic nematodes
Nematodes, pests, **102**, *102*
damage caused by, 31
description, 47
disease carriers, 61
predators, 127
spreading, *47*
symptoms, 51
Neodiprion. See Sawflies, conifer
Nicotine, 43
Nighthawks, 67
Nitrogen, 20, 53
deficiency, **146**, *146*
Noise for scaring birds, 71
Northern corn rootworm, **89**, *89*, 127
Nosema locustae, 93
Nuthatches, 67
Nutrient deficiency
damage caused by, 31
nitrogen, **146**, *146*
phosphorus, *52*, **148**, *148*
potassium, **149**, *149*
symptoms, 51, 53
Nutrients
balancing, 20
deficient (*see* Nutrient deficiency)
excessive, 53
imbalances, *48*
Nymphs, 27

Oak wilt, 51, **146**, *146*
Obliquebanded leafroller, 31, **102**, *102*
Oil spray, 41–42
dormant, 42
garlic, 42
with soap, 42
summer, 42
superior, 42
Oils, 41–42, *42*
Oleander scale, 107
Omnivores, 27
Onion
cat repellent, 73
protecting, 35
woodchuck repellent, 74
Onion maggot, 35, **103**, *103*
Onion thrips, 126
Oriental fruit moth, **103**, *103*
Oriole, 71, *71*
Orius. See Minute pirate bugs
Ostrinia nubilalis. See European corn borer
Otiorhynchus ovatus. See Strawberry root weevil
Otiorhynchus sulcatus. See Black vine weevil
Overhead sprinklers, 13, 21, *21*
Owls, 67, *67*
Ozone damage, 51, 53, **147**, *147*

PAN damage, 51, 53, **147**, *147*
Parasitic nematodes, 33, 40, *40*, 84, 88, 89, 90, 92, 96, 97, 103, 105, 106, 112, 116
Parasitic wasps, 28, 85, 86, 99, 100, 107, 108, 116. *See also* Braconid wasps; Ichneumon wasps
Parasitoids, 28
Parsley, *16*, 29
Parthenocissus quinquefolia. See Virginia creeper
Pathogens, 45
Peach leaf curl, **148**, *148*
diagnosing, 50
spraying, 63
symptoms, 51
Peach rosette, 51
Peachtree borers, 31, **104**, *104*
Pear psylla, 31, **104**, *104*
Peat pots, 16
Pediobius foveolatus, 100
Peroxyacetyl nitrate pollution, 51, 53, **147**, *147*
Pesticides. *See* Insecticides
Pests. *See* Animal pests; Insect pests
Petroleum oils, 41
Pheromone traps, 39, *39*
Philaenus spumarius. See Spittlebug
Phlox, 56–57
Phoebes, 67
Phosphorus deficiency, *52*, **148**, *148*
pH value of soil, 20, *20*
Phyllophaga. See June beetles
Phytophthora infestans. See Late blight
Phytoseiulus persimilis, 101, 126
Picea, 68
Pieris rapae. See Imported cabbageworm
Pillbugs. *See* Sowbugs
Pirate bugs, 114
Planning, 13, 16
Plant bugs
predators, 118, 121
spraying, 43
sticky traps, 38
Plant covers, 36
Planting patterns, 34–35
Plant screens, 33
Plants to attract beneficials, 29
Plasmodiophora brassicae. See Club root
Plum curculio, **105**, *105*
Podisus maculiventris. See Spined soldier bug
Pollination, 28
Pollution. *See* Air pollution
Popillia japonica. See Japanese beetle
Potassium deficiency, **149**, *149*
Potato beetle, Colorado. *See* Colorado potato beetle
Powders, 37
Powdery mildew, *46*, **149**, *149*
control by compost, 61
diagnosing, 50, *50*
spraying, 61, 62, 63
symptoms, 51
Praying mantid, *28*, **126**, *126*
Predators, 28, **66–67**, 101, 114
mites, 28, **126**, *126*
wasps (*see* Braconid wasps; Ichneumon wasps)
Protecting plants, 33
Pruning
diseased plants, 60, *61*
insect infestations, 38, *38, 39*
Prunus, 67
Pseudomonas. See Bacterial wilt
Psila rosae. See Carrot rust fly
Psylla, pear, 31, **104**, *104*
Purple martins, 28
Pyracantha, *50*
Pyrethrin, 43
Pyrethrum daisies, *41*

Rabbits, 36, *64*, **70**, *70*
Radishes, *35*
Railroad worms. *See* Apple maggot
Rainwater, 21, *21*
gauge, 21, *49*
Records, 15
Red scale, California, 107
Repellents, 65
deer, 68, 69
dogs and cats, 73
rabbits, 70
woodchucks, 74
Resistance to diseases, 34, 56–57, *56*
Rhagoletis pomonella. See Apple maggot
Rhododendrons, *20*
Robin, 71
Root rot, 51, **150**, *150*
Roots
damage, 31
diseases, 51
system, 16–17, *17*
Rootworm, northern corn, **89**, *89*, 127
Rosa rugosa, 68
Rose chafer, 31, **105**, *105*
Roses, *49*, 56
Rot. *See* Black rot; Blossom end rot; Botrytis fruit rot; Brown rot; Root rot
Rotation of crops, 14, **22–23**, 35, 57
Rotenone, 43
Roundheaded appletree borer, 31, **106**, *106*
Rove beetles, *24*, **127**, *127*
Row covers, 33, 36, 61, *70*, 74
Rugosa rose, 68
Rust, *44*, **150**, *150*
cedar-apple, 51, **136**, *136*
diagnosing, 50
spraying, 63
symptoms, 51
Rust fly, carrot, **84**, *84*

Sabadilla, 43
Sage, 68
Salt injury, 51, *53*, **151**, *151*
Saperda candida. See Roundheaded appletree borer
Sawflies
conifer, **106**, *106*
damage caused by, 31
larvae, *39*
leafminer, **107**, *107*
predators, 123, 128
Scab, apple. *See* Apple scab
Scales
armored, **107**, *107*
damage caused by, 31
handpicking, 38
predators, 123
soft, **108**, *108*
Scaring
animals, 65
birds, 71, *71*
rabbits, 70, *70*
Scavengers, 27
Scolytus multistriatus. See Elm bark beetles
Scorching. *See* Sunscald
Seedlings, 16–17, 31
Seeds, starting, 59
Septoria leaf spot, 51, **151**, *151*
Serviceberry, 67
Shelter for beneficial animals, 29
Silverfish, 27
Site, 57
Skunks, 67
Slime flux, 51, **152**, *152*
Slugs, **108–9**, *108*
copper barriers, 37, *37*
damage caused by, 31
dusts, 37
handpicking, 38
identifying, *30*
predators, 120, 121, 127
traps, 36, *36*, 38, 39, *39*
Smut, corn, **138**, *138*
Snails, **108–9**, *109*
copper barriers, 37
damage caused by, 31
dusts, 37
handpicking, *38*
identifying, *30*
predators, 121, 127
spraying, *41*
traps, 36, *36*, 39
Snakes, 66
Sneezeweed, *59*
Soap
deer repellent, 69
insecticidal, 33, 41
and oil spray, 42
spray, *41*
Sodium bicarbonate spray, 62
Soft scales, **108**, *108*
Soil, 13
dampness, 58
excessive nutrients, 53
fertility, 15, *15*
improving, **18–20**
nutrients (*see* Nutrients)
pH, 20
solarizing, 34, 60
testing, 20, *20*, 21
waterlogged, **154**, *154*
Solarizing, 34, 60
Soldier beetles, **127**, *127*
Soldier bug, spined, 100, **128**, *128*

Sooty mold, *48,* 51, *61,* **152**, *152*
Southwestern corn borer, **87**, *87*
Sowbugs, **109**, *109*
Spacing plants, *58*
Sparrows, 67, 71
Spider mites, **101**, *101*
  damage caused by, 31
  identifying, *30*
  oil sprays, *42*
  predators, 118, 125, 126
  spraying, 43
  water spraying, 38
Spiders, 28, *29*
Spined soldier bug, 100, **128**, *128*
Spittlebug, 31, **110**, *110*
Spot, bacterial, **131**, *131*
Spotted cucumber beetle, **89**, *89*
Spraying
  against deer, 68
  antitranspirants, 59
  diseases, 62–63
  insecticides, 41–43
  safety, 41
  with water, 38
Springtails, 127
Sprinklers, 13, 21, *21*
Spruce, 68
Spruce budworm, **110**, *110*
Squash, *35,* 36
Squash bug, **111**, *111*
  companion planting to prevent, *35*
  predators, 128
  spraying, 43
Squash vine borer, 31, **111**, *111*
Starling, 71
Stems
  damage, 31
  diseases, 51
Sticky traps, *36,* 38, *39*
  trunk bands, 33, 36, *36*
Stink bugs, **112**, *112,* 128
Strawberry root weevil, 31, **112**, *112*
Striped cucumber beetle, **90**, *90*
Sulfur, 63
Sulfur dioxide injury, 51, *52,* 53, **153**, *153*
Summer oil, 42
Sunlight. *See* Light
Sunscald, 51, 53, **153**, *153*
Superior oil, 42
Swallows, 67
Synanthedon. See Fruit borers
Synanthedon exitiosa. See Peachtree borers
Synanthedon pictipes. See Peachtree borers

Tachinid flies, **128**, *128*
Tagetes minutum, 102
Taphrina deformans. See Peach leaf curl
Tarnished plant bug, 31, **113**, *113*
Tar spot, *50*
Temperature of compost, 18–19
Temperatures, extremes, 52
Tent caterpillar, **113**, *113*
  predators, 128
  pruning off, 38
Thermometer, 18
Thrips, **114**, *114*
  damage caused by, 31
  predators, 121, 123, 125, 126
  spraying, 43
  sticky traps, 38
Thyridopteryx ephemeraeformis. See Bagworm
Tiger beetles, **129**, *129*
Tillage, 19
Timed planting, 35
Titmice, 67
Toads, 28, 66, *66*
Tomatoes, *48*
Tomato hornworm, **114**, *114*
Transplanting, 16, *16*
Trap cropping, 35, *35*
Traps, 33. *See also* Sticky traps
  earwigs, *36*
  meadow mice, 75
  moles and gophers, 72
  pheromone, 39, *39*
  slugs and snails, *36, 38–39,* 39
  trunk bands, 36
Treehoppers, 121
Trichogramma wasps, 85
Trichoplusia ni. See Cabbage looper
Trunk bands, 36, *36,* 37
Typhlodromus pyri, 101, 126

Ustilago maydis. See Corn smut

Vacuum cleaners for handpicking, 40
Valsa canker. See Cytospora canker
Vectors, 61
Venturia inaequalis. See Apple scab
Verbena, 56
Verticillium wilt, 50, 51, **154**, *154*
Vespula. See Yellow jackets
Vine weevil, black, 31, **81**, *81*
Vireos, 67
Virginia creeper, 67
Viruses, 46–47, *46, 49*
  carrier, 61
  leaf curl, 50
  plant disposal, 18
  symptoms, 51
Voles. *See* Meadow mice

Warbler, 71
Wasps. *See* also Parasitic wasps
  braconid, **119**, *119*
  gall (*see* Gall wasps)
  ichneumon, **123**, *123*
  metamorphosis, 27
  spraying, 43
Water
  attracting beneficial animals, 29
  lack of, 51
Watering, 13, **21**, 58
  excessive, 52
  repelling cats, 73
Waterlogged soil, 51, **154**, *154*
Weasels, 67
Weather
  extremes, *48*
Webworm
  damage caused by, 31
  fall, **115**, *115*
  garden, **115**, *115*
Weevil
  black vine, 31, **81**, *81*
  damage caused by, 31
  spraying, 43
  strawberry root, 31, **112**, *112*
Western flower thrips, 126
Wetwood, bacterial. *See* Slime flux
Whiteflies, **116**, *116*
  damage caused by, 31
  handpicking, 40
  identifying, *30*
  spraying, 43
  sticky traps, 38
Wilt
  bacterial (*see* Bacterial wilt)
  diagnosing, 50
  Fusarium, 50, 51, 141, *141*
  oak, 51, **146**, *146*
  spraying, 63
  Verticillium, 50, 51, **154**, *154*
Wind, *52,* 53
Wings, insects', *27*
Wintergreen, 73
Winter injury, **155**, *155*
Wireworms, 31, **116**, *116*
Woodchucks, **74**, *74*
Woodpeckers, 28, 67
Wrens, 67

Yarrow, 29, 68
Yellow jackets, **129**, *129*
Yellows, 51, **155**, *155*

Zinnias, 35

ACKNOWLEDGMENTS

Photo Credits

Heather Angel (Biofotos): page 117.

Ardea: photographer: P. Morris: opposite contents page; photographer: Bob Gibbons: page 21; photographer: John Mason: page 62; and photographer: Ian Beames: page 64.

Max E. Badgley: pages 11 (left and right), 80 (left and right), 87 (left and right), 89 (right), 90 (left), 92 (left), 93 (right), 95 (left), 98 (left), 100 (left and right), 107 (right), 111 (left), 112 (left), 115 (right), 118 (right), 123 (left), 124 (left and right), and 127 (right).

Charlton Photos Inc.: pages 79 (right), 83 (left), 92 (right), 105 (right), and 110 (right).

Bruce Coleman Ltd: photographer: Hans Reinhard: opposite title page, page 72 (top left); photographer: John Shaw: title page, pages 19 (top) and 94 (left); photographer: William S. Paton: contents page (bottom right); photographer: Gunter Ziesler: page 28 (top); photographer: Hans-Joachim Flugel: page 28 (center left); photographer: Jane Burton: pages 28 (center right), 41 (bottom), and 73 (top); photographer: Eric Crichton: page 38 (bottom); photographer: Neville Fox-Davies: page 40; photographers: Bob and Clara Calhoun: page 54; photographer: Robert P. Carr: page 58 (bottom); photographer: Andrew J. Purcell: page 72 (top right); photographer: Jeff Foott: page 72 (bottom); photographer: Dr. Frieder Sauer: page 121 (right); and photographer: Martini: page 135 (left).

Davey Tree Expert Company: photographer: D. L. Caldwell: pages 95 (right) and 154 (right).

Michael Dirr: page 150 (right).

Thomas Eltzroth: page 15 (top).

Garden Picture Library: photographer: Alan Bedding: back cover (top), page 20; photographer: Vaughan Fleming: back cover (center); photographer: Brian Carter: pages 16, 32, and 52 (bottom); photographer: Neil Holmes: page 17; photographer: J. S. Sira: pages 26, 39, and 76; photographer: John Glover: pages 34 (bottom) and 75 (bottom); photographer: Linda Burgess page 35 (left); photographer: Michael Howes: pages 36 (top), 50 (bottom left), and 70 (top); photographer: Mayer Le Scanff: page 59 (top); photographer: Clive Nichols: page 67 (top); photographer: Roger Hyam: page 71; and photographer: Mel Watson: page 73 (bottom).

George W. Hudler: pages 107 (left) and 134 (right).

Peter May: page 150 (left).

New York State Agricultural Experiment Station, Cornell University: pages 102 (right), 103 (left and right), 112 (right), and 133 (left).

NHPA: photographer: Anthony Bannister: page 24.

Oregon State University, Ken Gray Slide Collection: page 104 (right).

Oxford Scientific Films: page 81 (left); photographer: Alastair Shay: page 27; photographer: Michael Leach: 67 (bottom); photographer: Terry Heathcote: page 68; photographer: Niall Benvie: page 69 (top); photographer: Stan Osolinski: page 74; and photographer: David Fox: page 94 (right).

Papillio: photographer: Laura Sivell: copyright page; photographer: Ken Wilson: contents page (top left), pages 109 (left and right), 110 (left), and 123 (right); and photographer: Dennis Johnson: page 126 (right).

The Photo Library, Sydney: page 66.

Photos Horticultural: endpapers, pages 14 (top and bottom), 15 (bottom), 19 (bottom), 29 (right), 34 (top), 35 (right), 36 (bottom), 37, 42, 44, 46, 47 (top and bottom), 48, 49 (top left), 56, 57, 58 (top), 59 (bottom), 60 (top right), 61 (top left), 69 (bottom), 70 (bottom), 84 (left), 139 (right), 142 (left), 144 (right), 148 (right), and 149 (left).

Premaphotos Wildlife: photographer: K. G. Preston-Mafham: front cover, pages 38 (top), 49 (bottom), 50 (top right), 78, 81 (right), 82 (left), 93 (left), 98 (right), 106 (right), 108 (left and right), 113 (right), 118 (left), 119 (left and right), 121 (left), 122 (left and right), 128 (left and right), and 129 (left and right).

Ann F. Rhoads: pages 52 (top right), 132 (left), 136 (right), 147 (left), 151 (left), and 153 (left).

Rodale Stock Images: pages 113 (left), 114 (right), 136 (left), and 138 (left).

Edward S. Ross: page 106 (left).

David J. Shetlar: pages 86 (left), 89 (left), 90 (right), 91 (right), 96 (right), 104 (left), 105 (left), 111 (right), and 115 (left).

Harry Smith Collection: contents page (bottom left), pages 8, 49 (top right), 50 (bottom center), 60 (top left), 73 (center), 133 (right), 135 (right), 137 (left), 139 (left), 141 (left), 146 (left), 148 (left), and 155 (left).

Patrick Temple: page 147 (right).

Weldon Russell: page 12.

Weldon Trannies: contents page (top right), pages 41 (top), 50 (top center and bottom right), 52 (top left), 53 (top left and top right), 60 (bottom), 79 (left), 85 (left), 99 (left and right), 102 (left), 114 (left), 116 (left), 120 (left and right), 125 (left), 130, 131 (left and right), 134 (left), 140 (left), 141 (right), 142 (right), 143 (right), 145 (left), 149 (right), 151 (right), 152 (right), 153 (right), 154 (left), and 155 (right).

Ron West: half title page, back cover (bottom), pages 29 (left), 50 (top left), 53 (bottom), 61 (bottom right), 82 (right), 83 (right), 84 (right), 85 (right), 86 (right), 88 (left and right), 91 (left), 96 (left), 97 (left and right), 101 (left and right), 116 (right), 125 (right), 126 (left), 127 (left), and 140 (right).

Katharine D. Widin: pages 75 (top), 132 (right), 137 (right), 138 (right), 143 (left), 144 (left), 145 (right), 146 (right), and 152 (left).